THE COMPLETE IDIOT'S GUIDE® TO

Glycemic Index Snacks

by Lucy Beale and Julie Alles, R.D., L.D., C.L.T.

ALPHA

A member of Penguin Group (USA) Inc.

For Patrick

ALPHA BOOKS

Published by the Penguin Group

Penguin Group (USA) Inc., 375 Hudson Street, New York, New York 10014, USA

Penguin Group (Canada), 90 Eglinton Avenue East, Suite 700, Toronto, Ontario M4P 2Y3, Canada (a division of Pearson Penguin Canada Inc.)

Penguin Books Ltd., 80 Strand, London WC2R 0RL, England

Penguin Ireland, 25 St. Stephen's Green, Dublin 2, Ireland (a division of Penguin Books Ltd.)

Penguin Group (Australia), 250 Camberwell Road, Camberwell, Victoria 3124, Australia (a division of Pearson Australia Group Pty. Ltd.)

Penguin Books India Pvt. Ltd., 11 Community Centre, Panchsheel Park, New Delhi—110 017, India

Penguin Group (NZ), 67 Apollo Drive, Rosedale, North Shore, Auckland 1311, New Zealand (a division of Pearson New Zealand Ltd.)

Penguin Books (South Africa) (Pty.) Ltd., 24 Sturdee Avenue, Rosebank, Johannesburg 2196, South Africa

Penguin Books Ltd., Registered Offices: 80 Strand, London WC2R 0RL, England

Publisher: *Marie Butler-Knight*

Associate Publisher: *Mike Sanders*

Executive Managing Editor: *Billy Fields*

Senior Acquisitions Editors: *Paul Dinas, Brook Farling*

Senior Development Editor: *Christy Wagner*

Senior Production Editor: *Kayla Dugger*

Copy Editor: *Amy Borrelli*

Cover Designer: *Rebecca Batchelor*

Book Designers: *William Thomas, Rebecca Batchelor*

Indexer: *Joan Green*

Layout: *Ayanna Lacey*

Senior Proofreader: *Laura Caddell*

Contents

Part 1:   The Art of the Snack 1

1   Looking at Snacks in a New Light 3

Successful Snacking 3

When the Hunger Pangs Hit 4

Your Snacking Preferences 5

Your Food Preferences 6

Snack Size 6

The Ingenious Glycemic Index 6

Using the Glycemic Load 7

Healthful Benefits 8

Eat Better for Happier Moods 8

Eat Better for Less Inflammation 9

Eat Better for a More Radiant You 9

2   The Making of Good Snacks 11

Choosing Low-Glycemic Ingredients 11

Fantastic Flours 12

Bountiful Breads 13

Sugars and Sweeteners 13

Stocking Your Pantry 14

Staples to Keep on Hand 14

Let's Talk Herbs 15

Fresh or Frozen? 16

Don't Forget Dairy 16

Equipment 17

Storing Snacks 18

Part 2:   Mostly Meatless Snacks 19

3   Versatile Vegetables 21

Pick the Best Vegetables 21

Avocado Cups 22

Asian Vegetables with Peanuts 23

Cabbage Pecan Slaw 24

Blue Cheese Iceberg Salad 25

Tomato, Basil, and Mozzarella Salad 26

Cucumber, Bell Pepper, and Jicama Salad 27

Corn, Red Pepper, and Monterey Jack Salad 28

Broccoli Salad with Blue Cheese 29

Green Bean and Almond Salad 30

Southwestern Salad 31

Shoestring Carrot Patties 32

Chili Sweet Potato Fries 33

Twice-Baked Sweet Potatoes 34

Baked Sweet Potato Skins 35

Honey-Baked Acorn Squash 36

Asian Cakes with Cabbage 37

Spaghetti Squash with Spinach 38

Portobellos with Pepperoni and Walnuts 39

More-Than-Miso Soup 40

Vegetable Curry 41

Creamy Caraway Potato Salad 42

Thai Vegetable Rolls 43

Fennel, Apricot, and Carrot Wraps 44

Greek Salad Wraps 45

Broccoli and Corn Wraps 46

Eggplant Feta Rolls 47

Portobello Mushroom Pitas 48

4   Fantastic Fruit **49**

Granola Breakfast Sundaes 50

Orange Pistachio Parfait 51

Peach Parfait 52

Papaya Basil Parfait 53

Waldorf Salad Vinaigrette 54

Strawberry Iceberg Wedges 55

Minted Watermelon Salad 56

Pineapple Broccoli Slaw 57

Stuffed Dates 57

Banana Cream Cheese Roll-Ups 58

Raspberry Cottage Cheese 59

Frozen Cherry Almond Frosty 60

Grilled Pineapple Rings 60

Baked Apples with Yogurt 61

Peach and Pecan Stir-Fry 62

Sautéed Bananas and Raisins 63

Mango and Pineapple Freeze 64

5   Dips, Spreads, Salsas, and Sauces 65

The Art of the Dipper 65

Hot Chili Cream Cheese Dip 66

Bacon Cheddar Dip 67

Pepperoni Pizza Dip 68

Black Bean and Mango Dip 69

Five-Layer Mexican Dip 70

Cannellini Bean Dip 71

Chickpea, Basil, and Radish Dip 72

Creamy Artichoke Spinach Dip 73

Curried Carrot Dip 74

Greek Olive and Spinach Dip 75

Hummus with Lemon 76

Olive and Pimiento Cheese Spread 77

Creamy Salmon Spread 78

Sun-Dried Tomato Mediterranean Spread 79

Tomato Mango Salsa 80

Cucumber Lime Salsa 81

Garlic Basil Pesto 82

Sweet and Spicy Sesame Sauce 83

Moroccan Ketchup 83

Tzatziki 84

6   Cheese and Tofu Treats 85

Choose Cheese 85

Try Tofu 86

Mozzarella and Black Bean Salad 87

Feta, Fig, and Spinach Pizza 88

Mushroom and Artichoke Camembert 89

Jalapeño Cheddar Cheese Pizza 90

Brie with Blueberry Preserves 91

Artichokes and Olives on Cucumber 92

Monterey Jack Tacos 93

Green Olives with Feta and Celery 94

Cheese and Fruit Kabobs 95

Blue Cheese Pitas 96

Italian Pizza on a Pita 97

Gorgonzola Bites with Fresh Fruit 98

Layered Greek Pie 99

Olive Tapenade Roll-Ups 100

Bell Pepper and Tofu Kabobs 101

Japanese Tofu Skewers 102

Tofu and Green Pea Soup 103

Tofu Salad with Peanut Sauce 104

Part 3:   Heartier Fare 105

7   Beef, Pork, and Lamb 107

Beef and Black Bean Lettuce Wraps 108

Beef Gyros 109

Mexican Beef Tostadas 110

Zucchini with Beef and Peppers 111

Top Sirloin Kabobs 112

Mediterranean Beef Wraps 113

Beef and Blue Cheese Wraps 114

Moroccan Burgers 115

Steak Sandwiches with Peppers and Onions 116

Hot Dogs with Avocado-Chili Relish 117

New Orleans Quesadillas 118

Italian Sausage and Pesto Wraps 119

Italian Sausage and Turkey Patties 120

Classic Reuben with Pineapple 121

Deli Ham and Turkey Pitas 122

Ham, Corn, and Sweet Potato Patties.. 123

Pork Posole... 124

Caribbean Pork and Fruit Salad.. 125

Pulled Pork and Peach Wraps 126

Lamb Patties Piccata.. 127

8   Perfect Poultry **129**

Chicken and Brie Burgers... 130

Chicken Red Pepper Quesadillas.. 131

Chicken Satay with Peanut Sauce 132

Asian Chicken Lettuce Wraps 133

Chicken Wraps with Pears and Grapes..................................... 134

Creamy Chicken Wraps.. 135

Rosemary Honey Chicken Drumsticks....................................... 136

Pecan Coconut Chicken Fingers 137

Sesame Chicken Strips 138

Swiss Turkey Enchiladas.. 139

Turkey and Apple Pockets.. 140

Grilled Turkey and Cottage Cheese Burgers............................. 141

New Orleans Turkey and Sausage Kabobs................................. 142

9   Sensational Seafood **143**

Baja Fish Tacos 144

Open-Face Lemon Trout Sandwiches 145

Cajun Catfish Po'Boy... 146

Shrimp Po'Boy with Peaches.. 147

Tuna Salad with Mangoes and Avocado 148

Asian Tuna and Cabbage Salad 149

Tuna, Barley, and Black Bean Salad... 150

Southwestern Tuna Salad..151

Salmon with Sun-Dried Tomatoes.. 152

Salmon with Orange Slices 153

Parmesan Shrimp with Pine Nuts 154

Coconut Island Shrimp 155

Shrimp Fajitas... 156

Shrimp Tacos with Ginger Sauce 157

Crab Cakes 158

Baked Crab Enchiladas 159

Lobster Pitas 160

10   Excellent Eggs 161

Eggs and Your Health..161

The Basic Cooked Egg... 162

Marinara Vegetable Frittata 163

Spinach Cheese Squares... 164

Artichoke Squares...165

Ham and Cheese Pie 166

Crustless Vegetable Quiche 167

Cherry Almond Quiche... 168

Apple Dutch Quiche 169

Island Scrambled Eggs.. 170

Sweet Potato Honey Kugel 171

Norwegian Pancakes 172

Egg and Bacon Salad Pitas 173

Hard-Boiled Egg Spread.. 174

11   Bountiful Beans and Legumes............................ 175

The Delicious, Nutritious Legume............................175

Green Lentils with Feta... 177

Lentils with Spinach, Walnuts, and Parmesan........... 178

Artichokes with Chickpeas 179

Romaine Salad Tossed with Chickpeas..................... 180

Green Bean Salad with Edamame and Chickpeas 181

Chickpea Poppers.. 182

Chickpea Salad with Roasted Cumin....................... 183

Black-Eyed Pea and Ham Salad 184

Barbecued White Beans.. 185

Four-Cheese Black Bean Mash................................ 186

Sweet Potato and Black Bean Wraps........................ 187

Black Bean and Avocado Salad 188

Tuscan Bean Soup... 189

Great Northern Bean and Mushroom Burgers......................... 190

Guacamole with Green Peas and Tomato 191

Refried Bean–Stuffed Portobello Mushrooms 192

12   Great Whole Grains 193

Watch the Glycemic Load 193

Quinoa and Lentil Salad 194

Lentil Tabbouleh 195

Bulgur with Apples and Walnuts 196

Bulgur, Feta, and Olive Salad 197

Wheat Berry and Cabbage Salad 198

Fruit Salad with Wheat Berries 199

Creamy Swiss Grits 200

Polenta with Sausage and Mushrooms 201

Brown Rice Salad with Pecans 202

Cajun Dirty Rice 203

Barley Pilaf with Shrimp 205

Barley with Asparagus and Thyme 206

13   Crackers, Breads, and Muffins 207

Spiced Flax Cracker 208

Walnut Crackers 209

Parmesan Crisps with Garlic and Pepper 210

Oatmeal Flatbread Bars 211

Brie Biscuits 212

Ham and Cheddar Scones 213

Blueberry Banana Walnut Bread 214

Zucchini Apple Bread 215

Corn and Honey Muffins 216

Lemon Poppy Seed Muffins 217

Cranberry Pumpkin Seed Muffins 218

Date and Sunflower Seed Muffins 219

Part 4:   Sweet Treats 221

14   Nuts and Trail Mixes 223

Almonds with Rosemary and Cayenne 224

Orange Cashews 225

Berries with Pistachios 226

Spicy Pecan Nut Mix 227

Apricot Trail Mix 228

Peanut and Cracker Snack Mix 229

Peanut Butter Cranberry Wraps 230

High-Energy Protein Bars 231

Oats and Walnut Protein Bars 232

No-Bake Cranberry Balls 233

15   Puddings, Pies, and Cheesecakes 235

Sweet Snack Savvy 235

Bread Pudding with Chocolate and Cherries 236

Vanilla Pudding with Grilled Bananas 238

Crustless Lemon Cheesecake 239

No-Bake Chocolate Ricotta Cheesecake 240

No-Bake Cocoa Oatmeal Piecrust 242

Almond Nut Piecrust 243

Tarragon Custard 244

Berry Ginger Tofu Mousse 245

Chocolate and Espresso Mousse 246

Baked Berry Ricotta Puffs 247

Frozen Blackberry Coconut Dessert 248

Raspberry Yogurt Freezer Pops 249

16   Cookies, Brownies, Bars, and More 251

Low-Glycemic Baking 251

Oatmeal Cookies with Shaved Chocolate 253

Pecan Coffee Cookies 254

Gingerbread Drop Cookies 255

Ricotta Pistachio Cookies 256

Chocolate-Chip–Lace Cookies 257

Mint Chocolate Cookies 258

No-Bake Chocolate Chip Cookies 259

Oatmeal Raisin Cookies 260

Lemon Drop Cookies with Cornmeal 261

Coconut Pecan Cookies 262

Hazelnut Macaroons..*263*

Pine Nut Coriander Macaroons..............................*264*

Fudgy Brownies...*265*

Sweet Potato and Cinnamon Brownies....................*266*

High-Protein Chocolate Bars...................................*267*

Fruit and Nut Sticks *268*

Dried Fruit and Nut Cake *269*

Versatile Yellow Sponge Cupcakes..........................*271*

17   Delicious Drinks **273**

Apricot Tea...*274*

Raspberry Lemon Tea...*275*

Earl Grey Tea with Tarragon...................................*276*

Mexican Hot Chocolate *277*

Chocolate Raspberry Cocoa *278*

Pumpkin Holiday Nog *279*

Coconut Berry Cooler..*280*

Blackberry Cream Smoothie.....................................*281*

Green Garden Smoothie *282*

Piña Colada Smoothies *283*

Thai Ginger Smoothie *284*

Dairy-Free Chocolate Mint Shake *285*

Appendixes

A   Glossary **287**

B   Glycemic Index Values............................**301**

C   Resources **305**

Index **307**

Introduction

When you gotta snack, you gotta snack. And the good news is glycemic index snacks offer you the best results in a satisfying bite: sustained energy, delicious food that won't stretch your waistline, and high-quality healthy ingredients.

Say good-bye to your past snacking habits! Perhaps you grabbed something— anything—on the run; selected high-fat, high-starch, or high-sugar packages from a vending machine; or skipped snacks altogether, which left you fatigued and overly hungry at your next meal. With this cookbook, you can relax and eat snacks guilt-free.

The recipes in this book are designed to give you the best of eating and the best of snacking. You'll find light snacks for the times when you want vegetables, fruit, cheese, or tofu. Serve up heartier meat or legume snacks when you need long-term sustained energy. Enjoy sweet treats when your sweet tooth demands satisfaction, yet your mind reminds you to eat something healthy.

If you prefer to eat vegetarian fare, you'll find almost half of the recipes in these chapters meet your dietary preferences. Many recipes are also gluten-free and dairy-free so you can eat to meet your health needs.

The glycemic index is a time-tested way to eat healthy. You'll keep your blood sugar and insulin levels in a healthy range. This means you'll be enjoying fabulous foods while reducing inflammation, thus lessening the risk of chronic health issues. You'll be less likely to gain weight, and most likely, you'll even lose weight as you eat low-glycemic snacks.

I've taught groups about the glycemic index for more than 10 years, and I've eaten based on the glycemic index for nearly 15. I love the results in my energy levels, happy moods, and waistline. I hope you will, too!

How This Book Is Organized

This cookbook is divided into four parts:

In **Part 1, The Art of the Snack,** I discuss the health and weight-loss benefits of the glycemic index and the glycemic load. You'll use these well-researched guidelines to learn how to eat a healthy snack. All the recipes are low glycemic, with a calorie count that ranges from 100 to 300 and a glycemic load under 10. In these chapters, you also learn how to shop for and stock your pantry with low-glycemic ingredients.

Part 2, Mostly Meatless Snacks, offers you lighter-fare recipes for vegetables, salads, fruit, dips, sauces, salsas, and cheese. You'll find recipes for tofu here, too.

Part 3, Heartier Fare, gives you recipes for beef, poultry, seafood, pork, and lamb. These high-protein snacks give you long-term sustained energy. A special chapter on legumes offers you high-protein recipes that are both filling and economical. The chapter on breads and grains lets you fill your desire for starches with low-glycemic choices.

Finally, **Part 4, Sweet Treats,** presents a variety of cookies, cakes, cupcakes, custards, and puddings that will give you a sustained energy lift. You'll find recipes for trail mix and granola bars to take along on outdoor adventures. A beverage chapter helps you solve the problem of finding a refreshing beverage that tastes good and isn't filled with sugar, high-fructose corn syrup, or artificial sweeteners.

At the back of the book, I've included a glossary of the cooking terms used in this cookbook, a list of the glycemic index values and loads of carbohydrate ingredients called for in this cookbook's recipes, and resources for where to purchase some specialized ingredients online if you can't find them in your area.

Extras

I've included sidebars throughout to help guide you through using the glycemic index and attaining satisfying results with your cooking. Here's what to look for:

GLYCO-LINGO

With these definitions, you'll be glycemic index–conversant quickly!

HEALTHY NOTE

Gain information about ingredients, cooking methods, and using the glycemic index in these sidebars.

KITCHEN ALERT

Take heed of these cautions so you use only the best cooking and healthy eating techniques.

TASTY BITE

Use these tips to enhance your cooking experience and to create delectable snacks.

Acknowledgments

Many wonderful and generous people have given me support in numerous ways during the writing of this book. Thanks to Heather and Tessa Quinton for emotional and technical support; to my stepsons, Christopher and Patrick Partridge Jr., for editing assistance; and to my brilliantly supportive husband, Patrick Partridge, who managed to lend every kind of support I needed at exactly the perfect moment—from foot rubs to hiking trips to meal preparation and pep talks.

Special thanks to my positive and ever-encouraging agent, Marilyn Allen, and to my highly creative editor at Alpha Books, Paul Dinas.

Trademarks

All terms mentioned in this book that are known to be or are suspected of being trademarks or service marks have been appropriately capitalized. Alpha Books and Penguin Group (USA) Inc. cannot attest to the accuracy of this information. Use of a term in this book should not be regarded as affecting the validity of any trademark or service mark.

The Art of the Snack

Snacking is an essential part of eating. We enjoy mid-morning snacks, late-afternoon snacks, and snacks at parties and the ballpark. Now you can have your snack and eat it with pleasure and zero guilt!

Low-glycemic snacks give you the best of taste and the best of healthy eating. In Part 1, you learn more about the friendliness of the glycemic index and its companion, the glycemic load.

Looking at Snacks in a New Light

In This Chapter

- Snacking to meet your eating needs
- Snacking the glycemic index way
- Paying attention to glycemic load
- Promoting health and enjoyment

When was the last time you ate a snack? Most likely it was within the last 24 hours. Perhaps even several times today. If so, you're not alone.

Although we've heard many times from the experts that we're supposed to eat three square meals a day, few of us can manage our hunger well enough to do that. Instead, we grab a little something mid-morning, perhaps again in the late afternoon, and maybe after dinner and before bedtime.

Some folks call this grazing; others call it plain old common sense. After all, it's natural to eat when your stomach is hungry and sending you a message in the form of a hunger pang.

Successful Snacking

In a sense, this cookbook elevates the status of the snack to the importance that it deserves. After all, eating is important:

- It supplies your body with important nutrients to sustain your health.
- It gives you energy and stamina to live a full and active life.
- It gives you pleasure through your senses of taste, smell, sight, and touch.

Snacking is a major part of eating, and most people snack every day, so why not enjoy all the pleasure and nutrition you can?

By now you might be thinking, *Huh? What's so glamorous or important about grabbing a handful of potato chips for a snack?* Sure, it's easy to snack on readily available junk food. But ideally, a high-quality nutritional snack should contain low-glycemic carbs, healthy fats, and/or high-quality protein—the kind of nutrition that keeps you healthy and at your ideal size.

In reality, the snacks sold in a vending machine or in a gas station convenience store are mostly devoid of healthy nutrients. These types of snacks are high in greasy, high-glycemic, sugary starches with plenty of preservatives and mystery ingredients that can offer you negative nutrition. That kind of food may sustain life, but even that's not certain.

When the Hunger Pangs Hit

When you're between meals and your stomach signals that it needs feeding, it's time for a snack. Usually you feel a hunger pang. For most of us, the timing is predictable, such as late afternoon or mid-morning.

Your best choice for a snack is real food—the same food you'd eat for breakfast, lunch, or dinner—but in smaller amounts. Snack-size amounts.

Ideally, your snack has 100 to 300 calories. This amount of calories gives you enough fuel to keep your energy high until your next meal. It also prevents you from overeating between meals, and overeating is never a good idea.

Your snack should also be *low glycemic*. The snack shouldn't raise your blood sugar levels too fast or too high. This prevents an insulin rush and avoids weight gain, while giving you sustained, long-term energy levels and mental clarity. It should also have a *glycemic load* under 10. The amount is ideal for maintaining good health.

GLYCO-LINGO

The glycemic index is a way of measuring how much of a rise in circulating blood sugar a carbohydrate triggers, how fast a carbohydrate turns into sugar. **Glycemic load** indicates the amount of carbohydrates in a food that affects a blood sugar rise. The glycemic load includes the net amount of carbohydrates factored with the glycemic index value of the carbs. **Low glycemic** denotes a carbohydrate that does not trigger a quick rise in blood sugar levels. Instead, it's slowly digested and provides the body steady energy. High-glycemic carbohydrates trigger a quick rise in blood sugar levels and contribute to inflammation, mood swings, and weight gain.

Finally, be sure your snack offers good fats, high-quality protein, healthy carbohydrates, and fiber, or a combination of all four. Ideally, you'd get all the nutritional benefits of a complete mini-meal, or as many as possible.

Now, let's look more closely at your lifestyle needs in having a snack.

Your Snacking Preferences

You know how you like your snacks, and in this cookbook, I've included many choices so you can find something that meets your needs. Consider these lifestyle factors and determine which ones apply to you on which days:

- You need a snack you can take with you to work or on an outing.
- You have picky eaters in your family.
- Your children reject "adult" foods and prefer more simple fare.
- You don't have more than 5 to 10 minutes to prepare a snack.
- You have virtually no time to prepare a snack, but you can prepare some a few days ahead of time to eat later.
- You'd love to have recipes for more elaborate snacks to serve at parties, at potlucks, or for the soccer team.
- You don't have time to sit down and savor a snack.
- You want to prepare a "fancier" snack for guests or a social outing.
- You want to lose weight and improve your overall wellness.

For all these and other circumstances of your snacking needs, this book offers you many delicious choices.

HEALTHY NOTE

Many of the snacks in this book are nutritionally balanced, although some aren't. But they'll all give you sustainable energy levels until your next meal.

Your Food Preferences

You can make a snack from almost any ingredients. And in this cookbook, I have. You'll find chapters on vegetables, fruit, legumes, cheese, and eggs. If you want heartier fare, you'll find meat and seafood snacks. And if you have a sweet tooth that demands satisfaction, you'll find plenty of nutritious ways to satisfy it.

The sweets in the recipes don't come from ingredients that contain artificial sweeteners, either. Instead, recipes call for the sweetness of natural ingredients such as fruit, as well as the sweeteners stevia, honey, and on occasion, small amounts of table sugar.

Snack Size

Each recipe gives you a recommended serving size, and the nutritional counts in the recipes are based on the recommended serving size. How much you eat is always up to you, but to snack wisely and healthfully, eat the recommended amount of each snack or less.

I've designed each snack recipe to give you a calorie range of 100 to 300 calories per snack. In addition, each recipe is low glycemic and has a glycemic load under 10. This way, what you eat contributes to your overall health and weight control.

The Ingenious Glycemic Index

The concept of the glycemic index originated in the 1980s and has become more popular and pertinent every year since. It was first designed as a tool to help those with diabetes manage their blood sugar levels by keeping them in a healthy range. It's also the first food/health measurement tool that's been tested and verified on thousands of people.

The glycemic index measures how a specific carbohydrate food affects your blood sugar levels. The higher the value, the faster the carbohydrate raises your blood sugar. Over time, this quick rise in blood sugar has been shown to cause weight gain, insulin resistance, metabolic syndrome, general inflammation, diabetes, autoimmune disorders, allergies, arthritis, anxiety, depression, and even cancer.

High-glycemic-value carbohydrates are quickly absorbed and digested in the stomach, giving just a quick lift in blood sugar. Carbohydrates with a low-glycemic value take longer to digest and give a slow and steady rise, if any, to blood sugar levels. The latter usually contain more natural fiber, lower amounts of refined starches, and lower amounts of refined sugars than high-glycemic carbohydrates.

Here's the scale for glycemic index values:

> High: above 70
>
> Medium: 55 to 69
>
> Low: below 55

White potatoes, for example, are rated very high at 85 to 90. So eat those white and puffy Idaho spuds infrequently. If you have any of the chronic health conditions mentioned earlier, you may want to pass on white and fluffy potatoes altogether. Instead, enjoy a baked sweet potato, which has a low-glycemic index value of 46.

As a quick rule of thumb, white and fluffy starches and sugary foods are high glycemic, while vegetables and fruit are mostly low glycemic. Legumes contain slow-digesting carbohydrates and plenty of fiber, so they're low glycemic as well. Meat, fish, poultry, eggs, cheese, nuts, seeds, butter, and oils don't contain carbohydrates, so their glycemic index value is 0. In Appendix B, I give you a listing of common foods and their glycemic index value.

HEALTHY NOTE

Just because a snack is labeled "low glycemic" doesn't mean it lacks good taste or appetite satisfaction. As you glance through these recipes, you'll find delicious, mouthwatering foods you and your family will love.

Using the Glycemic Load

As research progressed on the glycemic index, it was discovered that simply eating low-glycemic carbohydrates wasn't enough to maintain healthy blood sugar levels. A person could still experience a spike in blood sugar if he or she ate too many low-glycemic carbohydrates at one time.

For example, you could whip up a smoothie with a bit of yogurt, a banana, a peach, blueberries, strawberries, and an apple. And you could feel proud for eating five fresh fruits that day with healthy yogurt. The only problem? It's heavy in carbs that turn into sugar in your body immediately.

Your body's reaction to this carb overload isn't healthy. Your blood sugar would spike, and as a result, you'd be hungry again within an hour or so—and you're likely to gain weight and experience more inflammation if you continue with this eating pattern. In other words, too many carbohydrates is still too many.

By adding the glycemic load factor, the glycemic index became more valuable. Here's the mathematical calculation for measuring the glycemic load of a food:

$$[(\text{glycemic index value}) \times (\text{grams carbohydrates} - \text{grams fiber})] \div 100$$

Let's look at the glycemic load of, for example, watermelon. Its glycemic index is pretty high, about 72. In a 120-gram serving, it has 6 grams carbohydrates available, so its glycemic load is pretty low: $72 \times 6 \div 100 = 4.32$, rounded to 4.

Your exact range varies based on your age, activity level, and size, but an ideal range of glycemic load per day is 80 to 120. If you want to lose weight, eat about 80 to 90 per day. If you're very active, you can eat at the higher range. To help you maintain your weight and enjoy your snacks without guilt, the suggested snack serving size of each recipe in this book is a glycemic load of 10 or less.

The glycemic load has emerged as the meaningful factor to keep in mind when considering low-glycemic eating.

Healthful Benefits

Eating low glycemic is becoming an important method for improving not only your waistline but also your health. Often, it's easy to eat nutritiously for breakfast, lunch, and dinner. However, it's the between-meal snacks that are a problem. After all, it's easy to overeat a snack, especially if it's junk food—either high in fat or sugar. The solution is simple. Eat high-quality food, and serve yourself a snack-size portion.

It's also easy to eat too quickly. You may be in a rush or trying to do too many things at once. As best you can, take a couple quiet minutes to enjoy your snack. You'll digest it better, and you'll feel more satisfied.

Additionally, it's easy to become less mindful and to use food to help calm you down or to cover up unpleasant emotions. Eat to satisfy stomach hunger *only*, not to avoid emotional or life concerns. You'll reap so many more benefits that way!

Eat Better for Happier Moods

It's true. You'll have happier moods if you eat low-glycemic foods. High-glycemic carbohydrates cause the body to quickly secrete high levels of the hormone insulin. Your body uses the insulin to help reduce high blood sugar levels. When this happens, your body also increases its levels of cortisol, the stress hormone. In a sense, insulin and cortisol are companion hormones and rise and ebb together. Too much cortisol leads to anxiety, depression, and mood swings. High levels of cortisol prevent you from losing weight and can actually cause you to gain weight.

The bottom line: eating white and fluffy starches and sugar-loaded foods—the high-glycemic carbohydrates—stresses you out and makes you gain weight.

You already know that you don't need any more stress in your life than you already have. So look for more happy, calm moods as you enjoy the delicious snacks featured throughout the following chapters.

Eat Better for Less Inflammation

Inflammation sounds so general, and it is. The body creates inflammation as a way to heal from injuries, and that's a good thing. But long-term inflammation—the kind that doesn't settle down and go away—causes a wide variety of chronic health conditions. Allergies, autoimmune disorders, arthritis, high blood pressure, high cholesterol, diabetes, metabolic syndrome, insulin resistance, weight gain, and even cancer are all possible with too much inflammation.

Anything you can do to reduce inflammation goes a long way toward improving virtually any health condition. Having too much of the stress hormone cortisol in your body increases inflammation. Eating low glycemic is a significant way to reduce inflammation because it helps keep cortisol levels in a healthy range.

Eat Better for a More Radiant You

Eating low glycemic as a way of life gives you more energy, higher stamina levels, and an all-around happier glow. And that's not to mention the good things it does for your hair, skin, and nails! Other benefits can include better muscle tone, better sleep, and more mental acuity.

You'll see small incremental positive changes within months, and those will extend over years.

The Least You Need to Know

- Low-glycemic snacks provide your body with steady energy to last until your next meal.
- Eat snacks that are between 100 to 300 calories and have a glycemic load of 10 or less.
- Eating low glycemic boosts your health and trims your waistline.
- Avoid mood swings and enjoy more relaxation by eating low glycemic.

The Making of Good Snacks

In This Chapter

* Starting with fresh and wholesome ingredients
* Staples for your pantry
* Storage tips

Cooking based on the glycemic index is the same as the cooking and food preparation you've always done. You'll use the same skills and techniques you already know and use. What will change are some of the staples you keep on hand in your pantry and freezer.

In this chapter, you learn what new items to keep in stock so you can cook delicious, flavorful snacks. You discover new tastes your whole family will enjoy. And you meet superb flour substitutes that let you enjoy low-glycemic baked snacks. You'll also learn how to store snacks for later, so you'll have some on hand when you're too busy to cook.

Choosing Low-Glycemic Ingredients

Take a tour of your grocery store, and you'll find specific areas that offer mostly low-glycemic ingredients. Visit the meat and fish counter, for example, and also the dairy, egg, and produce sections. Browse the health food section, too. Look for dried fruit, nuts, and whole-wheat pita bread and tortillas. Also pick up some wholesome, 100 percent stone-ground breads.

You won't need to spend much time in the sections that offer high-glycemic white and fluffy starches and sugary treats. And you'll seldom need to walk down the highly processed snack food and beverage aisles.

Fantastic Flours

Foods that contain white and finely milled wheat flour are usually high glycemic, so instead, stock up on healthful ingredients that make good flour substitutes. Most of the following are available in your local grocery or health food store, but if you can't find something locally, check online:

Coconut flour. This is simply coconut meat that's been ground into coarse flour. It's naturally sweet, low in carbohydrates, yet high in dietary fiber and protein. It offers a mild taste of coconut in baked goods, and it's especially good in cookies, cakes, and muffins. You can find it at health food stores and sometimes in the gluten-free section of the grocery store.

Oat bran. This heart-healthy soluble fiber adds texture and nutrition to baked goods. (Although the recipes in this book call for oat bran, you can substitute wheat bran or corn bran in any recipe.)

Chickpea (or garbanzo bean) flour. Made from ground chickpeas, this low-fat flour provides high fiber and high protein. It makes an excellent, neutral-tasting flour substitute. In the recipes in this book, chickpea flour is used along with other flour substitutes.

Nuts. You can make delicious flour from pecans, hazelnuts, almonds, or Brazil nuts. To make 1 cup nut flour, place $7/8$ cup nuts in a food processor. Pulse and process until the nuts turn into a flour. If you overprocess, you'll get nut butter, so watch carefully. Nuts are high in protein, are packed with healthy fats, and contain no carbohydrates, so they are zero glycemic.

Seeds. Sunflower and pumpkin seeds can be processed just like nuts are to make flour. They are zero glycemic and high in protein and healthy fats.

HEALTHY NOTE

Some health food stores sell nut and seed flours and do the processing for you. They're a bit more expensive than when you process the nuts yourself, but they save you time.

If you want to use wheat flour in the recipes, you can use coarsely ground whole-wheat flour, as in stone ground. But beware: the carbohydrate count will increase, as will the glycemic load.

Bountiful Breads

Some of the recipes in this book call for wheat-flour products and others suggest corn products. Most use low- to medium-glycemic baked products throughout. When combined with other ingredients in the recipes, the overall effect is low glycemic.

Here are some bread products you'll want to keep stocked:

Whole-wheat pita bread. Keep these on hand or in the freezer. They make great containers for sandwiches and spreads.

Whole-wheat tortillas. Use for making wraps and quesadillas. If you want, you can substitute reduced-carbohydrate tortillas, which are low glycemic.

Corn tortillas. These are naturally low glycemic. Use in place of pita bread and whole-wheat tortillas if you're gluten intolerant.

A couple recipes call for white bread or baguettes, often to maintain the authenticity of regional cooking styles, such as the recipes for po'boys.

Sugars and Sweeteners

With the ongoing controversy regarding the nutritional and health benefits and other concerns about sweeteners (they've been found to cause your body to produce insulin by making it think sugar is on the way, therefore, doing nothing to balance your insulin), I've chosen to avoid artificial sweeteners. Instead, recipes call for natural sweeteners in small amounts, such as these:

Table sugar. Small amounts of table sugar add sweetness. When combined with other ingredients, the recipes are low glycemic.

Honey. Small amounts add flavor and sweetness. Be sure you purchase 100 percent honey. Many products labeled as "honey" on the grocer's shelves are half high-fructose corn syrup and half honey. Don't buy those.

KITCHEN ALERT

We don't use agave nectar in our recipes because research on agave nectar shows some negative health results. At the time of this writing, many agave nectar products are blended with high-fructose corn syrup. High-fructose corn syrup is absorbed more quickly than regular sugar and enters your cells without any help, so avoid it as much as you can.

Molasses. Choose the depth of flavor you prefer: dark or light. If you don't like the taste of this all-natural syrup made from sugar cane, use honey instead.

Stevia. This natural herb originated in South America. We tried baking with stevia and its derivative, Truvia, but didn't like the taste in brownies and cakes. However, stevia is a great-tasting sweetener for beverages. But beware: it's very sweet, and a little goes a long way.

We generally don't use all-natural fruit juice as sweeteners in our recipes. However, some of the beverage recipes call for fruit juice blended with other ingredients.

Stocking Your Pantry

It's always helpful to have many of the ingredient staples on hand when you cook. We've made a list for you of the common staples called for in our recipes. Be sure to restock as you use up your supplies.

Staples to Keep on Hand

Here's a list of the ingredients you'll want to have stocked in your kitchen. These staples will keep in your pantry, refrigerator, or freezer for months:

- Grains like long-cooking rolled oats (not the instant kind).

- An assortment of your favorite herbal and caffeinated teas.

- Bottled organic unsweetened lemon and lime juices. Keep refrigerated after opening.

TASTY BITE

When shopping for bottled lemon and lime juices, look at your local health food store. You'll really enjoy and appreciate the pure taste of fresh lemon and lime juices in your snacks. Avoid purchasing the lemon and lime juices that contain preservatives. They distort the taste of your snack.

- Cans or packages of tuna fish.

- Canned beans. Keep a can or two of black beans, chickpeas (also known as garbanzo beans), and pinto beans. A can or jar of green beans is also good to have on hand.

- Dried beans. Choose a bag or two of your favorite mixes or a single variety.

- Cans or jars of vegetables such as diced or sliced black olives, diced green chiles, marinated artichoke hearts, whole or diced tomatoes, water chestnuts, olive tapenade, and minced garlic.

- Canned pineapple.

- Jars of peanut butter or your favorite nut butter and unsweetened fruit preserves.

- Dried fruit. Stock your pantry with raisins, cranberries, and dates. If you like, add figs and apricots.

- Nuts and seeds such as pecans, walnuts, almonds, and sunflower and pumpkin seeds.

- Chocolate chips.

- Extra-virgin olive oil.

- Vinegars.

- An assortment of spices, including ground cinnamon, salt, and black pepper.

You might already have many of these in your kitchen!

Let's Talk Herbs

While dried herbs are okay in a pinch, and we do recommend you have an assortment on hand, fresh herbs simply make foods taste better than their dry counterparts. We like the extraordinarily bright taste, but we sure don't like paying for grocery store packaged fresh herbs. To solve this problem, we grow our own!

Thank goodness it's not necessary to be a skilled gardener to grow herbs. You can grow them on a kitchen windowsill or in a flowerbed in your yard. They'll also easily grow in pots placed on a sunny porch or deck.

Here's a list of the easy-to-grow herbs called for in our recipes:

- Basil
- Cilantro
- Oregano
- Parsley
- Thyme

If you add in tarragon and sage, you'll have a wonderful spring-through-autumn supply for your snacks and other meals.

Fresh or Frozen?

Fresh fruit and vegetables are wonderful for our recipes, but you can certainly also use frozen. Frozen varieties offer good and sometimes better nutritional value than fresh. Unfortunately, this is because the soil may lack the vital nutrients needed for our health, unless you choose local or organically grown foods.

Don't Forget Dairy

Usually, our recipes call for low-fat dairy products. This keeps the saturated fat levels low, gives you great taste, and also has fewer calories. Here are a couple dairy products to keep on hand:

Butter, either salted or unsalted, adds wonderful flavor to your snacks. The recipes in this book call for real butter. Thinking of butter substitutes? Don't. Margarine or shortening are examples of trans fats or hydrogenated fats. They have been associated with weight gain, impaired metabolism, inflammation, and diabetes. It's best to avoid them.

Yogurt comes in many varieties—some healthy, some not so healthy. Many should be stocked in the dessert section because they contain sweeteners, flavorings, and preservatives. For that reason, the recipes in this book call for low-fat Greek-style yogurt. This yogurt is thick and creamy and contains active probiotics. We like it for what it doesn't contain: sweeteners, flavorings, and preservatives.

Add Parmesan cheese to your list of staples. Purchase it grated or shredded, and use it as a condiment like salt and pepper. Add a pinch to your breakfast eggs and dinner salads, and you'll really enjoy the added piquancy and flavor. It's also zero glycemic.

Add in your favorite cheeses, cottage cheese, and milk.

Equipment

The majority of the recipes in this book call for the basic kitchen equipment you might already have in your cupboards:

- Skillets

- Saucepans

- Baking dishes

- Utensils such as wooden spoons, whisks, spatulas, etc.

However, to prepare some of the recipes it would be helpful for you to have the following as well:

- Two baking sheets for cookies

- Parchment paper for lining baking dishes and cookie sheets

- Ramekins or custard cups for individual snack-size desserts

- Muffin tins and cupcake liners for baking muffins and cupcakes

- A food processor or blender

- An electric mixer, although you can mix by hand if you prefer

If you love other kitchen gadgets not listed here, feel free to use your favorites as well. Whatever makes you most comfortable and more likely to get in the kitchen!

TASTY BITE

You can get creative in packaging your snacks. Use fancy parfait glasses or simple small canning jars in place of ramekins and regular glassware.

Storing Snacks

When you prepare more servings of a snack than you and your family can eat, store the rest. How long you can store them depends on the type of snack.

If the snack contains fresh vegetables and fruit, it will hold in your refrigerator for a day or two. It probably won't freeze well. For meat and heartier snacks, you can store in the refrigerator for 3 or 4 days. You can also freeze in snack-size portions and defrost later. Store cookies and cakes in airtight containers in the pantry or refrigerator. Or freeze them in snack-size portions to enjoy later.

KITCHEN ALERT

If you aren't certain whether you should save and store a snack or not, err on the side of caution. Eat within a day, or throw it away.

The Least You Need to Know

- Use low-glycemic flour substitutes for preparing baked goods.
- Use small amounts of natural sweeteners to keep the glycemic value of a recipe low.
- Stocking flavorful condiments and specialty vegetables lets you easily prepare tasty snacks.
- Use fresh herbs, fruit, and vegetables when you can.

Mostly Meatless Snacks

When you need a light snack, look no further than Part 2. Thanks to the snacks in the following chapters, you'll gain enough energy to tide you over until your next meal, and you won't feel too full. Enjoy these snacks while you take a break to replenish your psychic, mental, and physical energy.

In Part 2, you'll find vegetable, fruit, dip, and cheese recipes that will satisfy your taste buds and nourish your body.

Versatile Vegetables

In This Chapter

- A colorful range of veggie snacks
- Sensational snack salads
- Cooked and raw vegetable bites
- Getting creative with spices and herbs

It's recommended that you get 5 to 10 servings of vegetables and fruit a day. Getting in all those veggies every day requires some menu planning creativity. If you shoot for two or three servings per meal, you'll meet your recommended intake. Or you can snack your way to your daily requirements. Even one or two servings a day can make a difference. (A serving is 1 cup raw vegetables or $\frac{1}{2}$ cup cooked.)

Vegetables are the perfect low-glycemic food. On the glycemic index scale of 0 to 100, with 0 to 55 being low, 56 to 69 being medium, and above 70 being high, virtually all vegetables are in the low category. The vegetables called for in this chapter range from 10 to 44, so you can be sure you'll benefit nutritionally from these recipes.

And as you'll find when you prepare these recipes, eating your vegetables will be far from boring. You'll look forward to your next veggie snack!

Pick the Best Vegetables

In the salad recipes, use fresh vegetables unless otherwise noted. In the cooked recipes, you can use either fresh or frozen. Often the frozen vegetables contain more vitamins and antioxidants because they were picked and processed at the height of ripeness. Fresh vegetables from the grocery store may have been harvested a week or two before you purchase them due to shipping and stocking time. If you want to eat the freshest produce possible, grow your own vegetables in the garden or shop at your local farmers' market during the summer and autumn months.

Canned vegetables, such as corn, olives, and chiles, retain their flavor well. Most other vegetables, like green beans and asparagus, lose their crispness and oomph when canned.

> **KITCHEN ALERT**
>
> White potatoes—the large ones used for baked potatoes—are high glycemic. To enjoy the taste and texture of potatoes without the high glycemic numbers, use sweet potatoes or red new potatoes in these recipes instead.

When you don't have time to prepare a vegetable snack, cut-up raw vegetables such as carrots, celery, radishes, sugar snap peas, jicama, broccoli, or cauliflower are handy to have in the crisper. If you want to add a bit more flavor, dip them—*sparingly*—into a small bowl of your favorite bottled salad dressing.

Avocado Cups

Creamy avocado is dressed with a tangy ranch dressing.

Snack servings:	Yield:	Prep time:	Serving size:
2	2 avocado cups	5 minutes	1 avocado cup
Each serving has:			
211 calories	2g protein	10g carbohydrates	7g fiber
20g fat	3g saturated fat	glycemic index: low	glycemic load: 1

1 avocado, cut in ½ and pitted (skin on)

2 TB. ranch-style salad dressing

1. Into each depression in each avocado ½, spoon 1 tablespoon ranch salad dressing.

2. Serve immediately.

Variation: Substitute your favorite salad dressing for the ranch. Try vinaigrette, blue cheese, Italian, and honey mustard.

Asian Vegetables with Peanuts

An Asian-style dressing with wasabi and ginger spices up coleslaw topped with peanuts.

Snack servings: 4	Yield: 4 cups	Prep time: 5 minutes	Serving size: 1 cup
Each serving has:			
180 calories	6g protein	8g carbohydrates	4g fiber
15g fat	2g saturated fat	glycemic index: low	glycemic load: 1

2 TB. cider vinegar

1 TB. sesame oil

2 TB. low-fat mayonnaise

1 tsp. fresh ginger, grated

2 tsp. wasabi paste

$\frac{1}{4}$ tsp. salt

$\frac{1}{8}$ tsp. ground black pepper

1 (16-oz.) pkg. shredded coleslaw mix

$\frac{1}{2}$ cup fresh cilantro, chopped

$\frac{1}{4}$ cup green onions, white and green parts, chopped

$\frac{1}{2}$ cup unsalted peanuts

1. In a large bowl, whisk together cider vinegar, sesame oil, mayonnaise, ginger, wasabi paste, salt, and pepper.

2. Add coleslaw mix, cilantro, and green onions, and toss.

3. Stir in peanuts just before serving.

TASTY BITE

If the taste of cilantro doesn't appeal to you, substitute an equal amount of fresh parsley instead.

Cabbage Pecan Slaw

Mellow roasted garlic, pecans, and parsley spice up apples and cabbage.

Snack servings:	Yield:	Prep time:	Cook time:	Serving size:
6	6 cups	15 minutes	30 minutes	1 cup

Each serving has:			
123 calories	1g protein	12g carbohydrates	3g fiber
9g fat	1g saturated fat	glycemic index: low	glycemic load: 3

2 large cloves garlic, unpeeled

2 TB. extra-virgin olive oil, plus 1 tsp. for drizzling

2 TB. water

2 TB. lemon juice

⅛ tsp. salt

⅛ tsp. ground black pepper

3 medium apples, your choice variety, cored and cut into thin strips (skin on)

2 cups green cabbage (about ½ head), very thinly sliced

⅓ cup pecans, toasted and chopped

3 TB. fresh parsley, chopped

1. Preheat the oven to 400°F.

2. Place garlic on a piece of aluminum foil, drizzle with 1 teaspoon extra-virgin olive oil, and wrap it up. Bake for about 30 minutes or until tender. Let cool slightly. Squeeze roasted garlic from its skin, and mash with a fork.

3. In a medium bowl, whisk together water, mashed garlic, lemon juice, remaining 2 tablespoons extra-virgin olive oil, salt, and pepper.

4. In a medium bowl, toss apples, green cabbage, pecans, and parsley. Add dressing, and toss well. Serve chilled.

HEALTHY NOTE

Roasting the garlic brings out its sweetness while diminishing some of its bite.

Blue Cheese Iceberg Salad

Crumbled bacon and Worcestershire sauce add flavor to this blue cheese–topped salad.

Snack servings:	Yield:	Prep time:	Cook time:	Serving size:
6	about 6 cups	10 minutes	5 minutes	about 1 cup

Each serving has:			
203 calories	8g protein	9g carbohydrates	2g fiber
14g fat	4g saturated fat	glycemic index: low	glycemic load: 1

½ cup low-fat mayonnaise

2 TB. ketchup

1 TB. prepared horseradish

1 or 2 dashes Worcestershire sauce

4 strips thick bacon

1 medium head iceberg lettuce, chopped in 1½-in. pieces

6 cherry tomatoes, halved

4 green onions, thinly sliced

¼ cup crumbled blue cheese

⅛ tsp. ground black pepper

1. In a small bowl, whisk together mayonnaise, ketchup, horseradish, and Worcestershire sauce until smooth.

2. In a large skillet over medium heat, add bacon. Cook for 5 to 10 minutes or until crisp. Using a slotted spoon, transfer bacon to a paper towel–lined plate. Drain bacon well and cut into 1-inch pieces.

3. In a serving bowl, toss lettuce with dressing, and top with cherry tomatoes and green onions. Sprinkle with bacon and blue cheese, season with pepper, and serve.

Variation: If you want to lower the fat content in this recipe, substitute soy-based bacon bits for the bacon.

Tomato, Basil, and Mozzarella Salad

Basil and garlic lend a Mediterranean twist to this fresh salad that tastes like it's straight from the garden.

Snack servings:	Yield:	Prep time:	Serving size:
6	5 cups	10 minutes	⅚ cup

Each serving has:			
154 calories	6g protein	4g carbohydrates	1g fiber
13g fat	5g saturated fat	glycemic index: low	glycemic load: 0

2 cups fresh parsley sprigs, lightly packed and coarsely chopped

2 cups Roma tomatoes (about 3 medium), chopped

1 cup low-fat mozzarella cheese, diced

2 TB. fresh basil, snipped

3 TB. balsamic vinegar

3 TB. extra-virgin olive oil

1½ tsp. minced garlic

⅛ tsp. salt

⅛ tsp. ground black pepper

1. In a large bowl, combine parsley, tomatoes, mozzarella cheese, and basil.

2. In a small bowl, combine balsamic vinegar, extra-virgin olive oil, garlic, salt, and pepper.

3. Pour dressing over salad, toss gently, and serve.

TASTY BITE

Instead of peeling and mincing garlic yourself, you can buy jars of minced garlic in the produce section of your grocery store. This saves preparation time and eliminates garlic-smelling hands.

Cucumber, Bell Pepper, and Jicama Salad

This fresh and crisp salad offers colorful vegetables dressed with lime vinaigrette.

Snack servings:	Yield:	Prep time:	Serving size:
6	about 6 cups	10 minutes	about 1 cup
Each serving has:			
71 calories	1g protein	7g carbohydrates	3g fiber
5g fat	1g saturated fat	glycemic index: low	glycemic load: 0

2 cups jicama (about ½ large), julienned

2 cups cabbage (about ½ large head), shredded

1½ cups cucumber (about 2 medium), julienned

¼ cup red onion (about ¼ medium), thinly sliced

1 cup red bell pepper (about 1 large), julienned

1 TB. fresh cilantro, finely minced

¼ cup lime juice or juice of 2 limes

2 TB. extra-virgin olive oil

⅛ tsp. salt

⅛ tsp. ground black pepper

1. In a large bowl, toss together jicama, cabbage, cucumber, red onion, red bell pepper, and cilantro.

2. In a small bowl, whisk together lime juice, extra-virgin olive oil, salt, and pepper.

3. Add lime juice mixture to cabbage mixture, and toss. Serve chilled.

TASTY BITE

If you or your family can't eat all three servings at once, you can half this recipe. Or make the full recipe and dress only the portions you'll eat for a snack. The undressed salad and remaining dressing will keep in the refrigerator for 3 or 4 days.

Corn, Red Pepper, and Monterey Jack Salad

Corn, celery, and red bell pepper are lightly spiced with jalapeño pepper cheese.

Snack servings:	Yield:	Prep time:	Serving size:
4	4 cups	10 minutes	1 cup

Each serving has:			
154 calories	8g protein	19g carbohydrates	3g fiber
6g fat	2g saturated fat	glycemic index: low	glycemic load: 0

2 cups corn, thawed if frozen

1 cup celery, diced

⅓ cup red bell pepper, finely chopped

¾ cup Monterey Jack cheese with jalapeño peppers, cut into ¼-in. cubes

3 TB. bottled vinaigrette salad dressing

2 TB. fresh parsley, snipped

1. In a large bowl, combine corn, celery, red bell pepper, and Monterey Jack cheese.

2. Add salad dressing, and toss. Stir in parsley before serving.

HEALTHY NOTE

The corn and cheese in this recipe offer plenty of stomach satisfaction and high-quality energy.

Broccoli Salad with Blue Cheese

Broccoli is dressed up with crunchy sunflower seeds and the sweet tastes of apple and raisins and then tossed with a blue cheese dressing.

Snack servings:	Yield:	Prep time:	Serving size:
5	4 cups	10 minutes	¾ cup

Each serving has:			
118 calories	3g protein	14g carbohydrates	2g fiber
6g fat	2g saturated fat	glycemic index: low	glycemic load: 7

2 TB. crumbled blue cheese

3 TB. low-fat mayonnaise

3 TB. low-fat sour cream

1 tsp. honey

2 tsp. lemon juice

½ tsp. ground black pepper

2 cups fresh broccoli, chopped

1 medium apple, your choice variety, chopped (skin on)

2 TB. raisins

¼ cup roasted sunflower seeds

1. In a large bowl, whisk together blue cheese, mayonnaise, sour cream, honey, lemon juice, and pepper.

2. Add broccoli, apple, and raisins, and toss.

3. Stir in sunflower seeds just before serving.

HEALTHY NOTE

This lower-fat version of a traditional broccoli salad is pepped up with a small amount of blue cheese crumbles.

Green Bean and Almond Salad

You'll enjoy these crunchy vegetables flavored with parsley, radishes, almonds, and lime vinaigrette.

Snack servings:	Yield:	Prep time:	Cook time:	Serving size:
4	4 cups	10 minutes	5 minutes	1 cup

Each serving has:			
126 calories	3g protein	9g carbohydrates	4g fiber
10g fat	1g saturated fat	glycemic index: low	glycemic load: 1

3 cups fresh green beans, trimmed	2 TB. extra-virgin olive oil
2 TB. water	2 TB. lime juice
⅓ cup fresh parsley, coarsely chopped	⅛ tsp. salt
4 radishes, chopped	⅛ tsp. ground black pepper
2 large stalks celery, chopped	¼ cup almonds, slivered

1. In a 2-quart microwave-safe bowl, combine green beans and water. Cover, and microwave on high for 5 minutes or until barely tender, stirring once. Drain, and transfer to a serving dish.

2. To beans, add parsley, radishes, and celery. Add extra-virgin olive oil and lime juice, and toss. Cover, and let stand at room temperature for up to 30 minutes.

3. To serve, sprinkle with salt, pepper, and almonds.

Variation: If radishes aren't your thing, substitute 1 green onion, chopped.

Southwestern Salad

This hearty salad features black beans and the delicious flavors of cayenne and cumin.

Snack servings:	Yield:	Prep time:	Serving size:
10	about 5 cups	15 minutes	½ cup
Each serving has:			
175 calories	10g protein	31g carbohydrates	7g fiber
2g fat	0g saturated fat	glycemic index: low	glycemic load: 10

1 (15-oz.) can black beans, drained and rinsed

1 medium jalapeño pepper, seeded and finely chopped

1 (15-oz.) can corn, drained

¼ cup red onion, chopped

½ cup red bell pepper, chopped

½ cup celery, chopped

1 TB. lime juice

1 TB. extra-virgin olive oil

½ tsp. cayenne

1 tsp. ground cumin

Pinch salt

1. In a large bowl, mix together black beans, jalapeño pepper, corn, red onion, red bell pepper, and celery.

2. In a small bowl, stir together lime juice, extra-virgin olive oil, cayenne, cumin, and salt. Drizzle lime mixture over bean mixture and toss. Serve chilled.

HEALTHY NOTE

The beans add to this recipe's glycemic load, but don't worry. Beans offer superb nutrition with plenty of fiber and vegetable protein. Plus they taste wonderful. This snack gives you quick energy and will stave off hunger for hours.

Shoestring Carrot Patties

Carrots taste sweet with a slight bite of spice in these pan-fried cakes.

Snack servings:	Yield:	Prep time:	Cook time:	Serving size:
6	6 patties	15 minutes	10 minutes	1 patty

Each serving has:			
186 calories	6g protein	25g carbohydrates	5g fiber
8g fat	2g saturated fat	glycemic index: low	glycemic load: 10

10 cups carrots, grated or shredded	¼ tsp. salt
¼ cup whole-wheat flour	¾ tsp. cayenne
4 large eggs	½ tsp. ground black pepper
1 TB. honey	2 TB. extra-virgin olive oil

1. In a medium bowl, combine carrots, whole-wheat flour, eggs, honey, salt, cayenne, and pepper. Mix well.

2. Form mixture into 6 patties.

3. In a skillet over medium-high heat, heat extra-virgin olive oil. Add patties (you might have to do this in batches), and cook 3 or 4 minutes per side or until golden brown.

HEALTHY NOTE

To lower the carbohydrate count and the glycemic load in this recipe, substitute coconut flour or chickpea flour for the whole-wheat flour.

Chili Sweet Potato Fries

Sweet potatoes deliver crunch with a salty, chili taste for a satisfying snack.

Snack servings:	Yield:	Prep time:	Cook time:	Serving size:
4	3 potatoes	10 minutes	50 to 60 minutes	¾ potato

Each serving has:			
146 calories	3g protein	26g carbohydrates	5g fiber
4g fat	1g saturated fat	glycemic index: low	glycemic load: 8

3 medium sweet potatoes, cut into
   1-in. strips (skin on)
1 TB. extra-virgin olive oil

1 TB. chili powder
¼ tsp. salt

1. Preheat the oven to 425°F.

2. In a large mixing bowl, combine potatoes, extra-virgin olive oil, chili powder, and salt. Gently toss until fries are evenly coated.

3. Spread out fries in a single layer on a rimmed baking sheet. Bake for 25 to 30 minutes, or until crispy on one side.

4. Turn fries using tongs or spatula, and cook for 25 to 30 more minutes or until golden brown.

HEALTHY NOTE

No one will miss regular french fries after they taste these delectable oven fries. They offer satisfying taste—with less fat, too!

Twice-Baked Sweet Potatoes

The sweetness of these potatoes is enhanced with honey, raisins, and cinnamon to satisfy your sweet cravings.

Snack servings:	Yield:	Prep time:	Cook time:	Serving size:
4	4 halves	10 minutes plus 10 minutes cool time	30 to 35 minutes	½ potato

Each serving has:			
177 calories	4g protein	25g carbohydrates	3g fiber
8g fat	2g saturated fat	glycemic index: low	glycemic load: 9

2 medium (10-oz.) sweet potatoes	¼ tsp. ground cinnamon
1 TB. honey	⅛ tsp. salt
¼ cup raisins	¼ cup walnut pieces
1 TB. butter, softened	

1. Preheat the oven to 350°F.

2. Scrub sweet potatoes, and pierce all over with a fork. Wrap each potato in a paper towel to help absorb moisture. Microwave on high for 6 to 9 minutes or until cooked throughout when pierced with a fork. Cool for 10 minutes.

3. Cut each potato in ½ lengthwise. Using a spoon, scoop pulp from each potato ½, leaving a ¼- to ½-inch shell. Place pulp in a medium bowl, and set aside shells.

4. Using a fork, mash potato pulp. Stir in honey, raisins, butter, ground cinnamon, and salt. Spoon potato mixture back into each shell. Place, filled sides up, in a large baking pan. Sprinkle with walnut pieces.

5. Bake for 20 to 25 minutes or until heated throughout.

Variation: Use molasses in place of the honey if you like that dark, aromatic flavor.

Baked Sweet Potato Skins

Savory flavors of garlic, bacon, and cheese give you the classic taste of potato skins with the low-glycemic advantage.

Snack servings:	Yield:	Prep time:	Cook time:	Serving size:
4	16 skins	10 minutes	80 minutes	4 skins

Each serving has:			
213 calories	9g protein	14g carbohydrates	2g fiber
14g fat	3g saturated fat	glycemic index: low	glycemic load: 5

4 medium sweet potatoes

2 TB. extra-virgin olive oil

1 tsp. garlic salt

$\frac{1}{2}$ tsp. chili powder

3 slices bacon, cooked crisp and crumbled

2 TB. green onions, thinly sliced

$\frac{1}{3}$ cup low-fat cheddar cheese, shredded

1. Preheat the oven to 350°F.

2. Place potatoes directly on the middle oven rack, and bake for 50 to 60 minutes or until tender.

3. When cool enough to handle, cut potatoes in quarters lengthwise. With a spoon, scoop pulp from skins, leaving $\frac{1}{4}$-inch-thick shells. Brush inside of shells with extra-virgin olive oil, and sprinkle with garlic salt and chili powder. (Skins may be refrigerated at this point for baking later.)

4. Increase the oven temperature to 450°F.

5. Place potatoes skin side down on 2 rimmed baking sheets. Bake for 15 to 20 minutes or until potatoes are hot and edges are crisp.

6. Remove from the oven, and sprinkle with bacon, green onions, and cheddar cheese. Bake for 5 more minutes or until cheese melts. Serve while hot.

Variation: Sprinkle 1 or 2 tablespoons of your favorite fresh herb, chopped, on the skins. Parsley, oregano, basil, cilantro, rosemary, or sage are all good options.

Honey-Baked Acorn Squash

The sweet taste of this acorn squash is enhanced with honey, cinnamon, and nutmeg.

Snack servings:	Yield:	Prep time:	Cook time:	Serving size:
4	1 squash	10 minutes	30 to 35 minutes	¼ squash

Each serving has:			
132 calories	2g protein	28g carbohydrates	3g fiber
3g fat	2g saturated fat	glycemic index: low	glycemic load: 9

1 (2-lb.) acorn squash	¼ tsp. ground cinnamon
1 TB. butter, melted	⅛ tsp. ground nutmeg
1 TB. honey	¼ tsp. ground black pepper

1. Preheat the oven to 450°F.

2. Wash squash and cut in half lengthwise. Remove and discard seeds. Place squash on an aluminum foil–lined jelly-roll pan.

3. In a medium bowl, stir together butter, honey, ground cinnamon, and ground nutmeg until blended. Brush squash evenly with butter mixture, and sprinkle with pepper.

4. Bake for 30 to 35 minutes or until tender. Serve warm. You can eat the skin, too!

Variation: You can also use spaghetti squash or butternut squash for this recipe. Or sprinkle the squash with ¼ cup chopped pecans after 20 minutes of baking.

Asian Cakes with Cabbage

These vegetable cakes are flavored with soy sauce, sesame oil, and ginger and served on a bed of coleslaw mix with Asian dressing.

Snack servings:	Yield:	Prep time:	Cook time:	Serving size:
6	12 cakes, 6 cups salad	10 minutes	20 minutes	2 cakes, 1 cup salad

Each serving has:			
180 calories	9g protein	23g carbohydrates	5g fiber
7g fat	3g saturated fat	glycemic index: low	glycemic load: 9

1 (14.1-oz.) can split pea soup	2 TB. toasted sesame oil
2 large eggs	2 tsp. low-sodium soy sauce
½ cup cornmeal	2 tsp. fresh ginger, grated
1 cup sugar snap peas, coarsely chopped	1 (16-oz.) bag coleslaw mix
2 cups carrots, *julienned* or grated	¼ cup bottled low-fat Asian dressing
1 cup green onions, chopped	

1. In a medium bowl, whisk together split pea soup and eggs. Stir in cornmeal, and add sugar snap peas, 1 cup carrots, ½ cup green onions, sesame oil, soy sauce, and ginger.

2. In another medium bowl, toss together coleslaw mix, remaining 1 cup carrots, and remaining ½ cup green onions. Toss with Asian dressing.

3. Heat a skillet coated with cooking spray over medium heat. Scoop pea mixture into the skillet in ¼-cup dollops, and cook for 5 minutes or until golden on one side. Flip, and cook for 5 more minutes. Transfer to a plate, and repeat with remaining pea mixture until you have 12 cakes.

4. Divide cabbage mixture among 6 plates. Top each plate with 2 cakes, and serve.

Variation: You could also serve alone without the coleslaw bed, tuck into a whole-wheat pita half, or serve wrapped in a lettuce leaf.

GLYCO-LINGO

To **julienne** a food means to slice it into very thin pieces.

Spaghetti Squash with Spinach

Here, spaghetti squash strands are tossed with a garlic-spinach sauce and topped with pine nuts.

Snack servings:	Yield:	Prep time:	Cook time:	Serving size:
4	about 3 cups	10 minutes	50 to 60 minutes	¾ cup

Each serving has:			
112 calories	4g protein	15g carbohydrates	2g fiber
6g fat	1g saturated fat	glycemic index: low	glycemic load: 5

½ (3-lb.) spaghetti squash, seeds scooped out (save remaining ½ for later use)

1 TB. extra-virgin olive oil

2 tsp. minced garlic

⅓ cup low-sodium vegetable broth, chicken broth, or water

⅛ tsp. salt

Pinch crushed red pepper flakes (optional)

1 (10-oz.) bag spinach

1½ tsp. pine nuts, toasted

1. Preheat the oven to 375°F. Coat a rimmed baking sheet with cooking spray.

2. Place squash, flesh side down, on the baking sheet, and bake for 50 to 60 minutes or until squash is easily pierced with a fork.

3. When squash is about 10 minutes from being done, place ½ tablespoon extra-virgin olive oil in a large skillet over medium heat. Add garlic, and sauté for 1 minute. Stir in vegetable broth, salt, and crushed red pepper flakes (if using). Add spinach, a handful at a time, and cook, stirring, until wilted. Cover to keep warm.

4. When squash is cooked, use a fork to separate strands into a medium bowl. Add remaining ½ tablespoon extra-virgin olive oil and toss gently.

5. Transfer "spaghetti" to plates or a platter, top with spinach mixture, garnish with pine nuts, and serve.

Variation: You can also sprinkle 1 tablespoon chopped fresh basil, oregano, or rosemary on top of each serving.

Portobellos with Pepperoni and Walnuts

Basil pesto and pepperoni flavor these Mediterranean-inspired stuffed mushrooms.

Snack servings:	Yield:	Prep time:	Cook time:	Serving size:
6	6 stuffed mushrooms	10 minutes	4 to 6 minutes	1 stuffed mushroom

Each serving has:			
105 calories	7g protein	3g carbohydrates	1g fiber
8g fat	2g saturated fat	glycemic index: low	glycemic load: 0

6 large portobello mushrooms (each about 4½-in. in diameter)

¼ cup purchased basil pesto

¾ cup bottled roasted red sweet pepper, cut into strips

1½ oz. sliced pepperoni, coarsely chopped

⅓ cup walnuts, chopped

⅛ to ¼ tsp. crushed red pepper flakes

½ cup low-fat Italian cheese blend or Parmesan cheese, shredded

1. Preheat the broiler to low.

2. Place portobello mushrooms, gill side up, in a 15×10-inch baking pan. Broil 3 or 4 inches from the heat for 4 minutes.

3. Meanwhile, in a medium bowl, combine basil pesto, roasted red sweet pepper, pepperoni, walnuts, and crushed red pepper flakes.

4. Divide pesto mixture evenly on top of mushrooms. Sprinkle with cheese.

5. Return mushrooms to the oven, and broil for 1 or 2 more minutes or until heated through and cheese is bubbly.

HEALTHY NOTE

It's amazing that these terrifically delicious stuffed mushrooms have no glycemic load. Enjoy a serving with confidence.

More-Than-Miso Soup

Miso soup with tofu and green onions offers a distinctively soothing taste while being filling and warm—great for a chilly day.

Snack servings:	Yield:	Prep time:	Cook time:	Serving size:
2	2 cups	3 minutes	5 minutes	1 cup

Each serving has:			
37 calories	3g protein	4g carbohydrates	1g fiber
1g fat	0g saturated fat	glycemic index: low	glycemic load: 0

2 cups water

1½ TB. miso paste

1 oz. firm tofu (about ¼ cup), diced

2 TB. green onions, diced

1. In a bowl or glass pitcher, microwave water on high for about 5 minutes or until boiling. Remove from the microwave, and whisk in miso paste.

2. Add tofu and green onions, and serve in large cups.

Variation: To enhance the Asian taste, add 1 teaspoon tahini and ½ teaspoon ground ginger. Or for an earthy, nutty kick, add 1 tablespoon marinara sauce.

Vegetable Curry

These vegetables cooked with Indian spices are a bowlful of summer's bounty.

Snack servings:	Yield:	Prep time:	Cook time:	Serving size:
4	4 servings	15 minutes	15 minutes	¼ recipe

Each serving has:			
146 calories	6g protein	22g carbohydrates	6g fiber
2g fat	0g saturated fat	glycemic index: low	glycemic load: 2

1 TB. extra-virgin olive oil	4 tsp. minced garlic
1 small yellow onion, finely diced	1 TB. curry powder
1 medium eggplant, cut into 1-in. cubes (skin on)	1 tsp. cumin
1 zucchini, cubed small (skin on)	2 tsp. ground coriander
2 medium carrots, sliced	½ cup water
1 bunch Swiss chard, woody stems discarded and leaves torn into big pieces	¼ tsp. salt
	¼ tsp. ground black pepper
¾ lb. plum tomatoes (about 2), diced	1 cup low-fat Greek-style yogurt

1. In a large, high-sided sauté pan or saucepan over medium-high heat, heat extra-virgin olive oil. Add onion, eggplant, zucchini, and carrots, and sauté for 10 minutes or until vegetables are soft.

2. Add Swiss chard, plum tomatoes, and garlic, and sauté for 5 more minutes. Add curry powder, cumin, 1 teaspoon coriander, and water. Bring mixture to a boil, reduce heat to medium-low, cover, and simmer for 10 minutes or until vegetables are cooked. Season with salt and pepper.

3. In a small bowl, mix together yogurt with remaining 1 teaspoon coriander. Cover and refrigerate until ready to use.

4. Ladle hot vegetable curry into bowls.

HEALTHY NOTE

With this stew, you can enjoy three or four servings of vegetables along with an exotic curry taste.

Creamy Caraway Potato Salad

Caraway, dill pickles, and eggs flavor this delicious potato salad.

Snack servings:	Yield:	Prep time:	Cook time:	Serving size:
12	6 cups	15 minutes	15 to 20 minutes	about ½ cup

Each serving has:			
169 calories	5g protein	18g carbohydrates	2g fiber
9g fat	1g saturated fat	glycemic index: low	glycemic load: 8

2½ lb. small red new potatoes (about 10), unpeeled

1 medium onion, chopped

1 tsp. minced garlic

5 large hard-boiled eggs, peeled and chopped

1 cup dill pickles, chopped

1 cup low-fat mayonnaise

3 TB. brine from pickles

½ tsp. celery seed

½ tsp. caraway seed

¼ tsp. ground black pepper

½ tsp. salt

1. Place potatoes in a large pot of lightly salted water. Set over medium-high heat, and bring to a boil. Boil for 15 to 20 minutes or until potatoes are tender. Drain well.

2. Cut potatoes in half or quarters. In a large bowl, gently combine potatoes, onion, garlic, hard-boiled eggs, and pickles.

3. In a small bowl, whisk together mayonnaise, brine, celery seed, caraway seed, pepper, and salt. Spoon mayo mixture into potato mixture, and stir gently.

4. Cover and refrigerate for 4 hours or overnight. Store extra snack servings in the refrigerator for up to 6 days.

KITCHEN ALERT

Be sure to use red new potatoes or a similar boiling-type potato for this recipe. Using a baking-type potato, such as an Idaho spud, significantly increases the glycemic index value and glycemic load.

Thai Vegetable Rolls

Here, rice noodles, apple, and vegetables are wrapped in lettuce leaves and topped with a sweet and spicy sesame sauce.

Snack servings:	Yield:	Prep time:	Cook time:	Serving size:
5	10 rolls	15 minutes	8 minutes	2 rolls

Each serving has:			
95 calories	1g protein	23g carbohydrates	2g fiber
0g fat	0g saturated fat	glycemic index: low	glycemic load: 10

3½ oz. thin dried rice noodles (also called rice vermicelli)

10 large red or green lettuce leaves

½ cup cucumber, finely diced

1 large carrot, finely diced

1 medium Granny Smith apple, finely diced

¼ cup fresh mint leaves

¼ cup fresh cilantro leaves

1 batch Sweet and Spicy Sesame Sauce (recipe in Chapter 5) or your favorite peanut sauce

1. Place rice noodles in a large bowl, and cover with just-boiling water. Let noodles sit for 5 to 8 minutes or until tender.

2. Drain noodles, and rinse with cold water. Spread noodles on a kitchen towel–lined baking sheet, and pat dry.

3. Divide noodles into 2 long cylindrical logs, and cut with scissors to total 10 equal portions.

4. Arrange lettuce leaves on your work surface. Mound 1 portion of noodles on top of lettuce followed by about ¹⁄₁₀ of cucumber, carrot, and apple slices. Top with about 3 mint leaves and 4 cilantro leaves.

5. Fold lettuce leaves over filling, and secure with toothpicks. Serve with Sweet and Spicy Sesame Sauce (recipe in Chapter 5) or your favorite peanut sauce or dressing.

HEALTHY NOTE

To lower the glycemic load of this recipe to 1, substitute bean sprouts for the rice vermicelli.

Fennel, Apricot, and Carrot Wraps

These creamy wraps are flavored with the gentle taste of fennel and the sweetness of apricots and carrots.

Snack servings: 5	Yield: 10 wraps	Prep time: 15 minutes	Serving size: 2 wraps
Each serving has:			
121 calories	2g protein	14g carbohydrates	3g fiber
8g fat	1g saturated fat	glycemic index: low	glycemic load: 3

1 small head red cabbage, shredded (about 6 cups)	3 TB. apple cider vinegar
2 medium bulbs fennel, cored and julienned	¾ cup low-fat mayonnaise
3 large carrots, grated	2 TB. prepared horseradish
½ cup dried apricots, chopped	⅛ tsp. salt
	10 large lettuce leaves

1. In a large bowl, combine cabbage, fennel, carrots, and apricots. Stir in apple cider vinegar, mayonnaise, horseradish, and salt.

2. Place about ½ cup salad on each lettuce leaf. Roll lettuce into a wrap, and serve.

HEALTHY NOTE

Lettuce leaves are the perfect low-glycemic wrap. They have a glycemic index value of 0 and add crunch and convenience.

Greek Salad Wraps

Greek yogurt coupled with mint and oregano lends a creamy and tart taste to these vegetable snacks.

Snack servings:	Yield:	Prep time:	Serving size:
6	3 tortillas	15 minutes	$\frac{1}{2}$ tortilla

Each serving has:			
128 calories	6g protein	21g carbohydrates	3g fiber
2g fat	0g saturated fat	glycemic index: low	glycemic load: 6

1 cup low-fat Greek-style yogurt

1 TB. fresh mint, chopped, or 1 tsp. dried

1 TB. fresh oregano, chopped, or 1 tsp. dried

$\frac{1}{4}$ tsp. salt

$1\frac{1}{2}$ cups carrots, shredded

$1\frac{1}{2}$ cups cucumber, diced

$\frac{1}{2}$ cup green peas, cooked

3 (10-in.) whole-wheat tortillas

2 medium plum tomatoes, halved and thinly sliced

1. In a medium bowl, combine yogurt, mint, oregano, and salt. Add carrots, cucumber, and peas.

2. Spoon $\frac{1}{3}$ of yogurt-vegetable mixture on each tortilla. Top with tomato slices, roll, and secure with toothpicks. Cut each tortilla in $\frac{1}{2}$ before serving.

Variation: To add more protein, substitute edamame for the green peas.

Broccoli and Corn Wraps

You'll love the crunchy texture and Asian flavor of these wraps.

Snack servings:	Yield:	Prep time:	Serving size:
4	4 cups	10 minutes	1 wrap

Each serving has:			
133 calories	6g protein	13g carbohydrates	2g fiber
8g fat	1g saturated fat	glycemic index: low	glycemic load: 3

4 romaine lettuce leaves

2 cups bean sprouts

2 green onions, sliced

2 stalks celery, cut into strips

½ cup corn kernels

¼ cup cooked or raw broccoli, chopped

2 TB. fresh cilantro, chopped

¼ cup bottled Asian-flavor salad dressing or Sweet and Spicy Sesame Sauce (recipe in Chapter 5)

2 TB. unsalted peanuts, chopped

1. Wash and trim lettuce, and arrange leaves on 4 individual serving plates.

2. In a medium bowl, combine bean sprouts, onions, celery, corn, broccoli, and cilantro. Add salad dressing, and toss.

3. Divide vegetable mixture evenly among lettuce leaves, and top each with ½ tablespoon peanuts. Serve at once.

Eggplant Feta Rolls

Black olive paste and feta cheese flavor these Greek-inspired rolls.

Snack servings:	Yield:	Prep time:	Cook time:	Serving size:
3	1 eggplant	5 minutes	20 minutes	⅓ recipe

Each serving has:			
106 calories	2g protein	6g carbohydrates	3g fiber
9g fat	2g saturated fat	glycemic index: low	glycemic load: 1

1 medium eggplant

2 TB. extra-virgin olive oil

⅛ tsp. ground black pepper

½ cup prepared black olive paste or tapenade

¼ cup feta cheese, crumbled

1. Preheat the oven to 425°F.

2. Cut eggplant into ½-inch vertical slices, and place on a large cookie sheet. Brush with extra-virgin olive oil, and sprinkle with pepper. Roast eggplant for 20 minutes or until tender. Cool.

3. Spread each slice with black olive paste, and sprinkle with feta cheese. Roll up and secure with toothpicks. Serve warm or at room temperature.

TASTY BITE

You can make these wraps ahead of time, store them in the refrigerator, and reheat them in the oven or microwave before serving.

Portobello Mushroom Pitas

Grilled portobello mushrooms have a meaty flavor that's enhanced by red onion.

Snack servings:	Yield:	Prep time:	Cook time:	Serving size:
4	2 pitas	10 minutes	12 minutes	½ pita

Each serving has:			
168 calories	5g protein	26g carbohydrates	4g fiber
6g fat	1g saturated fat	glycemic index: low	glycemic load: 11

4 large portobello mushroom caps

1 large red bell pepper, ribs and seeds removed, and quartered

1 (4½-in.) red onion, cut into thick slices

Cooking spray

2 TB. reduced-fat Italian dressing

2 TB. low-fat mayonnaise

2 whole-wheat pitas, split into rounds

4 lettuce leaves

4 slices tomato

1. Heat an outdoor grill or a large stovetop grill pan to medium-high.

2. Coat mushrooms, red bell pepper, and red onion with cooking spray. Place onion slices on the grill, and cook for 4 minutes per side, turning once, until lightly charred and tender. Grill mushrooms and peppers 5 or 6 minutes per side, turning once, until lightly charred and tender.

3. Meanwhile, in a small bowl, whisk together Italian dressing and mayonnaise until blended and smooth. Spread dressing mixture onto pita halves.

4. To assemble, top pita halves with 1 lettuce leaf, 1 tomato slice, 1 mushroom cap, 1 piece of red pepper, and onion. Serve at once.

Fantastic Fruit

In This Chapter

- Snacking on the natural sweetness of fruit
- Savory fruit snacks
- Low-glycemic treats

Fruit offers so many delights. It's delicious, sweet, and highly valued as an important nutritional component of your food intake. Fruit perks up many savory meals, as raisins can do in an Asian curry, and sweetens many healthful desserts, like peaches in ice cream.

Best of all, most varieties of fruit are low glycemic, with just a few ranging into the medium and high categories. Even then, when they're combined with other ingredients such as fat, nuts, or protein, the total glycemic value of the recipe is rated low. The medium-rated fruit varieties are pineapple, mango, raisins, papaya, and figs. Watermelon is rated the highest at 76, but because it's very light and contains lots of water, the overall glycemic effect of eating an average-size bowl of watermelon is low.

Nutritionally, fruit contains the natural sweetener fructose and lots of fiber. It's high in antioxidants, vitamins, and minerals. That's why nutritionists recommend you eat 5 to 10 servings of fruits and vegetables each day—they're good for you! The carbohydrate count of fruit is higher overall than that of vegetables, so you might want to limit your total servings of fruit to 3 to 5 per day.

Granola Breakfast Sundaes

Granola and strawberries top yogurt and bananas in this quick and tasty breakfast.

Snack servings:	Yield:	Prep time:	Serving size:
2	2 sundaes	5 minutes	1 sundae

Each serving has:			
171 calories	6g protein	27g carbohydrates	3g fiber
5g fat	1g saturated fat	glycemic index: low	glycemic load: 6

1 ripe banana, peeled, halved, and
    split lengthwise
½ cup low-fat Greek-style yogurt

¼ cup low-fat granola
¼ cup strawberries, sliced

1. Place 2 banana quarters in 2 separate bowls.
2. Top each with ¼ cup yogurt, 2 tablespoons granola, and 2 tablespoons
   strawberries.

Variation: If your child has milk allergies, substitute nondairy coconut milk yogurt
for the Greek-style yogurt called for in this recipe.

Orange Pistachio Parfait

The orange flavor of this breakfast parfait is refreshing any time of day.

Snack servings:	Yield:	Prep time:	Serving size:
1	1 parfait	5 minutes	1 parfait
Each serving has:			
251 calories	13g protein	38g carbohydrates	6g fiber
7g fat	2g saturated fat	glycemic index: low	glycemic load: 12

¾ cup low-fat Greek-style yogurt

1 tsp. orange zest

½ tsp. pure vanilla extract

1 tsp. flaxseeds

1 medium navel orange, peeled
   and separated into slices

1 TB. dried cranberries

1 TB. pistachio pieces

1. In a medium bowl, combine yogurt, orange zest, vanilla extract, and flaxseeds.

2. Spoon ½ of yogurt mixture into a parfait glass or tall drinking glass. Layer ½ of orange slices, ½ of cranberries, and ½ of pistachios on top.

3. Top with remaining yogurt mixture, and finish off with remaining orange slices, cranberries, and pistachios.

Variation: Substitute a tangerine or blood orange for the orange. Instead of pistachios, you can use pecans, slivered almonds, or walnuts.

Peach Parfait

This yogurt and peach parfait is spiced up with nutmeg.

Snack servings:	Yield:	Prep time:	Serving size:
4	4 parfaits	10 minutes	1 cup

Each serving has:			
133 calories	7g protein	21g carbohydrates	1g fiber
3g fat	2g saturated fat	glycemic index: low	glycemic load: 6

2 cups low-fat Greek-style yogurt	2 large ripe peaches, diced
1 TB. honey	2 TB. unsweetened shredded coconut, toasted
¼ tsp. ground nutmeg	

1. In a small bowl, combine yogurt, honey, and nutmeg.

2. Spoon equal amounts of peaches into the bottom of 4 small tumbler-style or parfait glasses.

3. Divide yogurt-honey mixture among glasses, and sprinkle with coconut. Serve chilled or at room temperature.

Variation: Increase the crunch of these parfaits by sprinkling them with 2 tablespoons chopped cashews.

Papaya Basil Parfait

Basil flavors this lovely medley of yogurt, nectarine, papaya, strawberries, and grapes.

Snack servings:	Yield:	Prep time:	Serving size:
4	5 cups	15 minutes	about 1¼ cups
Each serving has:			
127 calories	7g protein	21g carbohydrates	2g fiber
2g fat	1g saturated fat	glycemic index: low	glycemic load: 8

1 medium nectarine, diced

2 cups low-fat Greek-style yogurt

1 cup papaya, diced

½ cup strawberries, hulled and
  sliced

1 cup green grapes

2 TB. fresh basil, snipped

1. Place 2 tablespoons nectarine pieces in the bottom of 4 parfait glasses. Top each with 1 tablespoon yogurt.

2. In a medium bowl, combine papaya, strawberries, and grapes. Divide evenly among parfait glasses, layering alternately with yogurt.

3. Refrigerate until serving, garnished with fresh basil.

HEALTHY NOTE

The acid in the natural yogurt keeps the nectarines fresh looking and prevents the surface of the fruit from turning brown due to oxidation.

Waldorf Salad Vinaigrette

Apples, walnuts, grapes, and tangerines are tossed with a honey-cinnamon vinaigrette dressing to bring out the fruits' sweetness for a year-round treat.

Snack servings:	Yield:	Prep time:	Serving size:
6	6 servings	20 minutes	about 1 cup

Each serving has:			
145 calories	3g protein	18g carbohydrates	3g fiber
8g fat	1g saturated fat	glycemic index: low	glycemic load: 6

2 tsp. extra-virgin olive oil

2 tsp. apple cider vinegar

1 tsp. honey

⅛ tsp. salt

⅛ tsp. ground cinnamon

⅛ tsp. ground black pepper

2 medium Pink Lady apples (or Jonathan Gold, Gala, or Fuji), cored and cubed (skin on)

½ cup walnuts, toasted and coarsely chopped

2 large tangerines, peeled and sections cut in ½

1 cup seedless red or green grapes, cut in ½

1. In a small bowl, whisk together extra-virgin olive oil, apple cider vinegar, honey, salt, ground cinnamon, and pepper.

2. In a salad bowl, combine apples, walnuts, tangerines, and grapes. Pour dressing over fruit and nuts, and mix gently to coat.

TASTY BITE

This version of the classic Waldorf salad uses a light vinegar and oil dressing with honey and cinnamon in place of mayonnaise. You'll enjoy the fresh taste.

Strawberry Iceberg Wedges

Fruit brings a sweet and tangy taste for this summer salad dressed with poppy seeds.

Snack servings:	Yield:	Prep time:	Serving size:
6	6 iceberg wedges, 5 cups fruit	15 minutes	1 iceberg wedge with ⅚ cup fruit mix
Each serving has:			
151 calories	2g protein	19g carbohydrates	3g fiber
8g fat	1g saturated fat	glycemic index: low	glycemic load: 10

1 pt. fresh strawberries, hulled and sliced	1 medium head iceberg lettuce, cored and cut into 6 wedges
2 cups pineapple, cubed	¼ tsp. salt
2 cups cantaloupe, cubed	⅛ tsp. ground black pepper
2 TB. fresh mint, chopped	6 TB. bottled poppy seed dressing

1. In a large bowl, combine strawberries, pineapple, and cantaloupe with mint.

2. Arrange 1 lettuce wedge on each of 6 serving plates. Top evenly with fruit mixture. Season with salt and pepper, and drizzle 1 tablespoon poppy seed dressing over each salad.

Variation: Substitute fresh, pitted cherries or blueberries for the strawberries in this recipe.

Minted Watermelon Salad

This chilled, fresh summer salad is both sweet and tangy with a hint of bite from the watercress.

Snack servings:	Yield:	Prep time:	Serving size:
4	8 cups	15 minutes plus chill time	2 cups

Each serving has:			
120 calories	1g protein	13g carbohydrates	1g fiber
7g fat	1g saturated fat	glycemic index: low	glycemic load: 9

½ (13- to 14-lb.) oval seedless
watermelon

4 cups fresh watercress, snipped

½ medium red onion, cut into thin
wedges

2 TB. fresh mint, snipped

2 TB. extra-virgin olive oil

Dash salt

Dash ground black pepper

1. Cut watermelon into 1-inch cubes. Cover and chill if not already cold.

2. In a large bowl, toss together watercress, red onion, mint, extra-virgin olive oil, salt, and pepper. Sprinkle mixture over watermelon cubes, and serve cold.

HEALTHY NOTE

Watermelon is high glycemic, with a value of 76. However, it isn't a dense food, and when combined with low-glycemic vegetables and some oil, a snack serving of this salad is low glycemic.

Pineapple Broccoli Slaw

Green chiles add a hint of hot flavor to this sweet, colorful, and crunchy salad.

Snack servings:	Yield:	Prep time:	Serving size:
4	about 4 cups	10 minutes	1 cup
Each serving has:			
128 calories	2g protein	15g carbohydrates	2g fiber
7g fat	1g saturated fat	glycemic index: low	glycemic load: 6

½ (16-oz.) pkg. coleslaw mix

1 cup fresh pineapple chunks or ½ (20-oz.) can unsweetened pineapple chunks, drained

1 cup broccoli florets

2 TB. toasted sunflower seeds

1 TB. green chiles, diced

¼ cup mayonnaise or vinegar-and-oil salad dressing

⅛ tsp. crushed red pepper flakes

1. In a large bowl, combine coleslaw mix, pineapple, broccoli florets, sunflower seeds, and green chiles.

2. Add mayonnaise and crushed red pepper flakes, and toss. Toss again before serving.

Stuffed Dates

These dates are stuffed with cream cheese for a sweet, cheesy flavor.

Snack servings:	Yield:	Prep time:	Serving size:
2	6 stuffed dates	2 minutes	3 stuffed dates
Each serving has:			
84 calories	3g protein	20g carbohydrates	2g fiber
0g fat	0g saturated fat	glycemic index: low	glycemic load: 10

6 large dates, pitted

6 tsp. low-fat cream cheese

1. Open each date, and place 1 teaspoon cream cheese in cavity.

2. Serve immediately.

Variation: Instead of cream cheese, try some of these alternate fillings: peanut butter, almond butter, cheddar cheese, green olives, and pimientos.

Banana Cream Cheese Roll-Ups

Bananas and cream cheese are rolled up on toasted tortillas and flavored with cinnamon and nutmeg.

Snack servings:	Yield:	Prep time:	Cook time:	Serving size:
4	4 roll-ups	5 minutes	5 minutes	1 roll-up

Each serving has:			
165 calories	5g protein	24g carbohydrates	2g fiber
5g fat	1g saturated fat	glycemic index: low	glycemic load: 8

1 (3-oz.) pkg. low-fat cream cheese, softened

1 TB. honey

¼ tsp. ground cinnamon

¼ tsp. ground nutmeg

1 TB. extra-virgin olive oil

2 (10-in.) whole-wheat tortillas

1 large ripe banana, peeled and sliced

1. In a medium mixing bowl, combine cream cheese, honey, ground cinnamon, and ground nutmeg.

2. In a large skillet over medium heat, heat extra-virgin olive oil. Add 1 tortilla, and lightly toast for about 1 minute per side. Repeat with remaining tortilla.

3. Spread ½ of cream cheese mixture on each tortilla, and top with ½ of banana slices. Roll up tortillas, and cut each in ½ before serving.

Raspberry Cottage Cheese

Raspberries, apples, and grapes add sweet flavor to this almond-topped cottage cheese.

Snack servings:	Yield:	Prep time:	Serving size:
4	4 servings	10 minutes	about 1 cup

Each serving has:			
195 calories	10g protein	32g carbohydrates	5g fiber
4g fat	1g saturated fat	glycemic index: low	glycemic load: 9

1 medium apple, your choice variety, diced (skin on)

1 cup fresh or frozen raspberries

1 cup low-fat cottage cheese

1 cup green or red grapes

¼ cup raisins

¼ cup almonds, sliced

1. In 4 parfait glasses or serving dishes, layer apple, raspberries, cottage cheese, grapes, and raisins.

2. Sprinkle with almonds, and serve immediately.

HEALTHY NOTE

This is a perfect snack for when you're feeling fatigued or need a quick pick-me-up. The fruit adds both quick and sustained energy, while the protein in the cottage cheese fuels your activities for several hours.

Frozen Cherry Almond Frosty

This creamy chilled cherry frosty is sweetened with a hint of honey.

Snack servings:	Yield:	Prep time:	Serving size:
2	about 3 cups	10 minutes	1½ cups

Each serving has:			
160 calories	8g protein	23g carbohydrates	3g fiber
5g fat	2g saturated fat	glycemic index: low	glycemic load: 4

1 cup low-fat Greek-style yogurt	1 TB. flaxseed, ground
1 cup frozen unsweetened cherries	1 TB. honey
6 almonds	¼ to ½ cup ice

1. In a blender, place yogurt, cherries, almonds, ground flaxseed, and honey. Blend together, adding small amounts of ice as needed.

2. Freeze overnight before serving.

Grilled Pineapple Rings

Grilling brings out the sweetness of the pineapple and intensifies its tropical taste.

Snack servings:	Yield:	Prep time:	Cook time:	Serving size:
4	about 8 rings	2 minutes	4 to 6 minutes	2 rings

Each serving has:			
151 calories	2g protein	17g carbohydrates	3g fiber
10g fat	1g saturated fat	glycemic index: low	glycemic load: 11

1 medium pineapple, peeled, cored, and cut into ⅜-in. slices	¾ cup chopped pecans, toasted

1. Preheat grill to medium-high.

2. Place pineapple directly on the grill, and cook for about 2 or 3 minutes. Turn and grill for another 2 or 3 minutes.

3. Place grilled fruit in a serving dish, and sprinkle with chopped pecans. Serve warm.

Baked Apples with Yogurt

Cinnamon flavors these baked apples stuffed with fruit and nuts and topped with creamy yogurt.

Snack servings:	Yield:	Prep time:	Cook time:	Serving size:
4	4 apples	15 minutes	40 to 45 minutes	1 apple

Each serving has:			
154 calories	3g protein	29g carbohydrates	4g fiber
5g fat	1g saturated fat	glycemic index: low	glycemic load: 8

2 tsp. lemon juice

4 large, Jonagold, Pink Lady, Figi, Granny Smith, or your choice variety firm apples, cored, hollowed, and bottoms intact (skin on)

2 TB. roasted almond butter (or any natural nut butter such as peanut, hazelnut, pecan, or cashew)

1 TB. dried apricots, chopped

1 TB. pitted prunes, chopped

1 TB. raisins

2 tsp. honey

$\frac{1}{4}$ tsp. ground cinnamon

$\frac{1}{4}$ cup water

4 TB. low-fat Greek-style yogurt

1. Preheat the oven to 375°F.

2. Drizzle about $\frac{1}{8}$ teaspoon lemon juice inside each apple cavity, preserving remaining juice.

3. In a medium bowl, combine almond butter, apricots, prunes, raisins, honey, and ground cinnamon. Evenly divide mixture among apple cavities, and firmly press down stuffing into apple cavities. Place apples, cavity side up, in a shallow baking dish.

4. Mix together remaining lemon juice and water, and pour into the bottom of the baking dish around apples. Bake for 40 to 45 minutes or until apples are firm but tender.

5. Spoon 1 tablespoon yogurt over each warm baked apple, and serve warm. Apples can be reheated in a microwave.

Peach and Pecan Stir-Fry

Enjoy the blended flavors of sweet peaches, pecans, and basil in this fruity stir-fry.

Snack servings:	Yield:	Prep time:	Cook time:	Serving size:
4	3 cups	10 minutes	10 minutes	¾ cup

Each serving has:			
120 calories	2g protein	11g carbohydrates	2g fiber
9g fat	1g saturated fat	glycemic index: low	glycemic load: 3

1 TB. extra-virgin olive oil

¼ tsp. molasses

½ tsp. honey

4 ripe medium peaches (about 2 lb.), pitted and sliced

¼ cup pecans, chopped

½ tsp. vanilla extract

2 TB. fresh basil, snipped

1. In a large saucepan over medium heat, heat extra-virgin olive oil. Stir in molasses and honey. Add peaches and pecans, and sauté gently for 8 to 10 minutes or until mixture is fragrant.

2. Remove to a serving bowl, and stir in vanilla extract. Garnish with fresh basil before serving.

Variation: Use as a topping for ½ cup yogurt or cottage cheese. Both are low glycemic, and they add small amounts of fat and high amounts of protein to your snack.

Sautéed Bananas and Raisins

This naturally sweet warm snack is fragrantly flavored with bananas, walnuts, and raisins.

Snack servings:	Yield:	Prep time:	Cook time:	Serving size:
4	about 3 cups	5 minutes	5 to 10 minutes	¾ cup

Each serving has:			
144 calories	3g protein	18g carbohydrates	2g fiber
8g fat	1g saturated fat	glycemic index: low	glycemic load: 9

1 TB. extra-virgin olive oil	2 TB. raisins
2 medium ripe bananas, peeled and sliced	¼ cup walnuts, chopped

1. In a large saucepan over medium heat, heat extra-virgin olive oil. Add bananas, raisins, and walnuts, and sauté gently for 5 to 10 minutes or until mixture is hot throughout and fragrant.

2. Remove to a serving bowl, and serve immediately.

HEALTHY NOTE

This recipe tastes so sweet you'll think it contains added sugar. Be sure to savor every spoonful—eat slowly and be mindful of each taste.

Mango and Pineapple Freeze

Ginger spices up this icy fruit and ice cream freeze.

Snack servings:	Yield:	Prep time:	Serving size:
7	about 3½ cups	10 minutes plus 30 minutes freeze time	about ½ cup

Each serving has:			
73 calories	1g protein	16g carbohydrates	1g fiber
2g fat	1g saturated fat	glycemic index: low	glycemic load: 9

1 medium mango, peeled and sliced

½ fresh medium pineapple, cored, peeled, and chopped

1 tsp. crystallized ginger, chopped

½ cup premium vanilla ice cream (not artificially sweetened)

1. Place mango and pineapple on a large baking sheet, and freeze for 30 minutes.

2. In a food processor fitted with a chopping blade, or in a blender, process frozen mango and pineapple along with crystallized ginger and ice cream until chunky or smooth (your preference), stopping occasionally to scrape down the sides of the blender jar.

3. Serve immediately, or freeze for later.

Dips, Spreads, Salsas, and Sauces

In This Chapter

- Quick dip for quick energy
- Dips from varied cuisines
- Tasty spreads
- Super salsas

Dips, spreads, salsas, and sauces bring tasty delights to your palate for snacks and as an accompaniment to your meals. As you look through the recipes in this chapter, you'll find many different flavors, from international cuisines to local favorites.

The Art of the Dipper

It's time to switch up the way you think about dippers. First, avoid eating ordinary potato chips for dippers. Instead, add color to your snack with fresh-tasting vegetable scoopers. Nutritionally, they provide important fiber to your dip snack. That fiber makes your stomach feel fuller and more satisfied. With fewer calories, the vegetables actually lower the glycemic value and load of the recipe.

You can always use vegetable scoopers for the recipes in this chapter. Try carrot sticks, celery stalks, jicama rounds, broccoli and cauliflower florets, cucumber slices, radish slices, bell pepper slices, sugar snap peas, and raw green beans.

Some recipes specifically call for low-glycemic baked goods such as whole-wheat pita bread, corn tortillas, and corn chips. The nutritional counts in these recipes factor in the additional carbohydrates, thus increasing the glycemic load. If you want to reduce the glycemic load in those recipes, use vegetable scoopers instead.

HEALTHY NOTE

Very few crackers and baked goods are low glycemic, so I don't recommend you use those as a platform for the dips, spreads, and sauces in this chapter.

Hot Chili Cream Cheese Dip

This warm dip offers Southwestern flavor on corn tortillas.

Snack servings:	Yield:	Prep time:	Cook time:	Serving size:
8	4 cups dip	10 minutes	20 minutes	½ cup dip, 1 tortilla

Each serving has:			
138 calories	7g protein	19g carbohydrates	3g fiber
4g fat	1g saturated fat	glycemic index: low	glycemic load: 8

1 tsp. extra-virgin olive oil	1 cup salsa, your preference
½ cup yellow onion, finely chopped	1 (3-oz.) pkg. low-fat cream cheese, cubed
1 tsp. minced garlic	1 (2.25-oz.) can sliced ripe black olives, drained
1 (15-oz.) can chili with or without beans	8 (6-in.) corn tortillas

1. In a small skillet over medium heat, heat extra-virgin olive oil. Add onion and garlic, and sauté for 5 minutes or until tender. Stir in chili, salsa, cream cheese, and olives.

2. Reduce heat to low, cover, and cook, stirring occasionally, for 15 minutes or until heated through.

3. Serve with corn tortillas. Store leftovers in the refrigerator and reheat on the stove or in the microwave.

Bacon Cheddar Dip

Bacon and cheddar cheese flavor this dip made tangy with sour cream.

Snack servings:	Yield:	Prep time:	Serving size:
7	3½ cups dip	10 minutes plus 1 hour chill time	about ½ cup dip, 1 cup vegetables

Each serving has:			
195 calories	10g protein	7g carbohydrates	2g fiber
14g fat	8g saturated fat	glycemic index: low	glycemic load: 6

2 cups low-fat sour cream

1 cup low-fat cheddar cheese, finely shredded

1 (1-oz.) pkg. ranch salad dressing mix

2 strips bacon, cooked and crumbled

6 cups fresh vegetables: carrot sticks, celery stalks, jicama rounds, sliced cucumber, etc.

1. In a large bowl, combine sour cream, cheddar cheese, ranch salad dressing mix, and bacon. Cover and refrigerate for at least 1 hour.

2. Serve with fresh vegetables.

HEALTHY NOTE

To reduce the amount of fat and saturated fat in this recipe, use imitation bacon bits in place of the bacon.

Pepperoni Pizza Dip

Pepperoni adds zing to this dip flavored with pizza sauce and served on whole-wheat pita wedges.

Snack servings:	Yield:	Prep time:	Cook time:	Serving size:
12	about 4 cups dip	10 minutes	7 to 10 minutes	⅓ cup dip, ½ pita

Each serving has:			
211 calories	11g protein	22g carbohydrates	3g fiber
9g fat	3g saturated fat	glycemic index: low	glycemic load: 6

1 (8-oz.) pkg. low-fat cream cheese, softened

1 (4.25-oz.) can chopped black olives, drained

1 (4-oz.) can mushroom stems and pieces, drained and chopped

⅓ cup yellow or white onion, chopped

24 slices pepperoni, chopped

1 (8-oz.) can pizza sauce

1 cup shredded part-skim mozzarella cheese

6 whole-wheat pitas, toasted, split lengthwise, and cut into 6 wedges

1. Spread cream cheese in the bottom of a 9-inch microwave-safe pie plate. Top with black olives, mushrooms, onion, pepperoni, pizza sauce, and mozzarella cheese.

2. Microwave, uncovered, at 70 percent power for 7 to 10 minutes or until heated through and cheese is melted.

3. Serve with toasted pita wedges.

TASTY BITE

Enjoy this filling and tasty dip by eating slowly and savoring every bite.

Black Bean and Mango Dip

Enjoy the sweet and spicy note of black beans blended with mango salsa in this tasty dip.

Snack servings:	Yield:	Prep time:	Serving size:
12	about 3 cups dip	10 minutes	4 tablespoons dip
Each serving has:			
213 calories	13g protein	37g carbohydrates	9g fiber
3g fat	0g saturated fat	glycemic index: low	glycemic load: 10

1 (16-oz.) can black beans, drained and rinsed

1 TB. extra-virgin olive oil

½ cup mango salsa or other fruit salsa

¼ cup fresh cilantro, minced

1. Place beans and extra-virgin olive oil in a food processor fitted with a chopping blade. Pulse several times until beans are slightly chunky. Add mango salsa, and pulse until just blended.

2. Remove dip to a serving bowl, and stir in fresh cilantro before serving with vegetable scoopers such as celery, carrot sticks, broccoli florets, and cucumber slices.

Five-Layer Mexican Dip

In this dip, avocados are layered with pinto beans, cheddar cheese, sour cream, and tomatoes.

Snack servings:	Yield:	Prep time:	Serving size:
12	8 cups dip	20 minutes	about ⅔ cup dip

Each serving has:			
247 calories	13g protein	30g carbohydrates	8g fiber
9g fat	3g saturated fat	glycemic index: low	glycemic load: 8

3 medium plum tomatoes, seeded and chopped

1 small white onion, chopped

2 medium jalapeño peppers, seeded and chopped

¾ cup fresh cilantro leaves, chopped

¼ cup lime juice

2 medium ripe avocados, pitted and peeled

¼ tsp. salt

¼ tsp. ground black pepper

1 (15-oz.) can pinto beans, drained and rinsed

⅓ cup water, plus more as needed

1½ cups low-fat cheddar cheese, grated

1½ cups reduced-fat sour cream

1. In a medium bowl, combine tomatoes, onion, jalapeños, and ½ cup cilantro. Drizzle 2 tablespoons lime juice over tomato mixture, and set aside.

2. In a small bowl, and using a fork, break up avocado with remaining ¼ cup cilantro and remaining 2 tablespoons lime juice until slightly chunky. Season with salt and pepper, and set aside.

3. Place pinto beans and water in a food processor fitted with a chopping blade. Process to a slightly chunky purée, adding additional water 1 tablespoon at a time, to reach desired consistency. Season with salt and pepper, and stir.

4. Transfer beans to a 9×9-inch casserole dish or a large glass bowl, and spread into an even layer.

5. Sprinkle cheddar cheese evenly over beans. Dollop scoops of avocado mixture over cheese, and use a spatula to spread to a thin layer. Dollop scoops of sour cream over avocado, and spread into a thin layer. With a slotted spoon (to drain any liquid), spread tomato mixture evenly over sour cream.

6. Serve immediately with vegetable scoopers, or cover and chill for up to 4 hours.

> **TASTY BITE**
>
> This recipe is great for a large group. You can cut the recipe in half to serve a smaller group.

Cannellini Bean Dip

Mild beans are flavored with your choice of cilantro or parsley.

Snack servings:	Yield:	Prep time:	Cook time:	Serving size:
7	about 2½ cups dip	10 minutes	5 or 6 minutes	⅓ cup dip

Each serving has:			
208 calories	10g protein	33g carbohydrates	9g fiber
4g fat	0g saturated fat	glycemic index: low	glycemic load: 9

2 tsp. extra-virgin olive oil

½ cup red onion, finely chopped

2 tsp. minced garlic

¼ tsp. salt

¼ tsp. ground black pepper

1 (15-oz.) can cannellini (white kidney) beans, drained and rinsed well

1 tsp. chili powder

¼ cup water

¼ cup fresh cilantro or parsley, finely chopped

1. In a medium skillet over low heat, heat extra-virgin olive oil. Add red onion and garlic, and sauté for 5 or 6 minutes or until onion is very soft and golden. Season with salt and pepper.

2. Add onion mixture to the bowl of a food processor fitted with a chopping blade. Add cannellini beans, chili powder, and water. Pulse several times until mixture becomes slightly chunky. Transfer to a serving bowl, and stir in cilantro or parsley. Serve with vegetable scoopers.

Chickpea, Basil, and Radish Dip

Chickpeas, also known as garbanzo beans, are blended with fresh basil, garlic, and radishes in this Mediterranean-inspired dip.

Snack servings: 6	Yield: about 1½ cups dip	Prep time: 10 minutes plus 30 minutes chill time	Serving size: 4 tablespoons dip
Each serving has:			
209 calories	10g protein	32g carbohydrates	9g fiber
5g fat	1g saturated fat	glycemic index: low	glycemic load: 9

1 (15-oz.) can chickpeas, drained and rinsed, ½ cup liquid reserved

1 TB. extra-virgin olive oil

¼ tsp. salt

¼ tsp. ground black pepper

¼ cup fresh basil, coarsely chopped

4 radishes, chopped

1 tsp. minced garlic

2 TB. lemon juice

1. In a medium bowl, lightly mash chickpeas, extra-virgin olive oil, salt, and pepper until creamy but still chunky. Stir in basil, radishes, garlic, and lemon juice. Stir in reserved chickpea liquid, 1 tablespoon at a time, until dip holds together.

2. Refrigerate for at least 30 minutes. Serve with vegetable scoopers.

Creamy Artichoke Spinach Dip

This tasty artichoke and spinach dip is flavored with Swiss cheese and crushed red pepper flakes.

Snack servings:	Yield:	Prep time:	Cook time:	Serving size:
12	6 cups dip	10 minutes	1 hour	½ cup dip

Each serving has:			
163 calories	16g protein	11g carbohydrates	4g fiber
7g fat	4g saturated fat	glycemic index: low	glycemic load: 0

2 (14-oz.) cans water-packed artichoke hearts, drained, rinsed,
and coarsely chopped

1 (13.5-oz.) can spinach, well
drained, or 2 cups frozen spinach, defrosted and drained

1 (8-oz.) pkg. low-fat cream cheese,
cubed

1 cup Parmesan cheese, shredded

½ cup plain Greek-style yogurt

½ cup shredded low-fat Swiss
cheese

2 TB. lemon juice

1 tsp. crushed red pepper flakes

1 tsp. minced garlic

1. In a 3-quart slow cooker, combine artichoke hearts, spinach, cream cheese,
   Parmesan cheese, yogurt, Swiss cheese, lemon juice, crushed red pepper flakes,
   and garlic. Cover and cook on low for 1 hour or until heated through.

2. Serve warm with vegetable scoopers. Store in an airtight container in the refrigerator for up to 3 days.

HEALTHY NOTE

You can enjoy this healthy, lower-fat version of this all-time favorite dip without
guilt!

Curried Carrot Dip

Here, cannellini beans and carrots are spiced up with the flavors of curry and cumin.

Snack servings:	Yield:	Prep time:	Cook time:	Serving size:
6	about 4 cups dip	10 minutes	25 minutes	²⁄₃ cup dip

Each serving has:			
153 calories	4g protein	23g carbohydrates	5g fiber
6g fat	1g saturated fat	glycemic index: low	glycemic load: 6

3 cups carrots, sliced	1 TB. curry powder
2 TB. extra-virgin olive oil	1 tsp. ground cumin
½ cup white or yellow onion, chopped	1 (15-oz.) can cannellini beans, drained and rinsed
1 TB. minced garlic	½ tsp. salt

1. In a medium saucepan over high heat, bring a small amount of water to a boil. Add carrots, reduce heat to medium, cover, and cook for about 15 minutes or until carrots are very tender. Drain.

2. Meanwhile, in a small skillet over medium heat, heat extra-virgin olive oil. Add onion and garlic, and cook for 5 minutes or until tender. Stir in curry powder and cumin.

3. Transfer carrot and onion mixtures to a food processor fitted with a chopping blade. Add beans and salt, cover, and process until smooth. Transfer to a serving bowl, cover, and refrigerate for at least 4 hours or up to 3 days. Serve with vegetable scoopers.

HEALTHY NOTE

Heating the curry powder and cumin releases more fragrance and flavor from the spices.

Greek Olive and Spinach Dip

Oregano and garlic flavor this authentic Greek yogurt dip.

Snack servings:	Yield:	Prep time:	Cook time:	Serving size:
6	6 half pitas	10 minutes	3 minutes	$\frac{1}{2}$ pita

Each serving has:			
208 calories	9g protein	25g carbohydrates	4g fiber
10g fat	3g saturated fat	glycemic index: low	glycemic load: 6

2 TB. extra-virgin olive oil

4 green onions, chopped

1 TB. minced garlic

12 oz. spinach leaves, finely chopped

$\frac{1}{2}$ tsp. finely shredded lemon zest

2 tsp. lemon juice

1 cup low-fat Greek yogurt

$\frac{1}{2}$ cup finely crumbled feta cheese

$\frac{1}{4}$ cup black olives, sliced

2 TB. fresh oregano, snipped, or 2 tsp. dried

Dash ground black pepper

6 whole-wheat pitas, split lengthwise and toasted

1. In a large skillet over medium heat, heat extra-virgin olive oil. Add green onions and garlic, and sauté for about 1 minute or until fragrant. Add spinach, and sauté for about 2 minutes or until wilted. Remove to medium bowl.

2. To the bowl, add lemon zest, lemon juice, yogurt, feta cheese, black olives, oregano, and pepper. Stir lightly to mix.

3. Serve on toasted pita halves.

HEALTHY NOTE

Substitute cut-up vegetables for the pita bread, and you lower the glycemic load of this recipe to zero.

Hummus with Lemon

This traditional hummus recipe is flavored with garlic and enhanced with the taste of lemon.

Serving size:	Yield:	Prep time:	Serving size:
7	about 2½ cups hummus	10 minutes	⅓ cup hummus

Each serving has:			
184 calories	3g protein	12g carbohydrates	2g fiber
14g fat	2g saturated fat	glycemic index: low	glycemic load: 6

½ cup extra-virgin olive oil

3 TB. lemon juice

1 (15-oz.) can chickpeas, drained and rinsed

2 tsp. minced garlic

½ tsp. salt

1. In a food processor fitted with a chopping blade, combine extra-virgin olive oil, lemon juice, chickpeas, garlic, and salt. Cover and process until smooth.

2. Transfer to a small bowl. Serve with cut-up vegetable scoopers.

Variation: Add sliced black olives, diced mild green chiles, or diced raw vegetables such as bell peppers, celery, or radishes.

Olive and Pimiento Cheese Spread

Cream cheese is accented with the tangy taste of green olives and pimientos in this cheesy spread.

Snack servings:	Yield:	Prep time:	Serving size:
5	1¼ cups spread	10 minutes	¼ cup spread
Each serving has:			
129 calories	5g protein	3g carbohydrates	0g fiber
11g fat	7g saturated fat	glycemic index: low	glycemic load: 0

1 (8-oz.) pkg. reduced-fat cream cheese, softened

¼ cup chopped pimiento-stuffed olives

2 TB. olive juice

1. In a small bowl, combine cream cheese, olives, and olive juice.

2. Serve with vegetable scoopers.

HEALTHY NOTE

This recipe contains no fiber, so be sure to eat some by enjoying the vegetable scoopers. This recipe also has a strong flavor, so use mild-tasting scoopers like carrot sticks, celery stalks, and jicama slices.

Creamy Salmon Spread

Dill and green onions flavor this light salmon spread.

Snack servings:	Yield:	Prep time:	Serving size:
4	1 cup spread	10 minutes plus 1 hour chill time	¼ cup spread, ¼ celery

Each serving has:			
82 calories	12g protein	2g carbohydrates	0g fiber
2g fat	1g saturated fat	glycemic index: low	glycemic load: 0

½ cup low-fat cottage cheese

1 TB. water

4 green onions, white parts only, sliced

4 oz. smoked salmon, thinly sliced

1 (3-oz.) pkg. low-fat cream cheese

1 TB. fresh lemon juice

1 tsp. dried dill

Dash ground black pepper

3 stalks celery, cut into 2- or 3-in. lengths

1. Add cottage cheese and water to a food processor fitted with a chopping blade, and pulse until smooth. Add green onions, smoked salmon, cream cheese, lemon juice, dried dill, and pepper, and process until smooth and creamy. Refrigerate for at least 1 hour or overnight.

2. Spread on celery stalks, and serve.

Variation: You can use regular canned or packaged salmon in place of the smoked salmon.

Sun-Dried Tomato Mediterranean Spread

You'll taste the sunny Mediterranean flavors of oregano, black olives, and sun-dried tomatoes in every bite of this spread.

Snack servings:	Yield:	Prep time:	Serving size:
4	about 2 cups spread	10 minutes	$\frac{1}{2}$ cup spread

Each serving has:			
113 calories	5g protein	6g carbohydrates	0g fiber
8g fat	5g saturated fat	glycemic index: low	glycemic load: 6

$\frac{3}{4}$ cup low-fat Greek-style yogurt

$\frac{1}{2}$ cup low-fat cream cheese, softened

$\frac{1}{4}$ cup sun-dried tomatoes packed in oil, drained

3 TB. black olives, seeded and chopped

$\frac{1}{2}$ tsp. dried oregano

$\frac{1}{8}$ tsp. ground black pepper

1. In a medium bowl, stir together yogurt and cream cheese. Stir in sun-dried tomatoes, black olives, oregano, and pepper.

2. Serve with vegetable scoopers.

TASTY BITE

I favor the Greek-style yogurt because it doesn't contain additives and is thick and creamy. If you can't find this in the store, choose another type of additive-free yogurt.

Tomato Mango Salsa

This salsa combines a fresh-tasting blend of tomatoes and mangoes with chile, ginger, and coriander.

Snack servings:	Yield:	Prep time:	Cook time:	Serving size:
4	about 4 cups salsa	10 minutes	2 minutes	1 cup salsa

Each serving has:			
62 calories	1g protein	8g carbohydrates	1g fiber
4g fat	1g saturated fat	glycemic index: low	glycemic load: 3

½ lb. tomatoes, cut in wedges	1½ tsp. fresh ginger, minced
½ medium Serrano chile, very thinly sliced	1 TB. extra-virgin olive oil
¾ cup mango, chopped	1 tsp. coriander seeds, cracked
2 TB. red onion, finely chopped	2 TB. apple cider vinegar
	½ tsp. salt

1. In a medium bowl, combine tomatoes, Serrano chile, mango, red onion, and ginger.

2. In a small saucepan over medium heat, heat extra-virgin olive oil. Add coriander seeds, and cook, stirring, for about 1 minute or until medium brown. Remove from heat, and stir in vinegar and salt.

3. Pour warm spice mixture over tomato mixture, and let stand for 30 to 60 minutes for flavors to develop.

4. Serve with vegetable scoopers, serve over Mexican food, or place in a blender and chop for a delicious bowl of gazpacho.

Cucumber Lime Salsa

Here, the cooling taste of cucumber is mixed with spicy jalapeño.

Snack servings:	Yield:	Prep time:	Serving size:
4	2 cups salsa	10 minutes plus 2 hours chill time	$\frac{1}{2}$ cup salsa

Each serving has:			
77 calories	1g protein	4g carbohydrates	1g fiber
7g fat	1g saturated fat	glycemic index: low	glycemic load: 0

1 large cucumber, diced

1 tsp. minced garlic

1 medium jalapeño pepper, finely chopped

3 green onions, sliced

2 TB. fresh cilantro, minced

2 TB. lime juice

2 TB. extra-virgin olive oil

1 tsp. lime zest, grated

$\frac{1}{4}$ tsp. salt

$\frac{1}{4}$ tsp. ground black pepper

1. In a large bowl, combine cucumber, garlic, jalapeño pepper, green onions, cilantro, lime juice, extra-virgin olive oil, lime zest, salt, and pepper. Refrigerate for at least 2 hours before serving.

2. Serve with vegetable scoopers. You can also serve as a side condiment with Mexican-flavored meals, grilled meats, fruit salads, and fish.

Garlic Basil Pesto

Toasted almonds accent a blend of garlic, basil, and Parmesan in this pesto.

Snack servings:	Yield:	Prep time:	Cook time:	Serving size:
8	about 2 cups pesto	10 minutes	2 minutes	¼ cup pesto

Each serving has:			
37 calories	1g protein	0g carbohydrates	0g fiber
4g fat	1g saturated fat	glycemic index: low	glycemic load: 6

2 TB. raw almonds	¼ tsp. salt
2 cups packed fresh basil leaves	¼ tsp. ground black pepper
1 tsp. minced garlic	3 TB. extra-virgin olive oil
⅓ cup shredded Parmesan cheese	1 TB. water

1. In small, microwave-safe bowl or cup, microwave almonds on high for 1½ to 2 minutes or until lightly browned. Cool slightly.

2. In a food processor fitted with a knife blade, pulse almonds, basil, garlic, Parmesan cheese, salt, and pepper until finely chopped. With processor running, gradually pour in extra-virgin olive oil and water until blended.

3. Serve with vegetable scoopers. You can also serve as a condiment with grilled meats and fish, raw or cooked vegetables, salads, and Mediterranean-flavored foods.

Sweet and Spicy Sesame Sauce

Use this Asian-flavored sauce for dipping, as a salad dressing, or as a marinade for chicken or fish.

Snack servings:	Yield:	Prep time:	Serving size:
5	about 1 cup	5 minutes	$\frac{1}{5}$ cup

Each serving has:			
57 calories	1g protein	5g carbohydrates	1g fiber
4g fat	1g saturated fat	glycemic index: low	glycemic load: 0

3 TB. hoisin sauce	1 TB. toasted sesame oil
1 TB. toasted sesame seeds	1 TB. soy sauce
$\frac{1}{2}$ tsp. red chile flakes	$\frac{1}{2}$ cup hot water

1. In a small bowl, whisk together hoisin sauce, toasted sesame seeds, red chile flakes, toasted sesame oil, soy sauce, and hot water.

2. Serve as a dipping sauce.

Moroccan Ketchup

This ketchup is spiced up with exotic spices used in North African cuisine: cumin, coriander, cinnamon, and black pepper.

Snack servings:	Yield:	Prep time:	Serving size:
6	about 6 tablespoons	5 minutes	1 tablespoon

Each serving has:			
13 calories	0g protein	3g carbohydrates	0g fiber
0g fat	0g saturated fat	glycemic index: low	glycemic load: 0

$\frac{1}{3}$ cup ketchup	$\frac{1}{8}$ tsp. ground coriander
$\frac{1}{8}$ tsp. ground cumin	$\frac{1}{8}$ tsp. ground black pepper
$\frac{1}{8}$ tsp. ground cinnamon	

1. In a small bowl, combine ketchup, cumin, cinnamon, coriander, and pepper.

2. Can be stored in refrigerator for 1 month.

Tzatziki

This Greek yogurt dip is flavored with garlic, mint, and dill.

Snack servings:	Yield:	Prep time:	Serving size:
16	2 cups	10 minutes	2 tablespoons

Each serving has:			
25 calories	2g protein	4g carbohydrates	0g fiber
1g fat	0g saturated fat	glycemic index: low	glycemic load: 6

1 medium cucumber, peeled and seeded

1 cup low-fat Greek-style yogurt

½ tsp. minced garlic

1 TB. fresh dill, snipped, or 1 tsp. dried

1 TB. fresh mint, snipped, or 1 tsp. dried

Dash salt

Dash ground black pepper

Splash red wine vinegar

1. Finely grate cucumbers and place in center of a clean cloth dish towel. Gather up the ends of the towel, and twist over the sink to wring out liquid until cucumber is dry.

2. In a large bowl, gently fold cucumbers into yogurt. Mix in garlic, dill, mint, salt, pepper, and vinegar, and chill for at least 1 hour before serving. Dip will keep for up to 2 days in refrigerator.

TASTY BITE

Cucumbers can hold about ⅔ cup liquid, so be sure to squeeze out all the liquid before using. If they're added to the Tzatziki before they're dry, your dip will become watery.

Cheese and Tofu Treats

In This Chapter

- Naturally low-glycemic snacks
- Managing your saturated fat intake
- Melted cheese recipes
- Seasoning tofu for taste satisfaction

Cheese and tofu are two very different food items, yet both have much to offer in low-glycemic snacks. They both contain high levels of protein and can require minimal cooking. I've grouped them together in this chapter because most of the recipes are free of meat, fish, and poultry. Consider turning to these recipes when you want a meatless, high-protein snack.

Choose Cheese

Natural cheese is high in protein, but it's also high in both saturated and unsaturated fats. It doesn't contain carbohydrates, so you won't find cheese in the glycemic index lists. It's zero glycemic.

Because we want to provide you with recipes that are all-over good for your health, we aim to keep the saturated fat as low as we can in each recipe. That's why our cheese recipes call for low-fat or reduced-fat cheese as well as skim milk. We've made a few exceptions for soft and creamy cheeses such as Brie, but not many.

We've kept the flavor of the cheese recipes by using interesting combinations of condiments, spices, herbs, and vegetables.

Try Tofu

Tofu is made from fermented soybeans. Fermentation increases the digestibility and available protein of soybeans. It's an excellent source of vegetarian protein while being low in saturated fat. It contains some carbohydrates and is rated very low on the glycemic index.

Eaten plain, tofu is bland and lacks much flavor. Its popularity lies in its versatility. It takes on the flavors of the foods and seasonings it's paired with. It develops flavor as it marinates in such ingredients as ginger, soy sauce, toasted sesame oil, green onions, and virtually any marinade of your choosing.

Mozzarella and Black Bean Salad

Black beans, fresh mozzarella cheese, Italian dressing, and marinated artichoke hearts flavor this surprising salad.

Snack servings:	Yield:	Prep time:	Serving size:
12	about 12 cups	10 minutes	1 cup

Each serving has:			
241 calories	15g protein	30g carbohydrates	7g fiber
8g fat	3g saturated fat	glycemic index: low	glycemic load: 9

1 (19-oz.) can black beans, drained and rinsed

2 cups cherry tomatoes, halved

1 (9-oz.) pkg. cherry-size balls fresh mozzarella cheese

1 large cucumber, diced

1 (8.75-oz.) can kernel corn, drained and rinsed

1 (6-oz.) jar marinated artichoke hearts, drained

$^{1}\!/_{2}$ cup bottled Italian dressing

$^{1}\!/_{2}$ cup fresh parsley, chopped

12 lettuce leaves

1. In a large bowl, toss together black beans, cherry tomatoes, mozzarella cheese, cucumber, corn, artichoke hearts, Italian dressing, and parsley.

2. Place each lettuce leaf on a plate, and top with about 1 cup salad. Store leftovers in the refrigerator for 4 or 5 days.

HEALTHY NOTE

This is a superb snack salad for the times when you need to stave off hunger for several hours. The beans give you a full feeling in your stomach because they are high in fiber, and the cheese gives you high-quality protein.

Feta, Fig, and Spinach Pizza

Celebrate the festive taste of Mediterranean cuisine sparkling with the flavors of pine nuts and black olives.

Snack servings:	Yield:	Prep time:	Cook time:	Serving size:
4	2 tortillas	10 minutes	10 to 15 minutes	½ tortilla

Each serving has:			
287 calories	8g protein	32g carbohydrates	5g fiber
15g fat	5g saturated fat	glycemic index: low	glycemic load: 9

2 (10-in.) whole-wheat tortillas	6 fresh or dried figs, quartered
1 TB. extra-virgin olive oil	2 TB. pine nuts
1 cup feta cheese	3 TB. pitted Greek black olives, chopped
3 cups baby spinach leaves	

1. Preheat the oven to 400°F.

2. Place tortillas on a cookie sheet. Spread ½ tablespoon extra-virgin olive oil on each tortilla, and sprinkle with feta cheese. Top with spinach, figs, pine nuts, and black olives.

3. Bake for 10 to 15 minutes. Let stand 5 minutes before slicing and serving.

TASTY BITE

Whole-wheat tortillas are simple and easy to use as a base for pizzas. They're lower in glycemic value than a regular pizza crust, and they also offer fewer carbs and calories.

Mushroom and Artichoke Camembert

Marinated artichokes and sweet red peppers lend flavor and texture to this succulent and elegant cheese snack.

Snack servings:	Yield:	Prep time:	Cook time:	Serving size:
6	6 wedges	5 minutes	12 minutes	1 wedge, 2 sour-dough slices

Each serving has:			
134 calories	12g protein	7g carbohydrates	2g fiber
3g fat	2g saturated fat	glycemic index: low	glycemic load: 3

1 (4.25-oz.) pkg. low-fat Camembert or Brie cheese

1 (6-oz.) jar or ¾ cup marinated artichokes

2 cups crimini or button mush-rooms, quartered

¼ cup bottled roasted red sweet peppers, chopped

½ cup shredded low-fat Parmesan cheese

12 (¼-in.-thick) sourdough bread slices, toasted

1. Cut Camembert cheese into 6 wedges. Place 1 wedge on each of 6 small plates, and set aside.

2. Drain artichoke hearts, reserving liquid. Cut artichokes into thin slivers, and set aside.

3. In a large skillet over medium heat, heat reserved artichoke liquid. Add crimini mushrooms, and cook for 5 to 10 minutes or until tender. Stir in artichokes and roasted red sweet peppers, and heat through.

4. Spoon mixture on top of cheese wedges, and sprinkle with Parmesan cheese. Add 2 sourdough slices to each plate, and serve immediately.

HEALTHY NOTE

This recipe is a cheese lover's delight. It has lots of "adult" taste favorites, but don't be surprised if your children fall in love with it, too.

Jalapeño Cheddar Cheese Pizza

Pimiento and pickled jalapeño peppers flavor a tangy, cheddar cheese pizza.

Snack servings:	Yield:	Prep time:	Cook time:	Serving size:
6	6 pizzas	10 minutes	1 or 2 minutes	1 pizza

Each serving has:			
160 calories	13g protein	15g carbohydrates	2g fiber
5g fat	2g saturated fat	glycemic index: low	glycemic load: 5

1 cup low-fat extra-sharp cheddar cheese, shredded

1 (3-oz.) pkg. low-fat cream cheese, softened

1 (7-oz.) jar or 1 cup diced pimiento, drained

¼ cup drained pickled jalapeño pepper slices

2 TB. low-fat mayonnaise

1 TB. Worcestershire sauce

6 (6-in.) corn tortillas

1. Preheat the broiler to low.

2. In a food processor fitted with a chopping blade, blend extra-sharp cheddar cheese and cream cheese for 45 seconds or until well blended.

3. Add pimiento, jalapeño pepper slices, mayonnaise, and Worcestershire sauce, and pulse 5 or 6 times or to desired consistency.

4. Spread cheese mixture on corn tortillas. Place under the broiler for 1 or 2 minutes, and serve warm.

HEALTHY NOTE

Corn tortillas are a healthier choice than regular pizza dough as the base for these pizzas because corn tortillas are low glycemic and higher in fiber than regular white pizza dough.

Brie with Blueberry Preserves

Here, creamy warm Brie is flavored with thyme and blueberries.

Snack servings:	Yield:	Prep time:	Cook time:	Serving size:
6	1 Brie round	10 minutes	4 minutes	$\frac{1}{6}$ round

Each serving has:			
159 calories	9g protein	5g carbohydrates	0g fiber
12g fat	7g saturated fat	glycemic index: low	glycemic load: 0

$\frac{1}{4}$ cup sugar-free blueberry
   preserves

1 tsp. honey

$\frac{1}{4}$ tsp. dried thyme

1 (8-oz.) round Brie cheese

2 TB. walnuts, chopped

1. Preheat the oven to 450°F. Lightly coat a baking sheet with cooking spray.

2. In a small glass bowl, combine blueberry preserves, honey, and thyme. Set aside.

3. Cut Brie into 6 wedges. Place wedges close together on the baking sheet. Sprinkle with chopped walnuts.

4. Bake for 4 minutes or until cheese begins to soften in the center.

5. Meanwhile, microwave preserves mixture on high for 20 seconds or until thoroughly heated. Carefully remove Brie from the baking sheet, and place on a serving platter. Spoon melted preserves over Brie, and serve hot.

Artichokes and Olives on Cucumber

Cucumber slices hold a dollop of creamy filling seasoned with green chiles and Parmesan cheese.

Snack servings:	Yield:	Prep time:	Serving size:
8	about 24 *canapés*	10 minutes	3 canapés

Each serving has:			
181 calories	6g protein	8g carbohydrates	2g fiber
14g fat	4g saturated fat	glycemic index: low	glycemic load: 0

1 cup low-fat mayonnaise

1 cup freshly grated Parmesan cheese

1 (4-oz.) can green chiles, chopped

¼ cup black olives, chopped

1 cup artichoke hearts, chopped

2 medium cucumbers, sliced

1. In a medium bowl, mix together mayonnaise, Parmesan cheese, green chiles, black olives, and artichoke hearts.

2. Top each cucumber slice with 1 tablespoon artichoke mixture, and serve.

Variation: In place of the cucumbers, you can use jicama slices or celery stalks.

GLYCO-LINGO

Canapés are bite-size hors d'oeuvres. They're usually served on a small piece of bread or toast, but cucumbers work, too.

Monterey Jack Tacos

Corn tortillas are flavored with earthy tastes of the American Southwest: sautéed onions, chiles, and Monterey Jack cheese.

Snack servings:	Yield:	Prep time:	Cook time:	Serving size:
6	6 tacos	10 minutes	6 or 7 minutes	1 taco

Each serving has:			
112 calories	4g protein	13g carbohydrates	2g fiber
6g fat	3g saturated fat	glycemic index: low	glycemic load: 3

3 canned green chiles (your choice of heat)

1 TB. butter

1 small white onion, sliced

½ cup Monterey Jack cheese, shredded

6 (6-in.) corn tortillas

1. Cut chiles into thin strips. Set aside.

2. In a medium skillet over medium heat, heat butter. Add onion, and cook for 4 or 5 minutes or until softened. Stir in chile strips, and top with Monterey Jack cheese. Cover, reduce heat to low, and cook for about 2 minutes or until cheese melts.

3. Scoop chile mixture into tortillas, fold into tacos, and serve.

TASTY BITE

Cut down this recipe to two servings by using 1 chile, ¼ cup sliced onion, 1 teaspoon butter, 2½ tablespoons cheese, and 1 corn tortilla. This size is perfect for you and a friend for a late-night snack.

Green Olives with Feta and Celery

Tangy green olives in mild cheese are accented with fresh thyme.

Snack servings:	Yield:	Prep time:	Serving size:
4	20 stuffed celery pieces	10 minutes	5 stuffed celery pieces

Each serving has:			
120 calories	11g protein	4g carbohydrates	2g fiber
7g fat	4g saturated fat	glycemic index: low	glycemic load: 0

1 cup low-fat cottage cheese

½ cup feta cheese, lightly crumbled

½ cup pitted green olives, chopped

1 TB. fresh thyme, snipped

20 (3-in.) celery pieces

1. In a small bowl, mix cottage cheese and feta cheese.

2. Add green olives and thyme, and mix well.

3. Fill celery pieces with cheese mixture, and serve. Store any leftover cheese mixture in the refrigerator for 4 days for later use.

HEALTHY NOTE

You'll enjoy the taste of Greek flavors in every bite of this easy-to-make snack.

Cheese and Fruit Kabobs

This refreshing snack offers bites of cheddar and Swiss cheeses with fresh fruit.

Snack servings:	Yield:	Prep time:	Serving size:
8	8 kabobs	15 minutes	1 kabob

Each serving has:			
147 calories	15g protein	14g carbohydrates	2g fiber
4g fat	3g saturated fat	glycemic index: low	glycemic load: 9

½ lb. low-fat cheddar cheese, cut into 1-in. chunks

½ lb. low-fat Swiss cheese, cut into 1-in. chunks

2 cups fresh pineapple, peeled and cut into 1-in. chunks

2 cups seedless green or red grapes

1 pt. strawberries

8 (10-in.) wooden skewers

1. Thread chunks of cheddar cheese, Swiss cheese, pineapple, grapes, and strawberries alternately onto 8 wooden skewers.

2. Serve immediately.

 HEALTHY NOTE

These kabobs make great snacks for children because they'll love the novelty. Pack in a lunchbox as a snack or bring along to soccer or softball practice.

Blue Cheese Pitas

These pitas feature a creamy blue cheese spread accented with cayenne and black pepper.

Snack servings:	Yield:	Prep time:	Cook time:	Serving size:
8	8 half pitas	15 minutes	10 to 12 minutes	$\frac{1}{2}$ pita

Each serving has:			
195 calories	11g protein	19g carbohydrates	2g fiber
9g fat	4g saturated fat	glycemic index: low	glycemic load: 7

2 (3-oz.) pkg. low-fat cream cheese, softened

1 cup blue cheese, crumbled

1 TB. extra-virgin olive oil

$\frac{1}{4}$ cup skim milk

3 eggs

$\frac{1}{8}$ tsp. cayenne

$\frac{1}{8}$ tsp. ground black pepper

4 whole-wheat pitas, split into rounds

1. Preheat the oven to 375°F. Line 2 cookie sheets with parchment paper or aluminum foil.

2. In a small bowl, and using an electric mixer on medium speed or in a food processor fitted with a chopping blade, beat or process cream cheese and blue cheese for 30 to 60 seconds or until well blended. Add extra-virgin olive oil, skim milk, eggs, cayenne, and pepper, and beat or process for 30 to 60 seconds or until light and fluffy.

3. Place pita halves on the cookie sheets. Place $\frac{1}{8}$ of cheese mixture on each pita half and spread to edges.

4. Bake for 10 to 12 minutes or until golden brown. Serve warm.

Italian Pizza on a Pita

Italian seasoning flavors this mozzarella pita pizza.

Snack servings:	Yield:	Prep time:	Cook time:	Serving size:
6	6 half pitas	10 minutes	10 to 12 minutes	1 half pita
Each serving has:				
149 calories	10g protein	20g carbohydrates	3g fiber	
4g fat	2g saturated fat	glycemic index: low	glycemic load: 8	

3 whole-wheat pitas, split into rounds

$1\frac{1}{2}$ cups low-fat mozzarella cheese, shredded

3 tsp. Italian seasoning

$\frac{3}{4}$ cup red onion, sliced thinly

1 small tomato, sliced thinly

1. Preheat the oven to 350°F.

2. Place pita halves on an ungreased baking sheet. Sprinkle with mozzarella cheese and Italian seasoning. Top with red onion and tomato slices.

3. Bake for 10 to 12 minutes. Serve immediately.

Variation: Add any of your favorite pizza toppings: anchovies, pepperoni slices, hot peppers, mushrooms, etc.

Gorgonzola Bites with Fresh Fruit

Crisp bacon flavors this blend of Gorgonzola and cream cheese served with fresh fruit.

Snack servings:	Yield:	Prep time:	Serving size:
8	16 balls	15 minutes plus 1 hour chill time	2 balls, $\frac{1}{8}$ fruit slices

Each serving has:			
114 calories	7g protein	9g carbohydrates	2g fiber
6g fat	4g saturated fat	glycemic index: low	glycemic load: 0

$\frac{1}{2}$ (8-oz.) pkg. low-fat cream cheese, softened

1 (4-oz.) pkg. crumbled Gorgonzola cheese

$\frac{1}{2}$ tsp. Worcestershire sauce

$\frac{1}{4}$ tsp. ground black pepper

$\frac{1}{2}$ cup bacon, cooked and crumbled

1 medium apple, your choice variety, cored and sliced (skin on)

1 medium Bartlet pear, cored and sliced (skin on)

1 cup green grapes

1. In a food processor fitted with a chopping blade, combine cream cheese, Gorgonzola cheese, Worcestershire sauce, and pepper for 30 to 60 seconds or until well combined. Cover tightly and chill at least 1 hour or until firm. (You can prepare cheese mixture up to 3 days in advance.)

2. Roll cheese mixture into 16 round balls about the size of a truffle. Roll each ball in bacon. Serve immediately, or cover and chill until ready to serve. Serve with apple and pear slices and grapes.

Layered Greek Pie

This memorable Greek pie is flavored with garlic, hummus, and oregano.

Snack servings:	Yield:	Prep time:	Serving size:
8	1 (9-inch) pie	15 minutes plus 2 hours chill time	$\frac{1}{8}$ pie, 2 pita quarters

Each serving has:			
216 calories	12g protein	26g carbohydrates	4g fiber
8g fat	3g saturated fat	glycemic index: low	glycemic load: 6

1 cup low-fat cottage cheese

1 TB. lemon juice

1 tsp. dried oregano

$1\frac{1}{2}$ tsp. minced garlic

$1\frac{1}{2}$ cups hummus

1 cup cucumber, chopped

1 cup tomato, chopped

$\frac{1}{2}$ cup pitted kalamata olives, chopped

$\frac{1}{2}$ cup crumbled feta cheese

4 whole-wheat pitas, split into rounds, and cut in quarters

1. In a food processor fitted with a chopping blade, process cottage cheese, lemon juice, oregano, and garlic for 30 to 60 seconds or until smooth and combined.

2. Spread cottage cheese mixture into a deep 9-inch pie plate or shallow serving dish. Spread hummus evenly over cream cheese layer. Top with cucumber, tomato, olives, and feta cheese. Cover and refrigerate for 2 to 24 hours.

3. Serve with pita wedges for dipping.

Olive Tapenade Roll-Ups

Tangy olive tapenade and oregano flavor these cream cheese roll-ups.

Snack servings:	Yield:	Prep time:	Cook time:	Serving size:
4	4 half tortillas	10 minutes	4 minutes	1 half tortilla

Each serving has:			
128 calories	42g protein	11g carbohydrates	1g fiber
11g fat	1g saturated fat	glycemic index: low	glycemic load: 3

1 (3-oz.) pkg. cream cheese, softened

¾ cup olive tapenade

1 tsp. extra-virgin olive oil

2 (10-in.) whole-wheat tortillas

2 TB. fresh oregano, snipped, or 2 tsp. dried

1. In a medium bowl, and using an electric mixer on medium speed, beat cream cheese for 1 or 2 minutes or until smooth. Stir in olive tapenade.

2. In a large skillet over medium heat, heat extra-virgin olive oil. Add 1 tortilla to the skillet, and heat for 1 minute per side. Repeat with second tortilla.

3. Spread cheese mixture on tortillas. Top with oregano, and roll tortillas. Cut in half, and serve.

HEALTHY NOTE

Rolled tortillas, either whole wheat or corn, make perfect snacks. Spread a tortilla with your favorite combinations of beans, cheeses, vegetables, and condiments, roll it up, and you have a couple bites to eat quickly and easily.

Bell Pepper and Tofu Kabobs

Enjoy the taste of sesame seed–coated tofu kabobs with a sweet chile dipping sauce.

Snack servings:	Yield:	Prep time:	Cook time:	Serving size:
4	4 kabobs	15 minutes	10 to 12 minutes	1 kabob

Each serving has:			
208 calories	11g protein	17g carbohydrates	5g fiber
12g fat	2g saturated fat	glycemic index: low	glycemic load: 5

½ cup sesame seeds

1 (10.5-oz.) pkg. firm tofu, cut into 1-in. cubes

2 medium red bell peppers, ribs and seeds removed, and cut into 1-in. chunks

2 medium green bell peppers, ribs and seeds removed, and cut into 1-in. chunks

4 (10-in.) metal skewers

4 TB. bottled sweet chile dipping sauce

1. Preheat the broiler to medium. Line a broiler rack with aluminum foil.

2. In a blender or food processor fitted with a chopping blade, grind sesame seeds. Transfer to a plate.

3. Turn tofu cubes in nuts to coat.

4. Thread chunks of red bell peppers and green bell peppers on skewers, alternating with sesame seed–coated tofu. Place in the oven on the prepared broiler rack.

5. Broil kabobs, turning frequently, for 10 to 20 minutes or until bell peppers and sesame seeds begin to brown. Transfer kabobs to plates, and serve with sweet chile dipping sauce.

TASTY BITE

The tofu in this recipe absorbs the taste of the sesame seeds and the sweet chile dipping sauce. You'll enjoy the taste of Thai cooking with this simple recipe.

Japanese Tofu Skewers

Wasabi, soy sauce, and toasted sesame oil authentically flavor these tofu and mushroom skewers.

Snack servings:	Yield:	Prep time:	Cook time:	Serving size:
4	4 skewers	15 minutes	8 minutes	1 skewer

Each serving has:			
180 calories	10g protein	15g carbohydrates	2g fiber
11g fat	2g saturated fat	glycemic index: low	glycemic load: 4

½ cup reduced-sodium soy sauce

¼ cup mirin (sweet rice wine)

1 TB. toasted sesame oil

1 (15-oz.) pkg. tofu, cut into 1-in. cubes

16 small white mushroom caps

1 TB. extra-virgin olive oil

4 (10-in.) wooden skewers, soaked in water for 20 minutes

4 green onions, cut into 1½-in. lengths

⅔ cup reduced-sodium vegetable broth

2 tsp. wasabi paste

¼ cup lemon juice

1. Preheat the grill to medium.

2. In a small bowl, combine soy sauce, mirin, and sesame oil.

3. Add tofu cubes, and marinate for 10 minutes.

4. In a medium bowl, toss mushroom caps in extra-virgin olive oil to coat.

5. Drain tofu, preserving marinade. Slip tofu cubes onto the 4 wooden skewers, alternating with green onions and mushroom caps.

6. Spray grill grate with cooking oil. Grill tofu skewers, covered, turning once, for 6 to 8 minutes or until lightly browned.

7. In a small bowl, mix marinade with vegetable broth, wasabi paste, and lemon juice, and serve alongside skewers as a dipping sauce.

Tofu and Green Pea Soup

In this soup, green peas are cooked with chicken broth and flavored with miso, ginger, and watercress.

Snack servings:	Yield:	Prep time:	Cook time:	Serving size:
4	4 cups	5 minutes	10 minutes	about 1 cup

Each serving has:			
156 calories	11g protein	26g carbohydrates	9g fiber
1g fat	0g saturated fat	glycemic index: low	glycemic load: 6

4 cups frozen peas

3 cups low-sodium chicken broth

2 TB. green onion, diced

2 tsp. miso

2 tsp. fresh ginger root, coarsely chopped

½ cup watercress, coarsely chopped

½ cup firm tofu, crumbled

1. In a medium saucepan over medium heat, heat frozen peas with chicken broth. Cover, bring to a boil, and cook for about 10 minutes.

2. Add green onion, miso, ginger root, and watercress. Heat for 1 minute, and remove from heat.

3. Carefully pour mixture into a blender or food processor fitted with a chopping blade, and purée for about 1 minute or until smooth.

4. Pour into 4 bowls, and evenly divide crumbled tofu on top of each bowl. Serve hot, at room temperature, or chill and serve cold.

HEALTHY NOTE

Miso soup replenishes electrolytes and is all-over good for your body. Miso is a paste made by fermenting soybeans. Serve this soup at the onset of a cold or flu, after strenuous exercise, or when you need a remedy for fatigue and stress.

Tofu Salad with Peanut Sauce

Here, tofu and red bell peppers on a bed of lettuce are flavored with spicy garlic peanut sauce.

Snack servings:	Yield:	Prep time:	Cook time:	Serving size:
6	about 12 cups	15 minutes	10 to 12 minutes	2 cups

Each serving has:			
138 calories	9g protein	8g carbohydrates	3g fiber
9g fat	2g saturated fat	glycemic index: low	glycemic load: 0

3 TB. chunky peanut butter

2 tsp. minced garlic

2 TB. hot water

1 tsp. honey

1 TB. rice vinegar

2 tsp. low-sodium soy sauce

⅛ tsp. crushed red pepper flakes

1 large head iceberg lettuce, chopped (8 cups)

1 sweet red pepper, ribs and seeds removed, and thinly sliced

¼ cup green onions, thinly sliced

1 (14-oz.) pkg. firm tofu

1 TB. extra-virgin olive oil

1. In a small bowl, stir together chunky peanut butter, garlic, hot water, honey, rice vinegar, soy sauce, and crushed red pepper flakes.

2. In a large bowl, place lettuce, red pepper, and green onions.

3. Drain tofu and cut into 1-inch squares. Pat dry with paper towels.

4. In a large skillet over medium heat, heat extra-virgin olive oil. Add tofu, and cook for 10 to 12 minutes, turning often, until golden brown.

5. Add tofu to salad, and toss with peanut dressing.

HEALTHY NOTE

Tofu is an excellent source of low-fat protein. In this salad, you get the crisp taste of the sautéed tofu along with the crisp texture of the iceberg lettuce.

Heartier Fare

When your appetite yearns for a substantial snack, satisfy it with a recipe from Part 3. The calorie count of the recipes in these chapters ranges from 100 to 300 per snack while the flavors and textures give you big taste satisfaction.

You're going to love the meats, seafood, poultry, eggs, and legumes that fill you up while being watchful of your health and waistline. In addition to enjoying these snacks at home, serve them at parties, get-togethers, potlucks, and buffets. Everyone will enjoy your thoughtfulness!

Beef, Pork, and Lamb

In This Chapter

- Meaty snacks from around the globe
- Wraps, kabobs, burgers, and more
- Mixing meats for interesting tastes
- Cooking enough for a week's worth of snacks

For some people, meat makes all the difference. Whether it's beef, pork, or lamb, meat adds a delicious and high-quality protein to your snacks. The meaty recipes in this chapter will definitely satisfy your taste buds.

And forget about boring! With the Greek, Caribbean, Italian, Southwestern, Asian, and all-American recipes in this chapter, you'll take a culinary tour of the world with these and many other wonderful flavors in this chapter.

The most widely accepted way to eat a snack is with one's fingers, so we've created beef, pork, and lamb recipes that are delicious as wraps, sandwiches, and pitas. We also added some salads you'll need a fork for. But whether you eat them with your fingers or with utensils, we hope you love the meaty snacks in this chapter.

Many of the recipes make six or eight snacks. If that's too many servings for you or your family, you can store them for 2 or 3 days in the refrigerator, or freeze them for later in the week or month. If you plan to freeze them, freeze the fillings and add them to the tortillas, pitas, breads, lettuce, etc., when you're ready to eat.

Beef and Black Bean Lettuce Wraps

These tasty lettuce wraps are flavored with ginger, peanuts, and black bean salsa.

Snack servings:	Yield:	Prep time:	Serving size:
4	8 wraps	15 minutes plus 1 hour chill time	2 wraps

Each serving has:			
195 calories	20g protein	13g carbohydrates	3g fiber
8g fat	2g saturated fat	glycemic index: low	glycemic load: 2

1 (16-oz.) jar black bean and corn salsa, drained

1½ cups cooked beef, shredded

½ cup red bell pepper, chopped

¼ cup fresh cilantro, snipped

2 tsp. fresh ginger, grated

8 large butterhead or iceberg lettuce leaves

¼ cup salted peanuts, chopped (optional)

1. In a medium bowl, combine salsa, beef, red bell pepper, cilantro, and ginger. Cover and chill for 1 to 24 hours.

2. Spoon about 4 tablespoons beef mixture into each lettuce leaf. Top with peanuts (if using), roll up leaves, and serve.

TASTY BITE

For this snack, you can use leftover roast beef, packaged cooked beef, or deli-sliced beef.

Beef Gyros

You'll enjoy the complex flavors of Greek cuisine as you eat these gyros containing oregano, garlic, and lemon.

Snack servings:	Yield:	Prep time:	Cook time:	Serving size:
8	8 ½ pitas	15 minutes plus 30 minutes marinate time	14 to 20 minutes	½ pita

Each serving has:			
223 calories	21g protein	22g carbohydrates	4g fiber
7g fat	2g saturated fat	glycemic index: low	glycemic load: 8

1 tsp. dried oregano

¼ tsp. ground cumin

½ tsp. paprika

¼ tsp. ground black pepper

1 tsp. minced garlic

1 TB. lemon juice

2 tsp. extra-virgin olive oil

1 lb. eye round beef steak, trimmed of visible fat and sliced into 4 (4-oz.) lean beef tenderloins

1 large yellow or white onion, thinly sliced

2 medium red or green bell peppers, ribs and seeds removed, and thinly sliced

4 whole-wheat pitas

2 medium tomatoes, coarsely chopped

1 cup Tzatziki (recipe in Chapter 5) or Greek-style yogurt

1. In a small bowl, mix together oregano, cumin, paprika, pepper, garlic, lemon juice, and 1 teaspoon extra-virgin olive oil. Rub mixture onto steaks, place in a zippered plastic bag, and marinate for 30 minutes or overnight in refrigerator.

2. Preheat the broiler to high. Line a baking sheet with aluminum foil.

3. Remove steaks from marinade, place on the prepared baking sheet, and broil for 7 to 10 minutes. Remove from the oven and let cool for 5 minutes. Slice thinly.

4. Meanwhile, in a small skillet over medium-high heat, heat remaining 1 teaspoon extra-virgin olive oil. Add onion and bell peppers, and sauté for about 7 to 10 minutes or until soft.

5. To assemble, cut pitas in half, open pocket, and place 2 ounces steak, ½ cup bell pepper–onion mixture, and ½ cup tomatoes in each pita half. Top each half pita with Tzatziki, and serve.

Variation: Use lamb in place of the beef for another traditional Greek snack.

Mexican Beef Tostadas

These open-face beef tostadas are flavored with green chiles and topped with sour cream.

Snack servings:	Yield:	Prep time:	Cook time:	Serving size:
8	8 tortillas	11 minutes	4 minutes	1 tortilla

Each serving has:			
199 calories	21g protein	14g carbohydrates	2g fiber
6g fat	3g saturated fat	glycemic index: low	glycemic load: 6

8 (6-in.) corn tortillas

1 (17-oz.) pkg. refrigerated beef pot roast with juices or leftover pot roast

1 (14.5-oz.) can diced tomatoes and green chiles, with juice

1 medium green bell pepper, ribs and seeds removed, and cut into strips

½ cup low-fat sour cream

1 medium lime, cut into wedges

1. Wrap tortillas in paper towels, and microwave on high/100 percent power for 45 to 60 seconds or until warm. Cover and set aside.

2. Microwave beef according to the package directions.

3. Meanwhile, in a small saucepan over medium heat, heat tomatoes with juice for 4 minutes.

4. Cut meat into slices, and serve on warmed tortillas with tomatoes and green pepper strips. Top each with 1 tablespoon sour cream, and serve with lime wedges.

Zucchini with Beef and Peppers

Cinnamon and black pepper with raisins flavor this zucchini filled with beef and vegetables.

Snack servings:	Yield:	Prep time:	Cook time:	Serving size:
4	4 zucchini halves	15 minutes	20 minutes	$\frac{1}{2}$ zucchini

Each serving has:			
183 calories	21g protein	9g carbohydrates	2g fiber
6g fat	1g saturated fat	glycemic index: low	glycemic load: 2

2 medium zucchini

$\frac{1}{2}$ cup water

1 TB. extra-virgin olive oil

$\frac{1}{2}$ lb. ground beef

1 medium green bell pepper, ribs and seeds removed, and chopped

$\frac{1}{2}$ medium yellow or white onion, chopped

2 tsp. minced garlic

2 TB. golden raisins

$\frac{1}{8}$ tsp. salt

$\frac{1}{8}$ tsp. ground black pepper

$\frac{1}{8}$ tsp. ground cinnamon

$\frac{1}{4}$ cup shredded cheddar cheese

1 TB. pine nuts

1. Cut zucchini in $\frac{1}{2}$ lengthwise. Using a small spoon, carefully scoop out flesh, leaving a $\frac{1}{4}$-inch-thick shell around edges. Discard flesh.

2. Place each zucchini half cut side down in an 11x7x2-inch glass baking dish. Add water and cover lightly to vent and let air escape while heating. Microwave on high for 4 minutes. Place cooked zucchini in a large baking dish, and repeat with remaining zucchini.

3. Preheat the oven to 400°F.

4. In a large skillet over medium heat, heat extra-virgin olive oil and ground beef, stirring, for 10 to 15 minutes or until browned. Remove beef from the skillet and set aside. Drain the skillet.

5. Add green bell pepper, onion, and garlic, and cook, stirring occasionally, for 5 minutes. Stir in beef, golden raisins, salt, pepper, and cinnamon, and cook 2 minutes, stirring occasionally. Turn off heat, and stir in cheese.

6. Divide beef mixture among 8 zucchini halves. Sprinkle pine nuts over top, and bake for 10 minutes. Serve immediately.

TASTY BITE

Instead of pine nuts, you could use chopped hazelnuts or walnuts instead.

Top Sirloin Kabobs

These tender steak kabobs are gently flavored with thyme and garlic.

Snack servings:	Yield:	Prep time:	Cook time:	Serving size:
8	8 kabobs	10 minutes plus 30 minutes marinate time	10 to 12 minutes	1 kabob

Each serving has:			
256 calories	34g protein	0g carbohydrates	0g fiber
12g fat	3g saturated fat	glycemic index: low	glycemic load: 0

3 TB. extra-virgin olive oil

1 TB. minced garlic

1 TB. yellow or white onion, minced

1½ tsp. dried thyme, crushed

1 tsp. ground black pepper

½ tsp. salt

2 lb. beef top sirloin steak, trimmed of fat and cut into 1-in. cubes

8 wooden skewers, soaked for 20 minutes, or 8 metal skewers

1. In a large bowl, combine extra-virgin olive oil, garlic, onion, thyme, pepper, and salt. Add steak, and toss to coat evenly. Let stand at room temperature for 30 minutes.

2. Preheat the grill to medium.

3. Thread meat onto the skewers, leaving ¼ inch between pieces.

4. Grill skewers, covered, for 10 to 12 minutes for medium rare (145°F), turning to brown evenly. Serve at once.

TASTY BITE

These wonderfully flavored kabobs contain high-quality protein and fat but are missing fiber and carbohydrates. To eat a balanced snack, add vegetables or fruit as a side dish.

Mediterranean Beef Wraps

These convenient wraps are flavored with dill, garlic, and feta cheese.

Snack servings:	Yield:	Prep time:	Cook time:	Serving size:
8	4 wraps	10 minutes	7 to 9 minutes	$\frac{1}{2}$ wrap
Each serving has:				
211 calories	23g protein	13g carbohydrates	2g fiber	
7g fat	3g saturated fat	glycemic index: low	glycemic load: 3	

1 lb. ground beef round	$\frac{1}{2}$ tsp. ground black pepper
1 small red onion, chopped	$\frac{1}{4}$ tsp. salt
1 cucumber, finely diced	4 (8- or 10-in.) garden-spinach flatbread wraps
1 cup low-fat Greek-style yogurt	
1 tsp. minced garlic	3 plum tomatoes, finely chopped
1 tsp. dried dill	1 (4-oz.) pkg. crumbled feta cheese

1. In a large skillet over medium-high heat, cook beef and onion, stirring often, for 7 to 9 minutes or until beef crumbles and is no longer pink. Drain.

2. In a medium bowl, stir together cucumber, yogurt, garlic, dill, pepper, and salt.

3. Spoon 2 tablespoons cucumber mixture down center of each wrap. Top with beef mixture, tomatoes, and feta. Roll up. Serve with remaining cucumber mixture.

Variation: In place of the flatbread wraps, you could also use whole-wheat pita bread.

Beef and Blue Cheese Wraps

The luscious taste of blue cheese is wrapped with thyme and tomatoes.

Snack servings:	Yield:	Prep time:	Cook time:	Serving size:
8	4 tortillas	15 minutes	4 minutes	$\frac{1}{2}$ tortilla

Each serving has:			
200 calories	18g protein	19g carbohydrates	5g fiber
6g fat	2g saturated fat	glycemic index: low	glycemic load: 4

3 TB. reduced-fat mayonnaise

1 tsp. dried thyme, crushed

2 TB. yellow mustard

4 (8-in.) flour tortillas

12 oz. cooked roast beef, thinly sliced

$1\frac{1}{2}$ cups tomatoes, diced

$\frac{1}{3}$ cup crumbled blue cheese

4 cups mixed greens

1. In a small bowl, combine mayonnaise and dried thyme. Remove and set aside 1 tablespoon mayonnaise mixture. Stir yellow mustard into remaining mayonnaise mixture.

2. Spread one side of each tortilla with mayonnaise-mustard mixture. Evenly divide roast beef, tomatoes, and blue cheese among tortillas. Roll, and brush with reserved mayonnaise-dried thyme mixture.

3. In extra-large skillet over medium heat, lightly brown tortillas for about 2 minutes per side. Cut wraps in $\frac{1}{2}$.

4. Divide greens among salad dishes, and top with halved wraps.

Moroccan Burgers

These burgers blended with apricots and pine nuts sizzle with an exotic blend of spices.

Snack servings:	Yield:	Prep time:	Cook time:	Serving size:
6	6 burgers	10 minutes	14 to 18 minutes	1 burger

Each serving has:			
250 calories	27g protein	17g carbohydrates	1g fiber
8g fat	2g saturated fat	glycemic index: low	glycemic load: 8

1 lb. ground beef (85 percent lean)

1/3 cup dried apricots, finely snipped

2 TB. pine nuts, toasted

2 TB. fresh cilantro, chopped

2 tsp. minced garlic

1/4 tsp. salt

1/2 tsp. ground cumin

1/4 tsp. ground cinnamon

1/4 tsp. ground coriander

1/4 tsp. ground black pepper

4 kaiser rolls

8 TB. Moroccan Ketchup (recipe in Chapter 5)

4 red leaf lettuce leaves

1 medium tomato, sliced

1. Preheat the grill to medium.

2. In a large bowl, combine ground beef, apricots, pine nuts, cilantro, garlic, salt, cumin, cinnamon, coriander, and pepper. Shape mixture into 6 (3/4-inch-thick) patties.

3. Grill patties, uncovered, for 14 to 18 minutes or until done (160°F), turning once halfway through grilling.

4. Serve burgers on kaiser rolls topped with Moroccan Ketchup, lettuce, and tomato slices.

TASTY BITE

Moroccan spices, from northwest Africa, are cumin, coriander, and cilantro. They add an exotic flavor to your snack.

Steak Sandwiches with Peppers and Onions

Steak is served on a stone-ground baguette and smothered with peppers, onion, and tomatoes.

Snack servings:	Yield:	Prep time:	Cook time:	Serving size:
4	4 sandwiches	15 minutes plus 5 min-utes stand time	20 to 30 minutes	1 sandwich

Each serving has:			
222 calories	192g protein	19g carbohydrates	3g fiber
8g fat	2g saturated fat	glycemic index: low	glycemic load: 8

2 tsp. extra-virgin olive oil	8 oz. flank steak
2 medium green bell peppers, ribs and seeds removed, and sliced	1 (12- to 16-in.) stone-ground whole-wheat baguette, cut crosswise into 4 pieces
1 medium yellow onion, sliced	$\frac{1}{8}$ tsp. salt
1 (14.5-oz.) can diced tomatoes, drained	$\frac{1}{8}$ tsp. ground black pepper

1. In a large skillet over medium heat, heat 1 teaspoon extra-virgin olive oil. Add bell peppers and onion, and sauté for 5 minutes or until vegetables are tender.

2. Add tomatoes, bring to a simmer, and cook for 5 to 8 minutes or until slightly thickened.

3. Meanwhile, in another skillet over medium-high heat, heat remaining 1 tea-spoon extra-virgin olive oil. Add steak, and cook for 4 or 5 minutes or until browned. Turn and cook other side for 4 or 5 more minutes for medium rare. For medium, cook each side 5 or 6 minutes.

4. Transfer steak from the skillet to a cutting board, and let stand 5 to 10 minutes. Thinly slice steak against the grain.

5. Cut each baguette section horizontally and fill with steak, followed by vegetable mixture, and season with salt and pepper. Pierce sandwiches with toothpicks to hold together, if desired, and serve immediately.

HEALTHY NOTE

These small steak sandwiches are just the right size for a hearty snack that won't ruin your appetite for dinner.

Hot Dogs with Avocado-Chili Relish

Jalapeños spice up the avocado and tomato in this hot dog relish.

Snack servings:	Yield:	Prep time:	Cook time:	Serving size:
8	8 ½ hot dogs	15 minutes	10 minutes	½ hot dog

Each serving has:			
197 calories	9g protein	14g carbohydrates	3g fiber
12g fat	4g saturated fat	glycemic index: low	glycemic load: 6

2 TB. extra-virgin olive oil

1 or 2 medium jalapeño peppers, ribs and seeds removed, and thinly sliced

4 green onions, white parts only, thinly sliced

2 TB. lime juice

1 cup tomatoes, diced

1 avocado, peeled, pitted, and coarsely chopped

⅛ tsp. salt

⅛ tsp. ground black pepper

4 all-beef frankfurters or other bun-size sausages

2 TB. butter, softened

1 tsp. minced garlic

4 whole-wheat hot dog rolls, split in ½

1. Preheat the grill to medium.

2. In a small bowl, whisk together extra-virgin olive oil, jalapeños, green onions, and lime juice. Gently fold in tomatoes and avocado, and sprinkle lightly with salt and pepper.

3. Prepare frankfurters as desired.

4. In a small bowl, mix butter and garlic. Spread garlic butter on rolls.

5. Place rolls buttered side down on the grill, and toast for 2 or 3 minutes or until light golden. (Or place rolls on a baking sheet and broil in oven on low for 2 to 4 minutes.)

6. To serve, tuck frankfurters in toasted rolls, cut in ½, and top with avocado-chili relish. Serve immediately.

HEALTHY NOTE

In this snack, we've reduced the size of the frankfurter but made up for it by adding plenty of extra flavor!

New Orleans Quesadillas

Green olives with pimientos add flavor and zest to these baked salami, ham, and cheese quesadillas.

Snack servings:	Yield:	Prep time:	Cook time:	Serving size:
8	8 slices	10 minutes	15 minutes	1 slice

Each serving has:			
171 calories	10g protein	13g carbohydrates	1g fiber
8g fat	3g saturated fat	glycemic index: low	glycemic load: 4

4 (8- or 10-in.) whole-wheat tortillas

4 oz. thinly sliced Italian salami

1 cup part-skim mozzarella cheese, shredded

4 oz. thinly sliced Virginia ham

1/3 cup sliced pimiento-stuffed olives

1. Preheat the oven to 400°F.

2. Place 2 tortillas on a baking sheet.

3. Arrange quesadillas by overlapping slices of salami on 2 tortillas. Top each with 1/4 cup cheese, 1/2 of ham slices, 1/4 cup cheese, and 1/2 of olives. Top each prepared tortilla with 1 remaining tortilla.

4. Bake for 15 minutes or until golden. Remove to cutting board, cut each tortilla in 4 pieces, and serve.

TASTY BITE

The ingredients in these quesadillas—ham, salami, cheese, and olives—are used in New Orleans' famous muffaletta sandwiches.

Italian Sausage and Pesto Wraps

These wraps are packed with Italian-flavored vegetables, sausage, and cheese.

Snack servings:	Yield:	Prep time:	Cook time:	Serving size:
8	8 tortillas	10 minutes	15 to 20 minutes	1 tortilla

Each serving has:			
242 calories	14g protein	18g carbohydrates	4g fiber
13g fat	3g saturated fat	glycemic index: low	glycemic load: 4

8 oz. bulk mild Italian sausage

2 large yellow and/or red bell peppers, ribs and seeds removed, and cut into strips

1 medium white or yellow onion, sliced

1 (6-oz.) jar quartered marinated artichoke hearts, with liquid

¼ cup purchased basil pesto

8 (10-in.) flour tortillas

1½ cups low-fat Italian cheese blend, shredded

1. In a large skillet over medium heat, add sausage and cook, stirring, for 5 to 10 minutes or until brown. Drain fat from the skillet.

2. Add bell peppers and onion, and sauté for 3 or 4 minutes or until vegetables are crisp-tender. Add artichoke hearts with liquid and basil pesto, and cook for 5 minutes or until heated.

3. Divide sausage mixture among tortillas, top with cheese, roll, and serve.

Italian Sausage and Turkey Patties

Italian sausage adds spice and heat to these meat patties topped with a tasty ketchup-mayonnaise sauce.

Snack servings:	Yield:	Prep time:	Cook time:	Serving size:
8	8 burgers	5 minutes	10 minutes	1 burger

Each serving has:			
191 calories	12g protein	5g carbohydrates	1g fiber
14g fat	4g saturated fat	glycemic index: low	glycemic load: 6

3 TB. ketchup

3 TB. cup low-fat mayonnaise

½ lb. lean ground turkey

½ lb. sweet or hot Italian sausage, removed from casings

¼ cup yellow or white onion, minced

2 tsp. minced garlic

¾ tsp. ground black pepper

2 medium tomatoes, sliced

8 thin slices sweet onion

1. Heat an outdoor grill or stovetop grill pan to medium-high.

2. In a small bowl, mix ketchup and mayonnaise.

3. In a large bowl, mix ground turkey, sausage, minced onion, garlic, and pepper. Divide mixture into 8 portions, and form each into a ¾-inch-thick burger.

4. Grill patties, turning once, for 10 minutes or until cooked through.

5. Serve patties, topped with ketchup-mayonnaise sauce, tomato slices, and sweet onion slices.

Classic Reuben with Pineapple

This classic Rueben sandwich features sauerkraut, ham, turkey, and cheeses, and is sweetened with pineapple.

Snack servings: 8	Yield: 4 sandwiches	Prep time: 10 minutes	Cook time: 5 minutes	Serving size: ½ sandwich
Each serving has:				
210 calories	16g protein	9g carbohydrates	1g fiber	
12g fat	4g saturated fat	glycemic index: low	glycemic load: 4	

8 slices sourdough rye bread or whole-grain pumpernickel, toasted

½ cup bottled low-fat Thousand Island salad dressing

4 oz. sliced cooked turkey

4 oz. sliced cooked ham

4 slices low-fat Swiss cheese

1 cup canned sauerkraut, well drained

½ cup canned crushed pineapple, well drained

4 slices low-fat sharp cheddar cheese

4 slices red onion

1. Preheat the broiler to low.

2. Place bread slices on a large baking sheet. Spread one side of each slice with Thousand Island salad dressing. Top ½ of bread slices with turkey, ham, and Swiss cheese slices. Divide sauerkraut, crushed pineapple, cheddar cheese, and sliced onion equally among 8 slices.

3. Broil 5 inches from the heat for 5 minutes or until cheese is melted.

4. Remove from the oven, and carefully top turkey-topped bread slices with sauerkraut-topped slices, onion sides down, and serve.

Deli Ham and Turkey Pitas

Cheddar cheese, olives, and Italian dressing flavor these sliced meat-filled pitas.

Snack servings:	Yield:	Prep time:	Serving size:
8	8 ½ pitas	10 minutes	½ pita

Each serving has:			
227 calories	15g protein	23g carbohydrates	2g fiber
8g fat	2g saturated fat	glycemic index: low	glycemic load: 10

1 small cucumber, chopped

¼ cup white or yellow onion, chopped

1 (2¼-oz.) can sliced ripe black olives, drained

¼ cup low-fat Italian salad dressing

4 whole-wheat pitas, cut in ½

½ lb. thinly sliced deli ham

½ lb. thinly sliced deli turkey

4 slices low-fat cheddar cheese

1. In a small bowl, combine cucumber, onion, olives, and Italian salad dressing.

2. Fill pita halves with equal amounts of ham, turkey, cheddar cheese, and cucumber mixture, and serve.

TASTY BITE

To make 4 snack servings, cut the amount of each ingredient in this recipe in half.

Ham, Corn, and Sweet Potato Patties

Ham, corn, and sweet potato add a sweetness to these patties that's balanced with the tasty bite of garlic.

Snack servings:	Yield:	Prep time:	Cook time:	Serving size:
8	8 patties	15 minutes	28 minutes	1 patty

Each serving has:			
142 calories	10g protein	8g carbohydrates	2g fiber
8g fat	4g saturated fat	glycemic index: low	glycemic load: 1

1 large sweet potato	1 cup frozen corn kernels, thawed
1 tsp. minced garlic	1 large egg
2 cups ham, diced	3 TB. fresh parsley, chopped
⅔ cup low-fat pepper jack cheese, shredded	2 tsp. extra-virgin olive oil

1. With a fork, pierce skin of sweet potato in several places. Place potato in the microwave, and cook on high for 6 to 8 minutes or until a fork easily pierces potato. Remove from the microwave.

2. Slit potato in ½ lengthwise, and spoon out pulp into a medium bowl, breaking up pulp into small pieces with a fork. Stir in garlic, ham, cheese, corn, egg, and parsley. Shape mixture into 8 (½-inch-thick) patties.

3. In a large skillet over medium-high heat, heat 1 teaspoon extra-virgin olive oil. Add 4 patties, and cook for 5 minutes per side or until golden. Remove cooked patties to a serving plate. Repeat with remaining 1 teaspoon extra-virgin olive oil and remaining 4 patties.

TASTY BITE

Freeze any leftover patties. You can defrost them quickly in the microwave for another day's snack.

Pork Posole

This hearty soup exudes the flavors of the Southwest with a chili verde sauce and fresh cilantro.

Snack servings:	Yield:	Prep time:	Cook time:	Serving size:
8	about 5 cups	15 minutes	7 to 9 hours	⅝ cup

Each serving has:			
138 calories	16g protein	11g carbohydrates	2g fiber
3g fat	1g saturated fat	glycemic index: low	glycemic load: 4

1 lb. boneless pork loin roast

1 (15- or 16-oz.) can hominy, drained

1 (10-oz.) can green enchilada sauce

¾ cup yellow or white onion, chopped

2 tsp. minced garlic

1 tsp. ground cumin

½ tsp. salt

¼ tsp. ground black pepper

1 cup fresh cilantro, chopped

1 TB. fresh lime juice

1. In a 4-quart or larger slow cooker, combine pork, hominy, enchilada sauce, onion, garlic, cumin, salt, and pepper. Cover and cook on low for 7 to 9 hours or until pork is tender.

2. Remove pork to a cutting board. Using 2 forks, tear meat into bite-size shreds.

3. Spoon any fat from sauce.

4. Stir in cilantro and lime juice, and return meat to the slow cooker for a few minutes to warm through. Ladle *posole* into soup bowls, and serve.

GLYCO-LINGO

Posole is a soup that originated in pre-Columbian Mexico. Today we enjoy it for the spicy chili taste, interesting texture, and heart-warming healthfulness. You can turn up the heat in this posole by adding chili powder or a finely diced jalapeño pepper.

Caribbean Pork and Fruit Salad

This pork is spiced with Caribbean jerk seasoning and added to a pineapple and cantaloupe salad.

Snack servings:	Yield:	Prep time:	Cook time:		Serving size:
6	12 cups	15 minutes	30 minutes plus 10 minutes rest time		2 cups

Each serving has:			
152 calories	21g protein	11g carbohydrates	2g fiber
3g fat	1g saturated fat	glycemic index: low	glycemic load: 6

1 lb. *pork tenderloin*	¼ cup fresh lime juice
4 tsp. Caribbean jerk seasoning	1 TB. honey
1 (8-oz.) can pineapple chunks, with juice	8 cups mixed salad greens
1 tsp. freshly grated lime zest	½ cantaloupe, cut into chunks

1. Preheat the oven to 425°F.

2. Place pork in a roasting pan, and rub with 3 teaspoons Caribbean jerk seasoning.

3. Roast pork for 30 minutes or until a thermometer inserted in center registers 155°F. Remove pork to cutting board, cover loosely with aluminum foil, and let rest 8 to 10 minutes.

4. Drain pineapple juice into a large serving bowl. Add lime zest, lime juice, honey, and remaining 1 teaspoon Caribbean jerk seasoning, and whisk to blend.

5. Cut pork into ¼-inch-thick slices. Add to the serving bowl along with salad greens, cantaloupe, and pineapple chunks. Toss to mix, and serve.

GLYCO-LINGO

Pork tenderloin is an affordable cut of very tender meat that's low in fat and high in flavor. Find it already marinated—or not—in the meat section of your grocery store.

Pulled Pork and Peach Wraps

This slow-cooked pork has the sweet fruity taste of peaches and a light Italian seasoning.

Snack servings:	Yield:	Prep time:	Cook time:	Serving size:
10	5 cups	15 minutes	4 or 5 (or 8 to 10) hours	½ cup on 1 tortilla

Each serving has:			
225 calories	21g protein	18g carbohydrates	3g fiber
7g fat	3g saturated fat	glycemic index: low	glycemic load: 7

1½ lb. boneless pork shoulder roast, trimmed of fat

1 medium yellow or white onion, cut into wedges

¼ tsp. salt

¼ tsp. ground black pepper

1 TB. minced garlic

1 (12- to 16-oz. pkg.) frozen peaches

1 TB. honey

1 (14.5-oz.) can diced tomatoes with basil, garlic, and oregano, drained

10 (8- to 10-in.) whole-wheat tortillas

10 large red or leaf lettuce leaves

1. In a 3- or 4-quart slow cooker, combine pork and onion. Sprinkle with salt and pepper, and add garlic, peaches, and honey. Cover, and cook on low for 8 to 10 hours or on high for 4 or 5 hours.

2. Remove meat to a cutting board, reserving remaining mixture in the slow cooker. Using 2 forks, pull meat apart into bite-size pieces. Return meat to the slow cooker.

3. Add tomatoes, and stir to combine. Keep warm on lowest setting.

4. Line tortillas with lettuce leaves. Using a slotted spoon, spoon meat mixture onto tortillas. Roll up and serve. Meat mixture can be refrigerated or frozen for later use.

Lamb Patties Piccata

Lemon adds zing to this lean lamb piccata seasoned with parsley.

Snack servings:	Yield:	Prep time:	Cook time:	Serving size:
4	4 patties	10 minutes	10 to 12 minutes	1 patty

Each serving has:			
139 calories	17g protein	3g carbohydrates	0g fiber
6g fat	3g saturated fat	glycemic index: low	glycemic load: 1

8 oz. lean ground lamb

¼ cup plus 2 TB. minced fresh parsley

2 TB. plain breadcrumbs

1 TB. lemon zest

2 tsp. minced garlic

¼ tsp. salt

¼ cup cold water

3 TB. lemon juice

1 TB. water

2 tsp. butter

4 large lettuce leaves

1. In a medium bowl, combine lamb, ¼ cup parsley, breadcrumbs, lemon zest, garlic, salt, and cold water using your hands or a wooden spoon until well blended. Shape into four 4-inch patties.

2. Lightly coat a large skillet with cooking spray, and heat over medium heat. Add patties, and cook for 5 or 6 minutes per side or until cooked through. Remove to serving plate.

3. Drain fat from the skillet.

4. Stir in lemon juice and water, and bring to a boil. Add butter, and stir to melt and blend. Remove from heat, stir in remaining 2 tablespoons parsley, and pour mixture over patties.

5. Serve each patty on a lettuce leaf.

Perfect Poultry

In This Chapter

- Nutritious chicken and turkey dishes
- Varying flavors and tastes
- Getting energized with high-quality protein

When you prepare a snack with chicken or turkey as a main ingredient, you'll love the pick-me-up you get in return. Poultry offers high-quality complete protein with low to moderate amounts of saturated fat. The sustained energy you'll get from these snacks is thanks to the protein and healthy fat combined with ingredients that offer low-glycemic carbohydrates.

And because chicken and turkey are so easily adaptable flavor-wise, you might be surprised at all the options available when you cook with poultry, from mild to strong. In the following pages, you'll find Asian-, Thai-, Mexican-, and Italian-flavored recipes along with milder fare.

In this chapter, you also discover new ways of serving chicken and turkey—in smaller bites than a full meal, but still with all the flavor! The recipes also call for both cooked and uncooked poultry, based on the needs of each recipe. For cooked poultry, you can use the frozen packages from the grocer, cook your own, or use leftovers.

Chicken and Brie Burgers

Creamy and tangy Brie cheese is melted on these tasty chicken snack burgers served in pita bread.

Snack servings:	Yield:	Prep time:	Cook time:	Serving size:
6	6 burgers	5 minutes	10 to 12 minutes	1 burger and $\frac{1}{2}$ pita

Each serving has:			
290 calories	29g protein	17g carbohydrates	1g fiber
11g fat	5g saturated fat	glycemic index: low	glycemic load: 6

2 TB. snipped fresh parsley, or 2 tsp. dried

2 TB. snipped fresh basil, or 2 tsp. dried

$\frac{1}{4}$ tsp. ground black pepper

1 lb. uncooked ground chicken

4 oz. Brie cheese, thinly sliced

3 whole-wheat pitas, cut in $\frac{1}{2}$

6 large Bibb lettuce leaves

1. In a large bowl, combine parsley, basil, and pepper. Add ground chicken, and mix well. Using your hands, shape mixture into 6 patties.

2. Lightly coat a grill pan or large skillet with cooking spray, and set it over medium heat. Add patties, and cook for 10 to 12 minutes or until done (165°F), turning once halfway through cooking. Top each chicken patty with Brie cheese during the last minute of cooking.

3. Tuck 1 burger into 1 pita half lined with 1 lettuce leaf, and serve.

Variation: For **Chicken Italian Burgers,** substitute 2 teaspoons dried oregano for the parsley and basil, and substitute Parmesan cheese for the Brie. The nutritional counts are the same.

TASTY BITE

Fresh herbs add more taste and pizzazz to your recipe. If you need to use the dried versions, gently crush them in your hands to awaken the flavor before adding to the other ingredients.

Chicken Red Pepper Quesadillas

Warm, melted Monterey Jack cheese melds the flavors of roasted red peppers, cilantro, and chicken in these quick quesadillas.

Snack servings:	Yield:	Prep time:	Cook time:	Serving size:
4	4 quesadillas	5 minutes	5 minutes	4 wedges or 1 quesadilla

Each serving has:			
176 calories	10g protein	25g carbohydrates	4g fiber
4g fat	2g saturated fat	glycemic index: low	glycemic load: 10

8 (6-in.) corn tortillas	½ cup cooked chicken, shredded
1 (7-oz.) jar roasted red peppers, drained and sliced	¾ cup chopped fresh cilantro or parsley
¼ cup shredded Monterey Jack cheese	

1. Preheat the oven to 400°F.

2. Place 4 tortillas in a single layer on a large baking sheet. Place ¼ of roasted red peppers, Monterey Jack cheese, chicken, and cilantro on each tortilla. Top with remaining tortillas.

3. Bake for about 5 minutes. Cut each quesadilla into 4 wedges, and serve warm.

Variation: You can also substitute canned diced green chiles for the roasted red peppers. Choose the heat that best suits your taste buds: mild, medium, or hot. Or if you don't want any peppers, you can use 2 sliced fresh tomatoes instead of the peppers.

Chicken Satay with Peanut Sauce

This traditional Thai snack is salty and sweet and served with a spicy peanut dipping sauce.

Snack servings:	Yield:	Prep time:	Cook time:	Serving size:
8	16 skewers and 2½ cups sauce	15 minutes plus 1 or 2 hours marinate time	6 to 10 minutes	2 skewers

Each serving has:			
278 calories	27g protein	10g carbohydrates	2g fiber
15g fat	3g saturated fat	glycemic index: low	glycemic load: 2

1 cup low-fat Greek yogurt

2 tsp. ground ginger

1 tsp. minced garlic

1 TB. curry powder

1 lb. skinless, boneless uncooked chicken breast, cut in 4 (6×1¼×⅜-in.) strips

16 (10-in.) wooden skewers, soaked in water for 30 minutes

¾ cup smooth or chunky peanut butter

¼ cup low-sodium soy sauce

2 tsp. crushed red pepper flakes

2 tsp. honey

2 TB. lime juice, or juice of 1 lime

1. In a shallow bowl, combine yogurt, ginger, garlic, and curry powder. Add chicken strips, and marinate for 1 or 2 hours at room temperature. Discard marinade.

2. Preheat the grill to medium.

3. Thread chicken strips on the skewers, and place on an oiled grill pan. Grill for 3 to 5 minutes per side or until lightly browned and cooked through.

4. In a food processer fitted with a chopping blade, combine peanut butter, soy sauce, crushed red pepper flakes, honey, and lime juice, and process for 30 seconds to 1 minute or until smooth. (Add a small amount of water while processing if mixture is too thick.)

5. Serve satay hot or chilled with peanut dipping sauce on the side.

TASTY BITE

These skewers are great served cold. Refrigerate any leftovers for a snack later in the week.

Asian Chicken Lettuce Wraps

You'll savor the earthy flavors of soy sauce, teriyaki, and ginger paired with carrots and almonds in these Asian-inspired wraps.

Snack servings:	Yield:	Prep time:	Cook time:	Serving size:
6	6 wraps	15 minutes	3 to 6 minutes	1 wrap

Each serving has:			
180 calories	13g protein	17g carbohydrates	1g fiber
7g fat	1g saturated fat	glycemic index: low	glycemic load: 6

½ lb. boneless skinless chicken breasts, cut into 1-in. cubes

4½ tsp. extra-virgin olive oil

3 TB. Asian-style salad dressing

¼ tsp. garlic powder

⅛ tsp. crushed red pepper flakes

2 medium carrots, shredded (1½ cups)

1 (8-oz.) can water chestnuts, drained and diced

1 TB. fresh minced ginger root

6 leaves Bibb or iceberg lettuce

¼ cup sliced almonds

1. Coat a large nonstick skillet with cooking spray, and set over medium heat. Add chicken and 3 teaspoons extra-virgin olive oil, and cook for 3 to 6 minutes or until chicken is cooked throughout. Drain off oil, and set chicken aside.

2. In a small bowl, whisk salad dressing, garlic powder, crushed red pepper flakes, and remaining 1½ teaspoons extra-virgin olive oil. Stir in carrots, water chestnuts, ginger root, and chicken.

3. Spoon mixture onto lettuce leaves, and sprinkle with almonds. Fold sides of lettuce over filling, roll up, and serve.

 TASTY BITE

If you don't have fresh ginger root on hand, you can substitute dried ginger powder. It won't have quite the "bite" of fresh ginger root, but will add an Asian taste.

Chicken Wraps with Pears and Grapes

These refreshing fruit and chicken wraps are flavored with a light vinegar and oil dressing.

Snack servings:	Yield:	Prep time:	Serving size:
8	8 wraps	15 minutes	1 wrap

Each serving has:			
159 calories	11g protein	12g carbohydrates	2g fiber
8g fat	1g saturated fat	glycemic index: low	glycemic load: 5

2 cups cooked chicken, shredded

2 TB. finely diced green onions

1 cup red or green seedless grapes, cut in $\frac{1}{2}$

2 stalks celery, sliced

2 ripe pears, cored and cut in cubes

$\frac{1}{2}$ cup bottled vinegar and oil dressing

8 leaves romaine lettuce

1. In a large bowl, combine chicken, green onions, grapes, celery, and pears. Add vinegar and oil dressing, and toss to coat.

2. Place $\frac{1}{4}$ of mixture in each lettuce leaf. Fold and roll leaf into a wrap, and serve.

TASTY BITE

To make $\frac{1}{2}$ cup of your own vinegar and oil dressing, use $\frac{1}{3}$ cup extra-virgin olive oil and $\frac{1}{6}$ cup your favorite type of vinegar.

Creamy Chicken Wraps

In these tasty wraps reminiscent of chicken pot pie, each tortilla holds a creamy combination of flavorful mushrooms, carrots, peas, and chicken.

Snack servings:	Yield:	Prep time:	Cook time:	Serving size:
4	4 wraps	10 minutes	12 minutes	1 wrap

Each serving has:			
228 calories	21g protein	19g carbohydrates	3g fiber
7g fat	2g saturated fat	glycemic index: low	glycemic load: 8

2 tsp. extra-virgin olive oil	$\frac{1}{2}$ cup frozen peas, thawed
1 cup cooked chicken breasts, diced	1 TB. whole-wheat flour
1 (7-oz.) can sliced mushrooms, drained	$1\frac{1}{4}$ cups skim milk
	$\frac{1}{8}$ tsp. salt
$\frac{1}{2}$ cup fresh (1 medium carrot) or frozen carrots, diced	$\frac{1}{8}$ tsp. fresh ground black pepper
	4 (8-in.) whole-wheat tortillas

1. In a large skillet over medium-high heat, heat extra-virgin olive oil. Add chicken and mushrooms, and sauté for 3 minutes. Add carrots and peas, and sauté for about 5 more minutes.

2. Slowly stir in whole-wheat flour. Add skim milk, $\frac{1}{4}$ cup at a time, and cook, stirring constantly, for about 4 minutes or until sauce is thickened. Season with salt and pepper.

3. Pour $\frac{1}{2}$ to $\frac{3}{4}$ cup chicken-vegetable mixture into each tortilla. Roll up tortilla, and serve.

Rosemary Honey Chicken Drumsticks

Crushed rosemary flavors this slightly sweet chicken snack.

Snack servings:	Yield:	Prep time:	Cook time:	Serving size:
4	4 drumsticks	10 minutes	25 to 30 minutes	1 drumstick
Each serving has:				
169 calories	4g protein	45g carbohydrates	2g fiber	
6g fat	1g saturated fat	glycemic index: low	glycemic load: 1	

4 chicken drumsticks (1 lb.)   2 tsp. crushed dried rosemary
1 TB. honey

1. Preheat the oven to 450°F. Line a rimmed baking sheet with aluminum foil.

2. Arrange chicken in a single layer on the baking sheet.

3. In a small bowl, combine honey and crushed rosemary. Brush mixture on top of drumsticks.

4. Bake chicken on the lower oven rack for 25 to 30 minutes or until skin is light golden brown and juices run clear when chicken is pierced with fork. Drizzle any juices on baking sheet over chicken. Serve cold or hot.

Variation: You could use basil, oregano, or thyme instead of rosemary. Or for **Salsa Chicken Drumsticks,** add ½ cup bottled mild taco sauce and ¾ cup finely crushed tortilla chips in place of the honey and rosemary. *(Each variation serving has: 126 calories, 14g protein, 10g carbohydrates, 1g fiber, 3g fat, 1g saturated fat, glycemic index: low, glycemic load: 5.)*

Pecan Coconut Chicken Fingers

This extra-crispy sautéed chicken blends the flavors of coconut and pecans with a sweet and tangy dipping sauce.

Snack servings:	Yield:	Prep time:	Cook time:	Serving size:
8	16 fingers	15 minutes	4 to 10 minutes	2 fingers

Each serving has:			
245 calories	19g protein	12g carbohydrates	2g fiber
14g fat	4g saturated fat	glycemic index: low	glycemic load: 2

½ cup pecans, finely chopped	¼ cup honey
½ cup coconut flour	¼ cup water
¼ tsp. salt	2 TB. prepared white horseradish
1 large egg	1 TB. Dijon mustard
1½ TB. extra-virgin olive oil	2 TB. green onions, sliced
1 lb. chicken tenders (about 8), cut in ½ lengthwise	1 tsp. orange zest

1. In a shallow bowl, combine pecans, coconut flour, and salt.

2. In a separate shallow bowl, beat egg with a fork until frothy.

3. In a large nonstick skillet over medium-low heat, heat extra-virgin olive oil. When oil is hot, dip chicken tenders in egg and then in pecan mixture to coat. Add chicken to the skillet, and cook for about 4 minutes, turning once or twice, or until golden and cooked through.

4. Meanwhile, in a small bowl, combine honey, water, white horseradish, Dijon mustard, green onions, and orange zest. Serve alongside chicken as dipping sauce.

TASTY BITE

Make orange zest by grating the rind of an orange. You can also peel the rind from the orange, omitting the white part, and finely dice the peel. For convenience, you can even use orange peel from the spice rack.

Sesame Chicken Strips

Sesame lends a crunchy texture and aromatic flavor to these Asian-flavored chicken strips and dip.

Snack servings:	Yield:	Prep time:	Cook time:	Serving size:
8	about 16 strips	15 minutes	15 to 20 minutes	2 strips

Each serving has:			
251 calories	21g protein	6g carbohydrates	1g fiber
16g fat	3g saturated fat	glycemic index: low	glycemic load: 0

1 large egg

2 TB. plus 1/3 cup low-fat mayonnaise

1/4 cup grated Parmesan cheese

1/4 cup sesame seeds

Dash salt

Dash ground black pepper

1 lb. chicken breast, cut into finger-size strips

2 TB. *tahini*

2 TB. toasted sesame oil

1 1/2 tsp. lemon juice, fresh or bottled

1. Preheat the oven to 400°F. Line a 9×13-inch baking dish with aluminum foil or parchment paper.

2. In a small bowl, beat egg. Stir in 2 tablespoons mayonnaise.

3. In a shallow bowl, combine Parmesan cheese, sesame seeds, salt, and pepper.

4. Dip chicken strips into egg mixture and then into cheese mixture. Arrange coated strips in a single layer on the prepared baking dish.

5. Bake for 10 minutes, turn, and bake for 5 to 10 more minutes or until nicely browned and cooked through.

6. Meanwhile, in a small bowl, combine remaining 1/3 cup mayonnaise, tahini, toasted sesame oil, and lemon juice. Serve as a dipping sauce alongside chicken fingers.

GLYCO-LINGO

Tahini is a paste made from sesame seeds used to flavor many Middle Eastern recipes.

Swiss Turkey Enchiladas

Turkey and Swiss cheese are wrapped in corn tortillas and spiced with salsa and cilantro.

Snack servings:	Yield:	Prep time:	Cook time:	Serving size:
8	8 enchiladas	15 minutes	25 minutes	1 enchilada

Each serving has:			
197 calories	16g protein	15g carbohydrates	2g fiber
9g fat	4g saturated fat	glycemic index: low	glycemic load: 8

8 (6-in.) corn tortillas

1¼ cups green salsa

½ cup reduced-fat sour cream

¼ cup fresh cilantro, chopped

1½ cups diced cooked turkey
    breast

1½ cups shredded reduced-fat
    Swiss cheese

1 cup tomatoes, diced

1. Place tortillas on a cookie sheet in a cold oven, and preheat it to 425°F. Warm for 2 or 3 minutes. (Alternatively, place tortillas on a microwave-safe dish and microwave on high for 30 seconds.)

2. In a medium bowl, mix green salsa, sour cream, and cilantro. Spread ½ cup over the bottom of a 9×13-inch baking dish.

3. In another bowl, mix turkey, 1 cup Swiss cheese, and diced tomatoes.

4. Remove tortillas from the oven, and spoon ½ cup turkey mixture down center of each tortilla. Roll up tortillas, and place seam side down in baking dish. Pour remaining salsa mixture over top.

5. Cover with aluminum foil, and bake for 15 minutes or until bubbly. Uncover, sprinkle with remaining ½ cup Swiss cheese, and bake for 10 more minutes or until cheese has melted.

Variation: In place of the Swiss cheese, you could substitute Gouda, Brie, or herb-flavored cream cheese.

Turkey and Apple Pockets

Apple and sage lend a mildly sweet flavor to these pita pocket snacks.

Snack servings:	Yield:	Prep time:	Cook time:	Serving size:
6	6 pita ½ sandwiches	5 minutes	10 to 15 minutes	½ pita sandwich

Each serving has:			
216 calories	18g protein	20g carbohydrates	4g fiber
7g fat	2g saturated fat	glycemic index: low	glycemic load: 11

2 tsp. extra-virgin olive oil	¾ tsp. dried sage
1 lb. lean uncooked ground turkey	⅛ tsp. ground black pepper
1 medium apple (your choice variety), peeled, cored, and shredded	3 whole-wheat pitas, cut in ½

1. In a large nonstick skillet over medium heat, heat extra-virgin olive oil. Add turkey, and cook for 5 to 10 minutes or until lightly browned.

2. Add apple, sage, and pepper, and cook for 4 or 5 minutes, stirring often, until tender and browned. Remove from heat.

3. Divide turkey mixture into 6 equal portions. Spoon 1 portion turkey mixture into each pita pocket half, and serve warm.

Grilled Turkey and Cottage Cheese Burgers

Garlic lends a traditional grilling flavor to these turkey and cheese burgers.

Snack servings:	Yield:	Prep time:	Cook time:	Serving size:
8	8 burgers	10 minutes	8 to 12 minutes	1 burger

Each serving has:			
142 calories	17g protein	1g carbohydrates	0g fiber
8g fat	2g saturated fat	glycemic index: low	glycemic load: 0

1 lb. lean ground uncooked turkey	2 cloves garlic, minced
¼ cup low-fat cottage cheese	¼ tsp. salt
¼ cup fresh parsley, coarsely chopped	1 tsp. ground black pepper
2 tsp. fresh sage, finely chopped	1 tsp. extra-virgin olive oil

1. In a medium bowl, mix together turkey, cottage cheese, parsley, sage, garlic, salt, and pepper. Using your hands, shape mixture into 8 (½-inch-thick) patties.

2. In a large skillet over medium-high heat, heat extra-virgin olive oil. Add patties, and cook for 4 to 6 minutes on each side.

3. Serve on lettuce leaves or with cut-up carrots and celery.

Variations: For **Turkey and Chickpea Burgers,** use ¾ pound ground turkey; substitute 1 (15-ounce) can chickpeas, drained, rinsed, and mashed for the cottage cheese; and use 1 teaspoon cumin and ½ teaspoon paprika instead of the sage, garlic, and parsley. Add ½ cup green bell pepper, finely diced, too. *(Each variation serving has: 295 calories, 22g protein, 33g carbohydrates, 9g fiber, 9g fat, 2g saturated fat, glycemic index: low, glycemic load: 5.)*

For **Turkey and Pepperoni Burgers,** add 8 slices turkey or beef pepperoni, diced; ¼ cup roasted red peppers from a jar, sliced; ½ cup low-fat Italian 6-cheese blend; and 1 egg. Substitute marinara sauce for the cottage cheese, and 2 tablespoons basil and 2 tablespoons oregano for the parsley. *(Each variation serving has: 233 calories, 20g protein, 2g carbohydrates, 0g fiber, 16g fat, 4g saturated fat, glycemic index: low, glycemic load: 0.)*

TASTY BITE

Burgers are great for a snack. Wrap in a lettuce leaf or eat with a fork to keep the glycemic value low.

New Orleans Turkey and Sausage Kabobs

The spicy taste of andouille sausage is balanced with turkey and vegetables in this succulent kabob snack.

Snack servings:	Yield:	Prep time:	Cook time:	Serving size:
6	6 kabobs	15 minutes plus 30 minutes soak time for skewers	18 minutes	1 kabob

Each serving has:			
171 calories	20g protein	10g carbohydrates	4g fiber
6g fat	2g saturated fat	glycemic index: low	glycemic load: 1

¾ lb. turkey tenderloins, cut into 1½-in. chunks

¼ lb. andouille sausage, cut into ⅜-in. slices

1 (16-oz.) pkg. frozen whole okra, thawed

1 large red bell pepper, ribs and seeds removed, and cut in 1-in. pieces

2 medium yellow or white onions, cut into wedges

6 (12-in.) wooden skewers, soaked in water 30 minutes, or metal skewers

1½ tsp. Creole seasoning

1. Preheat the grill to medium-high (350°F to 400°F).

2. Thread turkey, sausage, okra, bell pepper, and onion wedges alternately onto skewers, leaving ¼ inch between pieces. Sprinkle with Creole seasoning.

3. Add kabobs to the grill, cover, and cook for 18 minutes or until done, turning every 6 minutes.

Variation: If andouille sausage is too hot to suit your taste, use a milder version. If okra doesn't appeal to you, substitute green bell peppers and/or pineapple cubes.

 KITCHEN ALERT

Be sure to soak the wooden skewers in water before grilling. The water keeps the skewers from charring, or worse, from catching on fire.

Sensational Seafood

9

In This Chapter

- High-protein, no-glycemic seafood
- Wraps, sandwiches, and salads from the sea
- Shellfish and seafood cakes, tacos, and fajitas
- Fresh, frozen, and canned seafood

If you live near the coast, or on a lake, where fresh seafood is readily and easily available, you're lucky! Otherwise, you probably purchase your seafood from the grocery store and it's usually frozen or canned. No matter where or how you purchase your seafood, the recipes in this chapter are easy to prepare, and they make your seafood sparkle with appetizing preparations, ingredients, and spices.

When shopping for seafood, don't overlook canned or frozen. You can keep cans or vacuum-packed containers of tuna, salmon, and crab in your pantry and cook seafood cakes or salads in minutes without an extra trip to the store. Also keep a 1- or 2-pound bag of large shrimp in your freezer. You can defrost as many shrimp as you crave quickly in a bowl under running cold water and have a superb snack ready in just 30 minutes.

If you live where fresh seafood is available, always purchase the fish with shiny eyes, and be sure the shellfish smells fresh.

Many grocery store fish counters offer quick-frozen fish that's defrosting as you look at it. Cook it within a day or two of purchasing it, and don't refreeze it. Refreezing fish ruins the taste.

Baja Fish Tacos

Baked halibut is flavored with avocado, salsa, and fresh cilantro and served on a corn tortilla.

Snack servings:	Yield:	Prep time:	Cook time:	Serving size:
8	8 tacos	15 minutes	15 minutes	1 taco

Each serving has:			
237 calories	17g protein	18g carbohydrates	4g fiber
11g fat	1g saturated fat	glycemic index: low	glycemic load: 5

1 small head red cabbage, thinly sliced (about 1½ cups)

½ cup fresh cilantro, roughly chopped

2 TB. lime juice

1 TB. honey

½ cup low-fat mayonnaise

¼ tsp. salt

1 lb. skinless halibut fillets, cut into 2×½-in. pieces

½ tsp. chili powder

¼ tsp. ground black pepper

8 (6-in.) corn tortillas

1 avocado, peeled, pitted, and sliced

½ cup fresh salsa

8 lime wedges

1. Preheat the oven to 400°F.

2. In a medium bowl, toss red cabbage, cilantro, lime juice, honey, mayonnaise, and salt.

3. Place fish in a shallow baking dish lined with aluminum foil. Sprinkle fish with chili powder and pepper, and bake for 15 minutes or until fish flakes.

4. Warm tortillas in a skillet over medium-low heat, or wrap tortillas in a damp cloth and microwave for 25 seconds.

5. Fill tortillas with equal amounts of fish, avocado, slaw, and salsa, and serve with lime wedges.

Variation: Substitute your favorite fish variety for the halibut in this recipe. Some choices include salmon, shrimp, crab, trout, and tuna.

Open-Face Lemon Trout Sandwiches

Lemon and dill enhance the flavor of this delicious grilled trout.

Snack servings:	Yield:	Prep time:	Cook time:	Serving size:
6	6 sandwiches	10 minutes	6 to 8 minutes	1 sandwich

Each serving has:			
248 calories	22g protein	12g carbohydrates	0g fiber
11g fat	2g saturated fat	glycemic index: low	glycemic load: 4

1 medium lemon

$\frac{1}{3}$ cup low-fat mayonnaise

2 TB. snipped fresh dill

$\frac{1}{4}$ tsp. salt

$\frac{1}{4}$ tsp. ground black pepper

1 lb. ruby or rainbow trout fillets (6 fillets)

3 ciabatta buns, halved

1. Preheat the grill to medium-high heat.

2. Finely shred peel and squeeze juice from $\frac{1}{2}$ of lemon, and thinly slice remaining $\frac{1}{2}$ and set aside.

3. In a small bowl, combine mayonnaise, lemon peel, lemon juice, dill, salt, and pepper.

4. Brush 2 tablespoons mayonnaise mixture on fish fillets. Place fish on the grill, skin side up, and cook for 1 minute. Carefully turn fillets skin side down, and grill for 5 to 7 more minutes or until fish flakes easily with a fork.

5. Add lemon slices and bun halves, cut side down, to the grill after turning fish.

6. Remove fish, buns, and lemon slices from the grill. Remove skin from fish, if desired, and cut fish into bun-size pieces. Top buns with some mayonnaise mixture, fish, and lemon slices, and serve with any remaining mayonnaise mixture.

HEALTHY NOTE

You can cook the trout on the grill, as recommended in the recipe, or you can pan-fry it in a skillet or even bake in the oven. Choose the approach that works best for you and your kitchen.

Cajun Catfish Po'Boy

A flavorful note of Cajun spices accents this catfish po'boy, which is a Louisiana submarine sandwich.

Snack servings:	Yield:	Prep time:	Cook time:	Serving size:
4	4 sandwiches	10 minutes	12 to 15 minutes	1 sandwich

Each serving has:			
174 calories	9g protein	16g carbohydrates	1g fiber
8g fat	1g saturated fat	glycemic index: low	glycemic load: 7

2 (3-oz.) catfish fillets

1 tsp. extra-virgin olive oil

1½ tsp. Cajun spices

2 TB. low-fat mayonnaise

1 (4-oz.) whole-wheat baguette, sliced lengthwise and toasted

4 slices red onion

4 (¼-in.-thick) slices tomato

2 Boston lettuce leaves

1. Preheat the oven to 400°F. Line a cookie sheet with aluminum foil.

2. Place catfish on the prepared cookie sheet. Brush with extra-virgin olive oil, and sprinkle with Cajun spices. Bake for 12 to 15 minutes or until fish flakes and is no longer translucent.

3. To assemble sandwiches, spread mayonnaise on one side of baguette slice, and top with catfish fillets, red onion slices, tomato slices, and lettuce leaves. Top with other baguette slice, and cut baguette into 4 slices. Cooked fillets can be stored in the refrigerator for 2 to 4 days.

Shrimp Po'Boy with Peaches

Peaches add sweetness to this spicy shrimp and bacon po'boy.

Snack servings:	Yield:	Prep time:	Cook time:	Serving size:
4	4 sandwiches	10 minutes	8 to 10 minutes	1 sandwich

Each serving has:			
295 calories	24g protein	25g carbohydrates	1g fiber
11g fat	2g saturated fat	glycemic index: low	glycemic load: 9

1 tsp. butter

$\frac{1}{2}$ tsp. minced garlic

$\frac{3}{4}$ lb. medium shrimp, peeled and deveined (12 to 16 shrimp)

1 small jalapeño, ribs and seeds removed, and thinly sliced

1 peach, halved and sliced

$\frac{1}{2}$ tsp. Cajun seasoning

$\frac{1}{4}$ cup low-fat mayonnaise

1 TB. lemon juice

1 tsp. ground black pepper

1 slice bacon, cooked crisp and crumbled

4 kaiser rolls

1. In a large skillet over medium heat, melt butter. Add garlic, shrimp, and jalapeño, and sauté for 3 to 5 minutes or until shrimp is cooked.

2. In a small bowl, gently combine peach slices, Cajun seasoning, mayonnaise, lemon juice, pepper, and bacon.

3. Divide shrimp among bottom layers of kaiser rolls. Top with peach-mayonnaise mixture and top layer of rolls, and serve.

Tuna Salad with Mangoes and Avocado

Mangoes lend a tropical taste to this tuna salad served with avocado.

Snack servings:	Yield:	Prep time:	Serving size:
4	4 salads	10 minutes	¼ tuna salad and ¼ avocado

Each serving has:			
226 calories	13g protein	14g carbohydrates	4g fiber
14g fat	2g saturated fat	glycemic index: low	glycemic load: 3

1 medium mango, peeled, seeded, and chopped

3 TB. red onion, chopped

2 TB. fresh cilantro, snipped

1 TB. extra-virgin olive oil

¼ to ½ tsp. ground cumin

¼ tsp. salt

⅛ tsp. cayenne

1 (6-oz.) can water-packed tuna, drained

1 large avocado, skin on, quartered, and pitted

1. In a medium bowl, stir together mango, red onion, cilantro, extra-virgin olive oil, cumin, salt, and cayenne. Add tuna, and stir gently to break up tuna. Cover and refrigerate up to 4 hours (if desired).

2. Spoon tuna mixture next to each avocado quarter on a plate, and serve immediately.

HEALTHY NOTE

Tuna salad tastes great with a wide variety of spices, fruit, vegetable, and nut combinations. This is one of our favorites. You can also use diced apples and walnuts, or raisins with curry seasoning.

Asian Tuna and Cabbage Salad

An Asian-style dressing highlights this quick tuna salad.

Snack servings:	Yield:	Prep time:	Serving size:
6	about 7 cups	10 minutes	1⅙ cups
Each serving has:			
169 calories	17g protein	5g carbohydrates	2g fiber
9g fat	2g saturated fat	glycemic index: low	glycemic load: 0

3 cups green or white cabbage, shredded

2 cups red cabbage, shredded

2 green onions, sliced

2 TB. almonds, sliced

2 tsp. toasted sesame seeds

2 (6-oz.) cans water-packed tuna, drained

3 TB. rice wine vinegar

1 TB. extra-virgin olive oil

1 tsp. sesame oil

1 tsp. honey

¼ tsp. salt

1. In a large bowl, combine green or white cabbage, red cabbage, onions, almonds, and sesame seeds. Add tuna, and stir gently, keeping tuna in large chunks.

2. In a small bowl, whisk together red wine vinegar, extra-virgin olive oil, sesame oil, honey, and salt. Pour over cabbage mixture, and toss. For greater flavor, refrigerate salad for 2 or 3 hours. Salad stores well in the refrigerator for 4 days.

Variation: If you like a bit more spice in your salad, add ¼ teaspoon wasabi to the dressing and substitute 1 teaspoon soy sauce for the salt.

Tuna, Barley, and Black Bean Salad

Beans, barley, and tuna are flavored with a Caribbean jerk dressing in this tasty salad.

Snack servings:	Yield:	Prep time:	Cook time:	Serving size:
6	about 6 cups	10 minutes	30 minutes	1 cup

Each serving has:			
271 calories	15g protein	33g carbohydrates	7g fiber
8g fat	1g saturated fat	glycemic index: low	glycemic load: 6

1 cup quick-cooking barley

1 (15-oz.) can black beans, drained and rinsed

1 small red bell pepper, ribs and seeds removed, and finely chopped

⅓ cup low-fat Caribbean jerk salad dressing

2 cups romaine lettuce, thinly sliced

1 (6.5-oz.) can water-packed chunk light tuna, drained

1. Prepare barley according to package directions. Cool, stirring occasionally, and set aside in a serving bowl.

2. Add black beans and red bell pepper, and toss with salad dressing.

3. Add romaine and tuna just before serving, and toss.

HEALTHY NOTE

This salad gives you a high amount of fiber with a spicy island flair.

Southwestern Tuna Salad

Tuna salad takes on a Southwestern flair with cilantro, jalapeño peppers, and lime juice.

Snack servings:	Yield:	Prep time:	Serving size:
4	about 4 cups	10 minutes	1 cup

Each serving has:			
146 calories	15g protein	18g carbohydrates	4g fiber
3g fat	1g saturated fat	glycemic index: low	glycemic load: 4

1 (7.06-oz.) pouch chunk white albacore tuna in water, drained

4 medium tomatoes, chopped

¼ cup red onion, finely diced

½ cup fresh cilantro, chopped

¼ cup lime juice

1 jalapeño pepper, minced (optional)

⅛ tsp. salt

1 head Boston lettuce

12 baked tortilla chips

1. In a medium bowl, place tuna, and break into large pieces using a fork. Add tomatoes, red onion, cilantro, lime juice, jalapeño (if using), and salt, and stir gently to mix.

2. Line plates with lettuce leaves, and top with tuna salad. Serve with tortilla chips.

Salmon with Sun-Dried Tomatoes

Salmon spread tastes sweet and savory with sun-dried tomatoes, garlic, capers, and anchovies.

Snack servings:	Yield:	Prep time:	Serving size:
8	8 ½ pitas	10 minutes	½ pita
Each serving has:			
212 calories	16g protein	19g carbohydrates	3g fiber
9g fat	2g saturated fat	glycemic index: low	glycemic load: 8

1 (14.75-oz.) can red sockeye
   salmon, drained and skin and
   bones removed

¼ cup oil-packed sun-dried tomatoes, drained and snipped

2 TB. lemon juice

2 TB. low-fat mayonnaise

2 tsp. minced garlic

1 tsp. capers, drained

1 tsp. anchovy paste (optional)

¼ tsp. ground black pepper

4 whole-wheat pitas, cut in ½

1. In a food processor fitted with a chopping blade, combine salmon, sun-dried tomatoes, lemon juice, mayonnaise, garlic, capers, anchovy paste (if using), and pepper. Process for 30 to 60 seconds or until smooth, adding additional mayonnaise for desired consistency if necessary.

2. Place ⅛ of mixture into each pita half, and serve.

Salmon with Orange Slices

Here, salmon is cooked simply with orange slices, fennel, and garlic. Delicious!

Snack servings:	Yield:	Prep time:	Cook time:	Serving size:
6	6 fillets	5 minutes	16 to 25 minutes	1 fillet

Each serving has:			
178 calories	17g protein	4g carbohydrates	1g fiber
10g fat	2g saturated fat	glycemic index: low	glycemic load: 0

2 tsp. minced garlic

1 tsp. fennel seed, crushed

1 tsp. extra-virgin olive oil

6 (1-in.-thick, 2.7-oz.) salmon fillets

$\frac{1}{4}$ tsp. salt

1 medium navel orange, sliced (skin on)

1 cup water

1. Coat a large skillet with cooking spray, and set over medium heat. Add garlic, fennel seed, and extra-virgin olive oil, and cook for 2 minutes.

2. Sprinkle salmon with salt, add salmon to the skillet, and increase heat to medium-high. Top salmon with orange slices, add water, and bring to a boil.

3. Reduce heat to medium-low, cover, and simmer for 8 to 12 minutes or until fish flakes easily with a fork.

4. Remove salmon from the skillet, and keep warm.

5. Simmer sauce, uncovered, for 6 to 9 minutes or until slightly thickened. Spoon sauce over fillets, and serve.

HEALTHY NOTE

This elegant snack is perfect to serve to guests at parties and other celebrations. It's also great for a special, everyday snack.

Parmesan Shrimp with Pine Nuts

Pine nuts, basil, and Parmesan cheese lend flavor to this shrimp sauté.

Snack servings:	Yield:	Prep time:	Cook time:	Serving size:
4	1 pound shrimp	10 minutes	4 to 6 minutes	4 shrimp
Each serving has:				
211 calories	26g protein	4g carbohydrates	1g fiber	
10g fat	2g saturated fat	glycemic index: low	glycemic load: 0	

1 lb. fresh or frozen jumbo shrimp, thawed if frozen (6 to 8 shrimp)

3 TB. fresh basil, snipped

1 TB. lemon juice

¼ tsp. salt

¼ tsp. ground black pepper

1 TB. extra-virgin olive oil

3 TB. pine nuts

2 TB. shredded Parmesan cheese

2 cups grape tomatoes

1 medium lemon, cut in wedges

1. Peel and devein shrimp, and remove tails. Rinse and drain shrimp, and set aside.

2. In a large bowl, combine 2 tablespoons basil, lemon juice, salt, and pepper. Add shrimp, and toss to coat. Cover and chill for 10 to 30 minutes.

3. In a large skillet over medium-high heat, cook ½ of shrimp in extra-virgin olive oil for 2 or 3 minutes or until shrimp are opaque, stirring often to cook evenly. Transfer cooked shrimp to a platter, and repeat with remaining ½ of shrimp.

4. Add pine nuts, Parmesan cheese, and tomatoes to shrimp, and toss to combine. Serve warm with lemon wedges and remaining 1 tablespoon basil.

Variation: If pine nuts aren't your thing, substitute chopped hazelnuts, pecans, or walnuts.

KITCHEN ALERT

If you don't prepare and eat defrosted seafood within 2 or 3 days of purchase, discard it or prepare it for eating later in the week. But be forewarned: reheated fish usually doesn't taste great unless it's been cooked into fish cakes. However, cooked shellfish recipes can often be reheated successfully without losing much taste.

Coconut Island Shrimp

Shrimp mingles with the spicy flavors of jerk seasoning and a crisp coating of coconut.

Snack servings:	Yield:	Prep time:	Cook time:	Serving size:
6	24 shrimp	15 minutes	12 minutes	4 shrimp

Each serving has:			
169 calories	19g protein	11g carbohydrates	2g fiber
5g fat	4g saturated fat	glycemic index: low	glycemic load: 4

1 lb. large raw shrimp (about 24), unpeeled

2 egg whites

¾ cup unsweetened flaked coconut

¾ cup whole-wheat breadcrumbs

1 TB. Caribbean jerk seasoning

1 tsp. paprika

1. Preheat the oven to 425°F. Coat a wire rack with cooking spray, and place inside a 15×10-inch jellyroll pan.

2. Peel shrimp, leaving tails on, and devein.

3. In a shallow bowl, whisk egg whites until frothy.

4. In a separate shallow bowl, stir together coconut, breadcrumbs, Caribbean jerk seasoning, and paprika.

5. Dip shrimp, 1 at a time, in egg whites and dredge in coconut mixture, pressing gently with your fingers. Arrange shrimp on the wire rack.

6. Bake for 10 to 12 minutes or just until shrimp turn pink, turning once after 8 minutes.

Shrimp Fajitas

Enjoy the lemon pepper, cumin, and garlic flavoring of these grilled shrimp, onion, and bell pepper fajitas.

Snack servings:	Yield:	Prep time:	Cook time:	Serving size:
6	6 fajitas	10 minutes	14 minutes	1 fajita

Each serving has:			
187 calories	18g protein	15g carbohydrates	3g fiber
6g fat	1g saturated fat	glycemic index: low	glycemic load: 4

6 (6-in.) corn tortillas

1 medium sweet onion, sliced

1 medium red bell pepper, ribs and seeds removed, and sliced

1 medium yellow bell pepper, ribs and seeds removed, and sliced

2 TB. extra-virgin olive oil

¼ tsp. garlic powder

¼ tsp. ground cumin

¼ tsp. lemon pepper seasoning

1 lb. large shrimp, peeled, deveined, and tails removed (12 to 18 shrimp)

1. Heat a grill to medium-high.

2. Wrap tortillas in heavy-duty aluminum foil, and place on the grill over indirect heat for 3 minutes to warm.

3. Lightly coat onions, red bell pepper, and yellow bell pepper with extra-virgin olive oil, and place on fine wire mesh rack. Sprinkle with garlic powder, cumin, and lemon pepper, and grill for 10 minutes over direct heat.

4. Add shrimp to vegetables on the rack, and grill for 4 minutes.

5. Serve tortillas, shrimp, and vegetables separately so snackers can prepare their own fajitas.

Shrimp Tacos with Ginger Sauce

These tasty shrimp tacos are served with a cherry-ginger sauce.

Snack servings:	Yield:	Prep time:	Cook time:	Serving size:
8	8 tacos	15 minutes	4 or 5 minutes	1 taco

Each serving has:			
153 calories	14g protein	19g carbohydrates	3g fiber
3g fat	1g saturated fat	glycemic index: low	glycemic load: 5

1 cup fresh or frozen sweet or tangy pitted cherries

1 or 2 jalapeño peppers, cut in $\frac{1}{2}$ and seeded (use 1 for mild and 2 for medium to hot)

1 (2-in.) piece ginger, peeled and quartered

3 tsp. honey

$\frac{1}{4}$ cup water

1 TB. extra-virgin olive oil

1 lb. large raw shrimp (about 24), shells and tails removed

8 (6-in.) corn tortillas

1 (16-oz.) pkg. coleslaw mix

1. In a food processor fitted with a chopping blade, or in a blender, combine cherries, jalapeños, ginger, honey, and water, and process for 30 to 60 seconds or until smooth.

2. In a large skillet over medium-high heat, heat extra-virgin olive oil. Add shrimp and cook for 2 or 3 minutes, turning occasionally, until shrimp are pink on the outside but not cooked through.

3. Reduce heat to medium, and carefully add cherry mixture. Simmer for about 2 minutes or until sauce reduces slightly and shrimp are cooked through.

4. Microwave tortillas for 30 to 40 seconds to warm.

5. Spoon 3 shrimp and 1 tablespoon cherry sauce into each taco, top with 4 tablespoons coleslaw mix, and serve immediately.

Crab Cakes

Cayenne and green onions flavor these classic crab cakes.

Snack servings:	Yield:	Prep time:	Cook time:	Serving size:
6	6 cakes	5 minutes	8 to 10 minutes	1 cake

Each serving has:			
190 calories	12g protein	12g carbohydrates	1g fiber
9g fat	1g saturated fat	glycemic index: low	glycemic load: 5

1 lb. fresh crabmeat or 1 (16-oz.) can crabmeat, drained

1 large egg

2 TB. low-fat mayonnaise

2 green onions, minced

1 stalk celery, minced

¾ cup whole-wheat breadcrumbs

½ tsp. ground mustard

⅛ tsp. cayenne

¼ tsp. salt

⅛ tsp. ground black pepper

2 TB. extra-virgin olive oil

1. In a medium bowl, combine crabmeat, egg, mayonnaise, green onions, celery, breadcrumbs, ground mustard, cayenne, salt, and pepper. Form mixture into 6 cakes.

2. In a large skillet over medium heat, heat extra-virgin olive oil. Add crab cakes, and cook for 8 to 10 minutes, flipping to ensure both sides are browned.

3. Serve warm or at room temperature.

Baked Crab Enchiladas

Garlic and chiles spice up these creamy and melted-cheesy crab snacks.

Snack servings:	Yield:	Prep time:	Cook time:	Serving size:
4	4 enchiladas	20 minutes	32 to 38 minutes	1 enchilada

Each serving has:			
267 calories	23g protein	24g carbohydrates	2g fiber
9g fat	4g saturated fat	glycemic index: low	glycemic load: 6

1 (3-oz.) pkg. low-fat cream cheese, softened

$\frac{1}{2}$ (1-oz.) pkg. ranch salad dressing mix

$\frac{3}{4}$ cup skim milk

$\frac{1}{4}$ cup red onion, diced

2 tsp. minced garlic

1 TB. extra-virgin olive oil

$\frac{1}{2}$ lb. fresh, frozen, or canned crabmeat, flaked and drained

1 (4-oz.) can chopped green chiles, drained

$\frac{1}{2}$ tsp. ground black pepper

$1\frac{1}{2}$ cups low-fat Monterey Jack cheese, shredded

4 (8-in.) flour tortillas, warmed

1 green onion, white and green parts, chopped (optional)

1 medium tomato, chopped (optional)

1 cup shredded lettuce (optional)

$\frac{1}{4}$ cup sliced ripe black olives (optional)

1. Preheat the oven to 350°F. Grease a 9×13-inch baking dish.

2. In a large bowl, combine cream cheese, ranch salad dressing mix, and $\frac{1}{2}$ cup skim milk until smooth. Set aside $\frac{3}{8}$ cup mixture for topping.

3. In a large skillet over medium heat, sauté red onion and garlic in extra-virgin olive oil for 2 or 3 minutes or until tender. Stir in crabmeat, green chiles, and pepper. Fold in remaining cream cheese mixture and 1 cup Monterey Jack cheese.

4. Spoon about $\frac{2}{3}$ cup crab mixture down the center of each tortilla. Roll tortilla, and place seam side down in the baking dish.

5. In a small bowl, combine remaining $\frac{1}{4}$ cup milk and reserved cream cheese mixture, and pour over tortillas.

6. Sprinkle tortillas with remaining Monterey Jack cheese, cover, and bake for 25 minutes. Uncover and bake for 5 to 10 more minutes or until heated through. Serve with green onions, tomatoes, lettuce, and olives (if using).

> **TASTY BITE**
>
> Keep small cans of sliced black olives stocked in your pantry. You can use them in many Mexican and Greek recipes.

Lobster Pitas

Lobster is accented with celery and red bell pepper and seasoned with paprika in this pita dish.

Snack servings:	Yield:	Prep time:	Cook time:	Serving size:
4	4 ½ pitas	10 minutes	12 to 18 minutes	½ pita

Each serving has:			
225 calories	21g protein	21g carbohydrates	2g fiber
6g fat	4g saturated fat	glycemic index: low	glycemic load: 4

2 whole-wheat pitas, split into rounds

½ lb. lobster meat

1 cup celery, diced

½ red bell pepper, ribs and seeds removed, and diced

3 TB. low-fat sour cream

½ tsp. paprika

3 oz. part-skim mozzarella cheese, grated (about 1 cup)

1. Preheat the oven to 350°F.

2. Arrange pita halves in a single layer on a baking sheet, and toast for 2 or 3 minutes or until crisp.

3. In a large bowl, combine lobster, celery, red bell pepper, sour cream, and paprika, and mix well.

4. Top pita halves with lobster mixture, sprinkle with mozzarella cheese, and bake for 10 to 15 minutes or until mozzarella melts and topping is warm. Serve immediately.

Excellent Eggs

In This Chapter

- The versatile egg
- Eggs: a perfect nutritional package
- Energy and protein from eggs
- Choosing whole eggs or whites

Eggs are friendly with all kinds of foods. They blend well with savory and strong-tasting foods like garlic, pepperoni, and spinach, and they also cozy up well to cherries, apples, and many varieties of fruits. All spices and herbs can enhance the comforting flavor of eggs. In this chapter, you'll find a dozen recipes for eggs prepared with vegetables, fruits, meats, spices, cheese, milk, and nuts—something for everyone!

Eggs and Your Health

Eggs might have gotten a bad rep for being unhealthy in the past, but let us set you straight on that. A large egg contains 70 calories, 6 grams complete protein, and 4.5 grams fat. The glycemic index value of eggs is zero, so they're great for a no- to low-glycemic snack. Eggs contain cholesterol; however, the amount of cholesterol is so minimal, it has no significant effect on the blood cholesterol.

The serving size for most recipes in this chapter is about 1 egg, so you'll be enjoying your egg snack while gaining sustained energy from the protein and fat.

The cholesterol is contained in the yolk only, so if your health practitioner has advised you to limit your overall cholesterol intake, you can substitute egg whites for the whole eggs in these recipes. Use 2 egg whites or ¼ cup cholesterol-free egg substitute in place of 1 whole egg.

The Basic Cooked Egg

A cooked egg is an excellent snack all by itself. You can cook an egg in less than 3 minutes. All you need is a small skillet, a tiny bit of butter, and an egg. It's your choice: scrambled, fried, sunny side up, or over easy.

Microwaving eggs takes even less time. Crack the egg into a small, microwave-safe bowl, and pierce the yoke with a fork or toothpick to avoid an explosion. Microwave the egg for 30 seconds, stir or flip it, and microwave for 30 more seconds. Voilà! You have a highly nutritious, delicious snack.

Hard-boiled eggs are an easy pack-along snack or perfect tucked into your briefcase for a workday snack break. Include a dash of salt and pepper, and you're ready to eat! Here's how to hard-boil eggs:

1. Place eggs in a saucepan and cover with water.

2. Set over high heat, and bring to a boil. Turn off heat, but keep the saucepan on the burner.

3. After 5 minutes, remove the saucepan from the burner, and run cold water over eggs.

When they've cooled, your eggs are ready to eat. Or you can refrigerate them for later use.

Marinara Vegetable Frittata

With just 1 slice, you'll savor the Mediterranean flavors of mozzarella and garlic with mushrooms and tomato sauce.

Snack servings:	Yield:	Prep time:	Cook time:	Serving size:
6	1 frittata	10 minutes	10 to 13 minutes	⅙ frittata

Each serving has:			
177 calories	14g protein	6g carbohydrates	1g fiber
11g fat	3g saturated fat	glycemic index: low	glycemic load: 1

1 TB. extra-virgin olive oil

2 cups zucchini, sliced

½ cup white or crimini mushrooms, sliced

½ cup red or green bell pepper, sliced (about 1 medium)

1 TB. garlic, minced

8 large eggs

1 cup low-fat mozzarella cheese, shredded

2 TB. fresh parsley, chopped, or 1 tsp. dried

¼ tsp. salt

¼ tsp. ground black pepper

½ cup marinara sauce, warm

1. Preheat the oven broiler to low.

2. In a large ovenproof skillet over medium-high heat, heat extra-virgin olive oil. Add zucchini, mushrooms, red bell pepper, and garlic, and sauté for 4 to 6 minutes or until almost tender.

3. In a medium bowl, whisk eggs, mozzarella cheese, parsley, salt, and pepper. Pour into the skillet, shaking the pan gently to distribute evenly.

4. Reduce heat to medium, and cook, without stirring, for 3 to 5 minutes or until eggs are set on the bottom and the sides. Eggs will be runny in center.

5. Broil 4 to 6 inches from the heat source for 2 minutes or until frittata is firm in the center.

6. Loosen edges with a spatula. Invert onto a serving platter, cut into wedges, and serve with heated marinara sauce.

Spinach Cheese Squares

Delicious warm or cold, these squares give you the succulent flavor of spinach, cheddar cheese, and Monterey Jack cheese.

Snack servings:	Yield:	Prep time:	Cook time:	Serving size:
6	12 squares	15 minutes	30 to 35 minutes	2 squares

Each serving has:			
143 calories	14g protein	8g carbohydrates	1g fiber
7g fat	4g saturated fat	glycemic index: low	glycemic load: 3

1 TB. butter, melted

¼ cup whole-wheat flour

½ tsp. baking powder

⅛ tsp. salt

¼ tsp. dried thyme

⅛ tsp. ground black pepper

2 large eggs

½ cup low-fat milk

1 (10-oz.) pkg. frozen chopped spinach, thawed and squeezed dry

1 cup low-fat cheddar cheese, shredded

1 cup low-fat Monterey Jack cheese, shredded

¼ cup yellow or white onion, chopped

1. Preheat the oven to 350°F. Brush the bottom and sides of an 8×8-inch baking dish with ½ tablespoon butter.

2. In a large bowl, stir together whole-wheat flour, baking powder, salt, thyme, pepper, eggs, milk, and remaining ½ tablespoon butter. Stir in spinach, cheddar cheese, Monterey Jack cheese, and onion. Pour into the prepared baking dish.

3. Bake for 30 to 35 minutes or until edges are lightly browned and a toothpick inserted near the center comes out clean. Cut into 12 squares.

Variation: Instead of the cheddar and Monterey Jack, you can substitute your favorite cheeses instead. Try Edam, Swiss, or Gouda.

Artichoke Squares

You'll love the unique flavor of marinated artichokes combined with cheddar cheese in these snack squares.

Snack servings:	Yield:	Prep time:	Cook time:	Serving size:
6	12 squares	10 minutes	30 to 35 minutes	2 squares

Each serving has:			
156 calories	17g protein	13g carbohydrates	3g fiber
5g fat	2g saturated fat	glycemic index: low	glycemic load: 2

4 large eggs

¼ cup fine, dry breadcrumbs

⅛ tsp. ground black pepper

⅛ tsp. dried oregano

⅛ tsp. hot pepper sauce

2 cups grated low-fat cheddar cheese

2 TB. fresh parsley, chopped, or 2 tsp. dried

2 (6-oz.) jars marinated artichoke hearts, drained and chopped

¼ tsp. salt

1. Preheat the oven to 325°F. Lightly grease a 9×9-inch baking dish.

2. In a medium bowl, whisk eggs. Stir in breadcrumbs, pepper, oregano, hot pepper sauce, cheddar cheese, parsley, artichokes, and salt.

3. Pour mixture into the prepared baking dish, and bake for 30 to 35 minutes until top is lightly browned and a toothpick inserted into the center comes out clean. Let cool for 10 minutes before cutting into 12 squares. Serve hot or cold.

Variation: If breadcrumbs aren't handy, you can substitute ¼ cup wheat or oat bran flakes.

Ham and Cheese Pie

Muenster cheese and fresh parsley add a comforting flavor to this eggy pie.

Snack servings:	Yield:	Prep time:	Cook time:	Serving size:
6	1 skillet pie	15 minutes	15 to 20 minutes	$\frac{1}{6}$ pie

Each serving has:			
178 calories	17g protein	2g carbohydrates	0g fiber
11g fat	4g saturated fat	glycemic index: low	glycemic load: 0

10 large eggs

Pinch cayenne

$\frac{1}{2}$ cup ham, chopped

1 cup grated Muenster cheese

$\frac{1}{4}$ cup fresh parsley, chopped

1 tsp. extra-virgin olive oil

1. Position a rack in the middle of the oven, and preheat the broiler to low.

2. In a large bowl, whisk eggs and cayenne. Fold in ham, $\frac{1}{2}$ cup Muenster cheese, and parsley.

3. In an ovenproof 6- to 8-inch skillet over medium-low heat, heat extra-virgin olive oil, swirling to coat the pan. Pour in egg mixture, and stir gently with a rubber spatula to distribute fillings. Cook for about 4 minutes or until bottom is just set.

4. Sprinkle remaining $\frac{1}{2}$ cup Muenster cheese on top, transfer to the oven, and broil for about 10 minutes or until pie is puffed and golden. Serve warm. Leftovers are good cold or warm.

Variation: For a little more kick, sauté a bunch of chopped green onions in the skillet before adding the egg mixture.

Crustless Vegetable Quiche

A vibrant medley of vegetables brings garden-fresh flavor to this quiche.

Snack servings:	Yield:	Prep time:	Cook time:		Serving size:
6	1 quiche	20 minutes	25 to 30 minutes plus 10 minutes stand time		$\frac{1}{6}$ quiche

Each serving has:			
152 calories	11g protein	7g carbohydrates	2g fiber
9g fat	3g saturated fat	glycemic index: low	glycemic load: 2

2 tsp. extra-virgin olive oil	1 cup skim milk
2 cups eggplant, chopped (skin on)	$\frac{1}{2}$ tsp. ground black pepper
1 cup zucchini, chopped	$\frac{1}{2}$ tsp. dried oregano
1 cup red bell pepper, chopped	$\frac{1}{2}$ cup fresh basil, torn in pieces
$\frac{1}{2}$ cup yellow onion, chopped	$\frac{3}{4}$ cup part-skim mozzarella cheese, shredded
2 cloves garlic, minced	
6 large eggs	

1. Preheat the oven to 425°F. Spray an 8-inch round or square glass pan with cooking spray.

2. In a large skillet over medium heat, heat extra-virgin olive oil. Add eggplant, zucchini, red bell pepper, onion, and garlic, and sauté for 10 minutes.

3. In a medium bowl, whisk eggs, skim milk, pepper, and oregano.

4. Add egg mixture, basil, and mozzarella to vegetable mixture in the skillet, and gently stir until eggs and mozzarella are evenly distributed among vegetables.

5. Pour egg-vegetable mixture into the prepared pan, and bake for 25 to 30 minutes. Remove from the oven, and let stand for 10 minutes to set quiche. Serve warm or at room temperature.

Variation: If you like, you can substitute other vegetables, such as chopped plum tomatoes, mushrooms, or black olives for the eggplant, zucchini, or red bell pepper.

HEALTHY NOTE

If you prefer egg whites to whole eggs, you can substitute $\frac{2}{3}$ cup egg whites for 5 of the 6 eggs in this recipe. (8 to 10 egg whites equal 1 cup.)

Cherry Almond Quiche

A perfect blend of creamy eggs enhance the sweet taste of cherries and the fresh aroma of toasted almonds in this flavorful quiche.

Snack servings:	Yield:	Prep time:	Cook time:	Serving size:
8	1 quiche	15 minutes	50 to 55 minutes	⅛ quiche

Each serving has:			
187 calories	6g protein	22g carbohydrates	2g fiber
10g fat	4g saturated fat	glycemic index: low	glycemic load: 10

1½ TB. butter	3 large eggs
1 cup whole milk	⅛ tsp. pure almond extract
½ cup whole-wheat or white flour, sifted	⅛ tsp. salt
¼ cup sugar	3 cups pitted cherries, fresh or defrosted
¼ cup heavy cream	½ cup almonds, sliced or slivered

1. Preheat the oven to 400°F. Grease a shallow, round, 11-inch quiche or gratin dish with ½ tablespoon butter.

2. In a medium bowl, combine whole milk, flour, sugar, heavy cream, eggs, almond extract, and salt, and whisk or beat for 5 minutes. Drain cherries, and stir liquid into batter.

3. Arrange cherries in the bottom of prepared baking dish, and pour in batter. Bake for 15 minutes.

4. Sprinkle almonds on top, and dot top with pieces of remaining 1 tablespoon butter. Bake for 35 to 40 more minutes or until puffed and golden brown and a toothpick inserted in the center comes out clean. Serve warm or at room temperature.

Variation: This quiche is perfect to use whatever fruit is in season. Try berries, apples, peaches, or pears in place of the cherries.

Apple Dutch Quiche

Baked eggs carry the sweet aromatic taste of apples and raisins enriched with the flavor of cinnamon in this tasty quiche.

Snack servings:	Yield:	Prep time:	Cook time:	Serving size:
6	1 pie	10 minutes	45 minutes	$\frac{1}{6}$ pie and apples

Each serving has:			
242 calories	7g protein	29g carbohydrates	3g fiber
12g fat	4g saturated fat	glycemic index: low	glycemic load: 12

2 tsp. extra-virgin olive oil	4 medium Golden Delicious, Cameo, or Pink Lady apples (skin on)
4 large eggs	$\frac{1}{2}$ cup raisins
$\frac{1}{4}$ cup whole-wheat or white flour	$\frac{1}{4}$ cup pecans, coarsely chopped
$\frac{2}{3}$ cup low-fat milk	$\frac{1}{2}$ tsp. ground cinnamon
2 TB. butter, cold	$\frac{1}{4}$ cup water
1 tsp. vanilla extract	

1. Preheat the oven to 450°F.

2. Pour extra-virgin olive oil into a 9-inch pie plate or dish, and heat in the oven 5 minutes.

3. In medium bowl, whisk together eggs, flour, milk, 1 tablespoon butter, and vanilla extract. Pour into the hot pie plate.

4. Bake for 20 minutes, without opening the oven door, or until sides of pie are puffed and high. Reduce oven temperature to 350°F, and bake 20 more minutes or until sides are browned and crisp.

5. Meanwhile, cut apples in $\frac{1}{2}$ and cut into thin wedges.

6. In a large skillet over medium-high heat, melt remaining 1 tablespoon butter. Add apples, raisins, pecans, and cinnamon, and cook, stirring, for 8 to 10 minutes or until apples are glazed and tender. Add water, 1 tablespoon at a time, if the pan becomes dry.

7. Remove pie from the oven, and cut into 6 wedges. Serve topped with apple mixture.

HEALTHY NOTE

Using unpeeled apples gives you more nutritional value—increased fiber—and more taste and flavor per bite.

Island Scrambled Eggs

These eggs are so sweet, they're scandalous! Yet they contain no added sugar—just a touch of honey.

Snack servings:	Yield:	Prep time:	Cook time:	Serving size:
6	6 eggs	10 minutes	5 to 8 minutes	1 egg, 1 pineapple slice, and $\frac{1}{6}$ banana-pecan mixture

Each serving has:			
215 calories	11g protein	17g carbohydrates	2g fiber
12g fat	4g saturated fat	glycemic index: low	glycemic load: 9

1 TB. butter

6 ($\frac{1}{4}$-in.-thick) slices ham

6 ($\frac{1}{4}$-in.-thick) slices pineapple

2 bananas, peeled and sliced

$\frac{1}{4}$ cup pecans, coarsely chopped

1 TB. honey

6 eggs, beaten

1. In a large skillet over medium heat, melt 1 teaspoon butter. Add ham, and sauté for 2 or 3 minutes or until brown on both sides. Remove from the skillet to a platter.

2. Add 1 teaspoon butter to the skillet. Add pineapple, bananas, pecans, and honey, and sauté for 3 to 5 minutes or until fruit is barely soft. Remove fruit to the platter with ham.

3. Add remaining 1 teaspoon butter to the skillet, and scramble eggs.

4. Arrange individual plates with 1 slice ham topped with 1 pineapple ring, 1 scrambled egg, and $\frac{1}{6}$ banana-pecan mixture.

HEALTHY NOTE

If you prefer, you can eliminate the honey in this recipe and still create a sweet and tropical taste for your eggs with the pineapple. As you sauté it, it becomes sweeter and more flavorful.

Sweet Potato Honey Kugel

The pecans, sweet potato, carrots, and apples are seasoned with cinnamon and nutmeg in this hearty kugel.

Snack servings:	Yield:	Prep time:	Cook time:	Serving size:
12	1 (9×13-inch) kugel	15 minutes	1 hour	1 (3×3-inch) square

Each serving has:			
196 calories	3g protein	22g carbohydrates	5g fiber
12g fat	5g saturated fat	glycemic index: low	glycemic load: 7

1 extra-large sweet potato, skin on and grated (4 cups)

4 large carrots, grated (3 cups)

2 large apples, your choice variety, finely diced (2 cups)

1 cup coconut flour

$\frac{1}{2}$ cup butter, melted

1 TB. honey

1 large egg, beaten

$\frac{1}{4}$ tsp. salt

$\frac{3}{4}$ tsp. ground cinnamon

$\frac{1}{4}$ tsp. ground nutmeg

$\frac{3}{4}$ cup toasted pecans, chopped

1. Preheat the oven to 325°F. Line a 9×13-inch baking dish with parchment paper or aluminum foil.

2. In a large bowl, stir together sweet potato, carrots, apples, coconut flour, butter, honey, egg, salt, cinnamon, nutmeg, and $\frac{1}{2}$ cup pecans. Spoon mixture into the prepared baking dish.

3. Bake, covered, for 45 minutes. Increase oven temperature to 350°F, uncover, and bake for 15 more minutes or until edges are golden brown.

4. Top evenly with reserved toasted pecans, and serve warm or chilled.

TASTY BITE

To toast nuts in the oven, arrange them in a single layer on a baking sheet. Bake at 350°F for 5 to 7 minutes or until lightly toasted and fragrant. To toast in the microwave, place nuts in small bowl, and cook for 60 seconds. Stir and cook 60 more seconds. Add more cook time, 30 seconds at a time, until nuts are lightly browned and fragrant.

Norwegian Pancakes

Brown and crispy on the outside and creamy on the inside, these pancakes taste both sweet and tangy.

Snack servings:	Yield:	Prep time:	Cook time:	Serving size:
4	1 pancake	5 minutes	4 to 6 minutes	¼ pancake

Each serving has:			
146 calories	7g protein	9g carbohydrates	0g fiber
10g fat	4g saturated fat	glycemic index: low	glycemic load: 2

4 large eggs	Dash ground black pepper
2 TB. cornstarch	½ tsp. ground nutmeg
¼ cup low-fat milk	1½ TB. butter
1½ TB. honey	3 TB. lemon juice
Dash salt	

1. In a medium bowl, whisk together eggs, cornstarch, milk, honey, salt, pepper, and nutmeg.

2. In a medium skillet over medium-high heat, melt ½ tablespoon butter.

3. Pour egg mixture into the skillet, and cook for 2 or 3 minutes or until eggs are set. Turn and cook on the other side for 2 or 3 more minutes until pancake has slightly browned sides.

4. Remove to a serving dish. Top with remaining 1 tablespoon butter cut into small pieces, sprinkle with lemon juice, and serve at once.

Variation: For a sweeter taste, replace the lemon juice with unsweetened fruit preserves or defrosted, frozen berries.

Egg and Bacon Salad Pitas

Bacon and eggs are enhanced with the flavors of Dijon mustard and basil.

Snack servings:	Yield:	Prep time:	Cook time:	Serving size:
8	4 pitas	5 minutes	5 to 10 minutes	$\frac{1}{2}$ pita

Each serving has:			
226 calories	10g protein	20g carbohydrates	1g fiber
12g fat	3g saturated fat	glycemic index: low	glycemic load: 8

3 slices bacon

$\frac{1}{2}$ cup low-fat mayonnaise

2 tsp. Dijon mustard

6 hard-boiled eggs, peeled and
   chopped

12 to 16 basil leaves

1 medium tomato, chopped

1 medium cucumber, chopped

4 whole-wheat pitas, cut in $\frac{1}{2}$ and
   lightly toasted

1. In large skillet over medium-high heat, cook bacon for 5 to 10 minutes or until crisp. Drain, pat with a paper towel to remove excess fat, and chop coarsely.

2. In a medium bowl, whisk together mayonnaise and Dijon mustard. Stir in eggs, bacon, basil leaves, tomato, and cucumber.

3. Stuff pita pockets with equal amounts of egg mixture, and serve.

TASTY BITE

Prepare your bacon as healthfully as possible to capture the bacon's wonderful taste and reduce the amount of fat. Cook until crisp, so less fat remains in the bacon. Drain well, and pat with a paper towel to remove the excess fat.

Hard-Boiled Egg Spread

What a great way to enjoy hard-boiled eggs—covered with sour cream and green onions.

Snack servings:	Yield:	Prep time:	Serving size:
9	about 3 cups	15 minutes plus chill time	about ⅓ cup

Each serving has:			
153 calories	9g protein	3g carbohydrates	0g fiber
12g fat	6g saturated fat	glycemic index: low	glycemic load: 0

6 large hard-boiled eggs, peeled
2 TB. butter, softened
⅛ tsp. salt
2 TB. green onions, thinly sliced

½ cup low-fat sour cream
½ cup low-fat cream cheese, softened

1. In a medium bowl, or in a food processor fitted with a chopping blade, finely chop or mash eggs. Add butter and salt, and mash or process until well blended. Spoon into a 3- to 5-cup serving dish, and spread in an even layer. Cover and refrigerate for 1 hour or until firm.

2. Sprinkle egg mixture with green onions.

3. In a small bowl, mix or process sour cream and cream cheese until well blended. Spoon over green onions and egg mixture, and spread evenly without disturbing them. Cover and chill for 1 hour.

4. Serve with your choice of cut vegetables such as celery sticks, carrot sticks, or cucumber slices.

Variation: For a different flavor, substitute sun-dried tomatoes packed in oil or caviar for the green onions.

Bountiful Beans and Legumes

In This Chapter

- Legumes: inexpensive nutrition powerhouses
- Tips for digesting legumes
- Legume-rich recipes with healthy fats
- Quick and easy canned legumes

Legumes are a satisfying snack you can enjoy for just pennies per serving. But eating legumes for snacks isn't just about the economics. It's also about enjoying some of the tastiest food there is.

Legumes are easy to prepare, even when you don't have the time to boil a pot full. That's when you'll be glad you've stocked your pantry with some extra cans of legumes. Just open a can of these wonderfully high-nutrition gems, add to your recipe, and voilà, you and your family are deliciously reviving your energy for the next several hours.

The Delicious, Nutritious Legume

Legumes are often called beans, and vice versa. Legumes include beans, peas, and lentils, but not the vegetable variety of green or string bean found raw in the grocery store. Most of the legumes called for in this chapter (with the exception of edamame) are dried. You can cook them yourself or purchase them already cooked in cans.

A mere handful of legumes provides you with top-drawer nutrition. Every variety is very high in protein. Plus, they offer virtually no fat, so if you want to lower your fat intake, enjoy legumes. We've added healthy fats to these recipes so your snack has a delicious texture and you can taste more flavor in each bite.

Legumes are high in carbohydrates, so when you read the nutritional information with each recipe, don't panic. Check out the high amount of fiber and then subtract that amount of fiber from the amount of carbohydrates. That number is called the *effective carbohydrate* and is used to determine the recipe's glycemic load. The glycemic load in the legume recipes, as in all the recipes in this cookbook, is usually 10 or lower.

Don't let any concerns about digestion of legumes get in your way of enjoying these recipes. If your body feels bloated and gassy after eating them, there's a biological reason—your body doesn't make the digestive enzymes a person needs to digest legumes easily. To remedy this, you can take a special digestive enzyme for legumes such as Beano whenever you eat them. The recommended amount is to chew 1 or 2 tablets with your first bites of legumes, but read the package instructions carefully.

TASTY BITE

Although each recipe calls for a specific type of bean, feel free to vary the type. You may want to mix bean types, eat the ones you like best, or use whatever cans of beans you have in your pantry.

Green Lentils with Feta

Green lentils get a jazzy boost with sun-dried tomato paste and feta cheese.

Snack servings:	Yield:	Prep time:	Cook time:	Serving size:
8	4 cups	10 minutes	25 minutes	about $\frac{1}{2}$ cup

Each serving has:			
201 calories	13g protein	25g carbohydrates	12g fiber
4g fat	4g saturated fat	glycemic index: low	glycemic load: 3

$1\frac{1}{2}$ cups green lentils	5 TB. sun-dried tomato paste
$2\frac{1}{2}$ cups water	$\frac{1}{4}$ cup fresh parsley, chopped
$\frac{1}{4}$ tsp. salt	$\frac{1}{4}$ tsp. ground black pepper
7 oz. feta cheese (about 2 cups)	

1. In a heavy saucepan over high heat, combine green lentils, water, and salt. Bring to a boil, reduce heat to medium-low, and cover. Simmer gently for about 20 minutes or until lentils are just tender and most of the water has been absorbed. Drain.

2. Crumble $\frac{1}{2}$ of feta cheese into the saucepan, and stir in sun-dried tomato paste, parsley, and pepper.

3. Transfer lentil mixture to plates or bowls, crumble remaining feta cheese on top, and serve immediately.

KITCHEN ALERT

The cooking time for the lentils in this recipe is given for cooking at sea level. If you live in the mountains, where water boils at a lower temperature than at sea level, increase the cook time. Here in Utah, at 4,500 feet elevation, the lentils take 30 to 35 minutes to become tender.

Lentils with Spinach, Walnuts, and Parmesan

Lentils are delicious combined with dill, Parmesan cheese, and walnuts in this tasty, satisfying snack.

Snack servings:	Yield:	Prep time:	Cook time:	Serving size:
6	about 4 cups	15 minutes	32 to 43 minutes	$^2/_3$ cup

Each serving has:			
222 calories	13g protein	23g carbohydrates	11g fiber
9g fat	1g saturated fat	glycemic index: low	glycemic load: 3

1 cup lentils, drained and rinsed	$^1/_2$ cup carrot, diced
2$^1/_2$ cups water	5 oz. baby spinach (about 1$^1/_2$ cups)
$^1/_4$ tsp. salt	$^1/_4$ cup lemon juice
2 tsp. extra-virgin olive oil	2 TB. fresh dill, finely chopped, or 2 tsp. dried
$^1/_2$ cup walnuts, chopped	$^1/_4$ cup Parmesan cheese, shredded
$^1/_2$ cup yellow or white onion, diced	

1. In a medium saucepan over high heat, combine lentils, water, and salt. Bring to a boil, cover, and simmer for 20 to 30 minutes or until lentils are tender. Drain.

2. Meanwhile, in a large skillet over medium heat, heat extra-virgin olive oil. Add walnuts, and cook, stirring, for about 4 or 5 minutes or until fragrant and slightly browned. Remove to a side dish.

3. Add onion and carrot to the skillet, and sauté for about 8 minutes or until onions are lightly browned. Add spinach, stir until wilted, and remove from heat.

4. Add lentils, lemon juice, and chopped dill to the skillet, and stir gently to mix.

5. Spoon lentil mixture on individual serving plates, sprinkle with Parmesan cheese and walnuts, and serve.

Artichokes with Chickpeas

Basil flavors this tasty stir-fry of artichokes and chickpeas.

Snack servings:	Yield:	Prep time:	Cook time:	Serving size:
8	6 cups	5 minutes	25 to 30 minutes	¾ cup

Each serving has:			
248 calories	12g protein	40g carbohydrates	13g fiber
6g fat	1g saturated fat	glycemic index: low	glycemic load: 9

1 TB. plus 1 tsp. extra-virgin olive oil

½ medium yellow or white onion, diced

1 (15-oz.) can artichoke hearts in water, drained

2 tsp. minced garlic

2 medium tomatoes, drained and diced

1 tsp. whole fennel seed

2 TB. oil-packed sun-dried tomatoes, drained and chopped

1 (15-oz.) can chickpeas, drained and rinsed

2 TB. fresh basil, lightly chopped

Dash salt

Dash ground black pepper

1. In a large skillet over medium heat, heat 1 teaspoon extra-virgin olive oil. Add onion, and sauté for about 10 minutes or until lightly caramelized.

2. Add artichokes, garlic, tomatoes, fennel seed, and sun-dried tomatoes, and stir. After 1 minute, reduce heat to low, and simmer for 15 to 20 minutes.

3. Add chickpeas, basil, and remaining 1 tablespoon extra-virgin olive oil, and combine. Season with salt and pepper, and serve.

HEALTHY NOTE

In addition to garbanzo beans, chickpeas are also known as Indian peas, ceci beans, and Bengal grams.

Romaine Salad Tossed with Chickpeas

This tangy salad with romaine lettuce hosts tomatoes, green olives, anchovy paste, and chickpeas.

Snack servings:	Yield:	Prep time:	Serving size:
4	about 6 cups	15 minutes	1½ cups

Each serving has:			
218 calories	6g protein	20g carbohydrates	6g fiber
14g fat	2g saturated fat	glycemic index: low	glycemic load: 5

1 large head romaine lettuce, torn	½ cup green olives
1 cup cherry tomatoes, halved or quartered	1 in. anchovy paste (about ½ tsp.)
	1 TB. balsamic vinegar
½ cup canned chickpeas, drained and rinsed	3 TB. extra-virgin olive oil

1. In a serving bowl, place lettuce, tomatoes, chickpeas, and olives.

2. In a small bowl, combine anchovy paste, balsamic vinegar, and extra-virgin olive oil.

3. Pour dressing over salad, toss well, and serve immediately.

Green Bean Salad with Edamame and Chickpeas

This terrific variation on a three-bean salad is flavored with celery seed and onions in a vinaigrette dressing.

Snack servings:	Yield:	Prep time:	Cook time:	Serving size:
12	about 6 cups	10 minutes	15 minutes	about $\frac{1}{2}$ cup

Each serving has:			
214 calories	10g protein	26g carbohydrates	8g fiber
8g fat	1g saturated fat	glycemic index: low	glycemic load: 6

2 tsp. lemon zest

$\frac{1}{4}$ cup extra-virgin olive oil

$\frac{1}{4}$ cup red wine vinegar

$\frac{1}{2}$ tsp. celery seed

$\frac{1}{4}$ tsp. salt

$\frac{1}{2}$ tsp. honey

1 (10-oz.) pkg. frozen shelled edamame

1 (15-oz.) can chickpeas, drained and rinsed

2 cups fresh green beans, cut into 1-in. pieces

6 green onions, thinly sliced diagonally

1. In a serving bowl, whisk together lemon zest, extra-virgin olive oil, red wine vinegar, celery seed, salt, and honey. Set aside.

2. In a large saucepan fitted with a steamer basket over medium-high heat, bring 1 inch water to a boil. Add edamame to the basket, and steam, covered, for 3 minutes.

3. Add chickpeas, and steam, covered, for 4 or 5 minutes or until heated through. Remove edamame and chickpeas to a colander, and drain well. Add to the serving bowl.

4. In the same saucepan, bring another 1 inch water to a boil. Add green beans to the basket, and steam, covered, for 4 or 5 minutes or until tender-crisp. Pour into the colander, and drain well.

5. Add green beans and onions to chickpea mixture, and toss to coat with dressing. Serve warm, or refrigerate and serve chilled.

Chickpea Poppers

These chickpeas are baked and then sprinkled with your choice of zesty seasoning.

Snack servings:	Yield:	Prep time:	Cook time:	Serving size:
2	$\frac{1}{2}$ cup	5 minutes	1 hour	$\frac{1}{4}$ cup

Each serving has:			
202 calories	10g protein	30g carbohydrates	9g fiber
5g fat	1g saturated fat	glycemic index: low	glycemic load: 9

$\frac{1}{2}$ cup canned chickpeas, drained, rinsed, and patted dry

1 tsp. extra-virgin olive oil

$\frac{1}{2}$ tsp. your choice of seasonings: chili powder, black pepper, cumin, coriander, cinnamon, cloves, allspice, etc., or combination of seasonings

$\frac{1}{4}$ tsp. salt (optional)

1. Preheat the oven to 400°F. Line a 9×13-inch baking dish with aluminum foil.

2. In a small bowl, mix chickpeas with extra-virgin olive oil. Spread chickpeas in the baking dish, and bake for 1 hour.

3. Toss chickpeas with seasonings and salt (if using).

TASTY BITE

These poppers are delicious and can easily satisfy your desire for a spicy and crunchy finger-food snack. Make plenty for a party. Your guests will love them.

Chickpea Salad with Roasted Cumin

Roasted cumin lends an earthy and rich Mediterranean flavor to these chickpeas and vegetables.

Snack servings:	Yield:	Prep time:	Cook time:	Serving size:
8	about 4 cups	15 minutes	1 minute	½ cup

Each serving has:			
243 calories	11g protein	36g carbohydrates	10g fiber
7g fat	1g saturated fat	glycemic index: low	glycemic load: 9

¾ tsp. cumin

2 TB. lime juice

2 TB. extra-virgin olive oil

¼ cup yellow or white onion, chopped

1 cup celery, sliced

1 medium tomato, seeded and chopped

1 (15-oz.) can chickpeas, drained and rinsed

2 TB. fresh oregano, chopped, or 2 tsp. dried

Dash salt

Dash ground black pepper

1. In an 8-inch skillet over medium heat, add cumin and toast 1 minute or until fragrant. Remove from heat.

2. In a small bowl, whisk together lime juice, extra-virgin olive oil, and toasted cumin.

3. In a serving bowl, place onion, celery, tomato, chickpeas, and oregano. Add lime juice dressing, and toss to coat. Sprinkle with salt and pepper, and serve.

TASTY BITE

The key to preparing this recipe is to toast the cumin. It adds fragrance and flavor.

Black-Eyed Pea and Ham Salad

Garlic, hot sauce, and honey enliven this chilled salad.

Snack servings:	Yield:	Prep time:	Cook time:	Serving size:
8	6 cups	15 minutes plus 8 hours chill time	4 or 5 minutes	¾ cup

Each serving has:			
233 calories	8g protein	17g carbohydrates	4g fiber
16g fat	2g saturated fat	glycemic index: low	glycemic load: 6

1 TB. honey

¼ cup cider vinegar

2 tsp. minced garlic

1 tsp. hot sauce

½ cup extra-virgin olive oil

3 cups canned black-eyed peas, drained and rinsed

1 medium green bell pepper, ribs and seeds removed, and diced

½ cup red onion, diced

1 large stalk celery, diced

1 cup cooked ham, chopped

1. In a large bowl, whisk together honey, cider vinegar, garlic, hot sauce, and extra-virgin olive oil. Add black-eyed peas, green bell pepper, red onion, and celery, and toss to coat. Cover and chill for 8 hours.

2. In a small skillet over medium-high heat, add ham and sauté for 4 or 5 minutes or until lightly browned. Stir into chilled pea mixture just before serving.

Variation: Substitute other varieties of legumes—such as black beans, red beans, or kidney beans—for the black-eyed peas.

Barbecued White Beans

These baked beans are creamy and sweet with the flavors of ham and the bite of crushed red pepper.

Snack servings:	Yield:	Prep time:	Cook time:	Serving size:
6	3 cups	15 minutes	10 to 14 minutes	$\frac{1}{2}$ cup

Each serving has:			
275 calories	19g protein	45g carbohydrates	18g fiber
3g fat	1g saturated fat	glycemic index: low	glycemic load: 6

$1\frac{1}{2}$ tsp. extra-virgin olive oil	1 TB. prepared mustard
1 small yellow or white onion, chopped	1 TB. apple cider vinegar
1 tsp. minced garlic	$1\frac{1}{2}$ tsp. pure maple syrup or honey
$\frac{1}{2}$ cup cooked ham, cut in strips	$1\frac{1}{2}$ tsp. Worcestershire sauce
1 (15-oz.) can cannellini beans (white kidney beans), drained and rinsed	$\frac{1}{8}$ tsp. crushed red pepper flakes

1. In a large saucepan over medium heat, heat extra-virgin olive oil. Add onion and garlic, and sauté for 3 or 4 minutes or until tender.

2. Add ham, and cook for 2 or 3 more minutes or until browned.

3. Add cannellini beans, mustard, cider vinegar, maple syrup, Worcestershire sauce, and crushed red pepper flakes, and cook for 5 to 7 minutes or until heated through.

4. Serve immediately. Store leftovers in the refrigerator. You can reheat them on the stove or in the microwave for a quick and hearty snack.

Four-Cheese Black Bean Mash

Jalapeño pepper heats up this creamy refried bean dish.

Snack servings:	Yield:	Prep time:	Cook time:	Serving size:
8	3 cups	10 minutes	10 minutes	⅜ cup

Each serving has:			
212 calories	13g protein	34g carbohydrates	8g fiber
3g fat	1g saturated fat	glycemic index: low	glycemic load: 9

1 (15-oz.) can black beans, drained and rinsed

2 TB. water

1 TB. extra-virgin olive oil

¼ cup yellow or white onion, chopped

1 jalapeño pepper, seeded and minced

1 tsp. minced garlic

½ cup shredded low-fat Mexican four-cheese blend

1. In a food processor fitted with a chopping blade, process black beans and water for 10 to 15 seconds or until smooth.

2. In a large skillet over medium heat, heat extra-virgin olive oil. Add onion and jalapeño pepper, and sauté for 4 or 5 minutes or until tender. Add garlic, and sauté for 1 more minute.

3. Add black bean purée, and stir until blended. Cook, stirring frequently, for 3 minutes or until bean mixture is thoroughly heated.

4. Stir in cheese until melted, and serve immediately with cut vegetables.

KITCHEN ALERT

Jalapeño peppers can be too hot to handle. Wash your hands carefully after chopping, and don't touch your eyes or other sensitive body parts while handling them. If jalapeños are too hot for your taste buds, substitute a milder, green chile.

Sweet Potato and Black Bean Wraps

Mango highlights these Caribbean-flavored wraps.

Snack servings:	Yield:	Prep time:	Cook time:	Serving size:
6	6 wraps	15 minutes	11 to 16 minutes	1 wrap

Each serving has:			
188 calories	7g protein	28g carbohydrates	6g fiber
6g fat	1g saturated fat	glycemic index: low	glycemic load: 9

1 medium sweet potato (skin on)	6 tsp. extra-virgin olive oil
½ cup canned black beans, drained and rinsed	6 (6-in.) corn tortillas
2 tsp. chili powder	¼ cup low-fat cheddar cheese, shredded
1 tsp. minced garlic	1 cup mango, diced

1. Scrub sweet potato, and pierce all over with a fork. Place on a microwave-safe plate, and microwave, uncovered, on high for 9 to 12 minutes or until tender, turning once.

2. Slit potato, scoop pulp into a small bowl, and mash pulp with a fork. Stir in black beans, chili powder, and garlic.

3. In a large skillet over medium heat, heat 2 teaspoons extra-virgin olive oil. Add 2 corn tortillas, and cook for 1 or 2 minutes, turning once, until warm and softened. Repeat with remaining oil and corn tortillas.

4. Place ⅓ cup sweet potato filling on each tortilla. Roll up and place on microwave-safe plate. Sprinkle with cheese. Microwave on high for 1 or 2 minutes until warmed throughout. Serve with mango.

TASTY BITE

Instead of the mangoes, you can substitute peaches or nectarines, which have a similar flavor. Sliced bananas also work well as a topping for these wraps.

Black Bean and Avocado Salad

Lime juice and garlic add zing to this bean and corn salad.

Snack servings:	Yield:	Prep time:	Serving size:
14	about 7 cups	15 minutes plus 2 hours chill time	about ½ cup

Each serving has:			
230 calories	10g protein	33g carbohydrates	9g fiber
8g fat	1g saturated fat	glycemic index: low	glycemic load: 6

2 medium ripe avocados, peeled, pitted, and diced

2 TB. lime juice

1 (15.25-oz.) can whole kernel corn, drained

1 (15-oz.) can black beans, drained and rinsed

1 medium sweet red pepper, ribs and seeds removed, and chopped

6 green onions, chopped

2 TB. fresh parsley, minced

3 tsp. minced garlic

2 TB. extra-virgin olive oil

1 tsp. red wine vinegar

½ tsp. salt

¼ tsp. ground black pepper

1. In a large bowl, combine avocados and lime juice. Let stand for 5 minutes.

2. In another large bowl, combine corn, black beans, sweet red pepper, onions, parsley, and garlic.

3. In a small bowl, whisk together extra-virgin olive oil, red wine vinegar, salt, and pepper.

4. Pour dressing over corn mixture, and toss to coat. Gently fold in avocado mixture, cover, and refrigerate for 2 hours or until chilled.

TASTY BITE

Be sure to coat the avocado well with the lime juice and the dressing. The acids in the lime juice and vinegar prevent the avocado from oxidizing, or turning brown.

Tuscan Bean Soup

Carrots and tomatoes with Italian seasoning add flavor to this cannellini bean soup.

Snack servings:	Yield:	Prep time:	Cook time:	Serving size:
6	about 6 cups	10 minutes	15 minutes	1 cup

Each serving has:			
280 calories	18g protein	48g carbohydrates	19g fiber
3g fat	0g saturated fat	glycemic index: low	glycemic load: 9

1 TB. extra-virgin olive oil

1 cup peeled baby carrots, coarsely chopped

$\frac{1}{2}$ cup white or yellow onion, chopped

1 (15-oz.) can cannellini beans (white kidney beans), drained and rinsed

1 (14.5-oz.) can Italian-flavored diced tomatoes, drained

2 cups water

1 tsp. Italian seasoning

$\frac{1}{8}$ tsp. ground black pepper

1. In 4-quart saucepan or Dutch oven over medium-high heat, heat extra-virgin olive oil. Add carrots and onions, and sauté for 3 minutes.

2. Add cannellini beans, tomatoes, water, and Italian seasoning, and bring to a boil. Slightly mash beans, and simmer, uncovered and stirring occasionally, for 8 minutes.

3. Remove from heat, ladle soup into individual serving bowls, sprinkle with pepper, and serve.

Great Northern Bean and Mushroom Burgers

The flavor of mushrooms and sage keynotes these burgers.

Snack servings:	Yield:	Prep time:	Cook time:	Serving size:
8	8 burgers	15 minutes	12 minutes	1 burger

Each serving has:			
221 calories	14g protein	34g carbohydrates	9g fiber
5g fat	1g saturated fat	glycemic index: low	glycemic load: 6

2 TB. extra-virgin olive oil

²⁄₃ cup white or crimini mushrooms, finely chopped

2 tsp. minced garlic

1 (15-oz.) can Great Northern beans, drained and rinsed

3 TB. lemon juice

¼ cup fresh parsley, finely chopped

2 tsp. fresh sage, snipped, or ½ tsp. dried

¼ tsp. salt

¼ tsp. ground black pepper

½ cup wheat or oat bran

1 large egg, beaten

8 large Bibb or leaf lettuce leaves

1. In a medium skillet over medium-high heat, heat 1 tablespoon extra-virgin olive oil. Add mushrooms and garlic, and sauté for 5 minutes or until tender. Remove from the heat.

2. In a food processor fitted with a chopping blade, purée Great Northern beans with lemon juice. Transfer to a medium bowl, and stir in mushroom mixture, parsley, sage, salt, pepper, wheat bran, and egg.

3. Shape mixture into 8 (½- to ¾-inch-thick) patties.

4. In a large skillet over medium heat, heat 1 remaining tablespoon extra-virgin olive oil. Add patties, and cook for 4 minutes on each side, being very careful when turning. Serve on individual lettuce leaves.

HEALTHY NOTE

Burgers are a favorite snack food. Bean burgers offer a delicious and meatless high-energy snack.

Guacamole with Green Peas and Tomato

This high-protein version of guacamole is flavored with green chiles and tomato.

Snack servings:	Yield:	Prep time:	Serving size:
8	4 servings	10 minutes	about $\frac{1}{2}$ cup

Each serving has:			
203 calories	4g protein	17g carbohydrates	10g fiber
15g fat	2g saturated fat	glycemic index: low	glycemic load: 3

1 cup frozen green peas, defrosted and drained	1 medium tomato, chopped
2 TB. lime juice	$\frac{1}{4}$ cup canned diced green chiles, drained
2 large ripe avocados, peeled and pitted	1 TB. red onion, chopped
	$\frac{1}{8}$ tsp. salt

1. In a food processor fitted with a chopping blade, or in a strong blender, pulse peas with lime juice until smooth.

2. Place avocados in a medium bowl. Add blended peas, tomato, green chiles, onion, and salt. Mix gently with a fork, using enough pressure to bring ingredients together, but not so much that the avocados lose all their chunkiness.

3. Serve immediately on small serving plates.

Refried Bean–Stuffed Portobello Mushrooms

The flavor of avocado accents these mushrooms stuffed with refried beans and cottage cheese.

Snack servings:	Yield:	Prep time:	Cook time:	Serving size:
2	2 mushrooms	5 minutes	2 or 3 minutes	1 mushroom

Each serving has:			
251 calories	13g protein	17g carbohydrates	9g fiber
16g fat	3g saturated fat	glycemic index: low	glycemic load: 3

2 portobello mushrooms, stems removed

4 TB. refried beans

1 cup spinach leaves

$\frac{1}{2}$ cup low-fat cottage cheese

1 medium avocado, pitted and sliced

1. Turn mushrooms upside down on a microwave-safe dish. Spread $\frac{1}{2}$ of refried beans on each mushroom, and place $\frac{1}{2}$ of spinach on top. Cover with cottage cheese.

2. Microwave on high for 2 or 3 minutes. Top with avocado slices, and serve.

Great Whole Grains

In This Chapter

- Whole-grain comfort foods
- Fill-you-up snacks
- Combining grains with fruit, meats, and legumes

Good-for-you whole grains are low glycemic. When grains are processed into light and fluffy flours, they become high glycemic. That's why you won't find many recipes that call for light and fluffy flours in this cookbook.

Ah, but those whole grains—they taste great in salads, pilafs, and stews, as you'll see by the recipes in this chapter.

Watch the Glycemic Load

Whole grains are low glycemic, but they're very high in carbohydrates. They offer you moderate amounts of fiber, but not enough to offset the high carbohydrate count. That means the glycemic load of whole grains can get too high for your daily count. The recommended glycemic load count for a person ranges from 80 to 120 per day. The variation accounts for a person's activity level, age, and size. That's why we've kept the glycemic load of each recipe serving size at or below 10.

Note, too, that the recipe nutritional information suggests modest serving sizes. As you follow your personal health, fitness, and eating plan, be sure to eat enough of your snack, as recommended, but not too much. Otherwise, your glycemic load could soar too high.

Quinoa and Lentil Salad

The crisp and fluffy texture of *quinoa* and creamy lentils serve as a base for avocado, fennel, and tomatoes in this tasty salad.

Snack servings:	Yield:	Prep time:	Cook time:	Serving size:
4	about 4 cups	15 minutes	20 minutes	1 cup

Each serving has:			
260 calories	10g protein	35g carbohydrates	12g fiber
10g fat	1g saturated fat	glycemic index: low	glycemic load: 9

½ cup quinoa	½ cup cherry tomatoes, cut in ½
½ tsp. salt	¼ cup fresh cilantro, chopped
7 cups water	6 radishes, sliced
½ cup lentils	1 fennel bulb, thinly sliced
¼ cup Italian vinaigrette dressing	
1 small avocado, peeled, pitted, and diced	

1. In a medium saucepan over medium heat, combine quinoa, ¼ teaspoon salt, and 4 cups water. Bring to a simmer, cover, and cook for about 15 minutes.

2. Meanwhile, in a separate medium saucepan over medium heat, combine lentils, remaining 3 cups water, and remaining ¼ teaspoon salt. Bring to a simmer, uncovered, and cook for about 20 minutes or until lentils are tender and water has been absorbed. Cool.

3. Place quinoa and lentils in a serving bowl, and toss with 2 tablespoons Italian vinaigrette dressing.

4. In a large bowl, combine avocado, cherry tomatoes, cilantro, radishes, and fennel. Toss with remaining Italian vinaigrette dressing.

5. Arrange vegetable salad over bed of quinoa and lentils, and serve immediately.

GLYCO-LINGO

Quinoa, a whole grain, was originally cultivated in the Andes Mountains of South America. It contains a good balance of essential amino acids, or protein, and it's high in dietary fiber while being gluten-free.

Lentil Tabbouleh

Lentils and bulgur are blended with the tastes of mint and onions in this classic salad.

Snack servings:	Yield:	Prep time:	Cook time:	Serving size:
4	6 cups	20 minutes	15 to 20 minutes	1½ cups
Each serving has:				
220 calories	11g protein	40g carbohydrates		13g fiber
4g fat	1g saturated fat	glycemic index: low		glycemic load: 9

3 cups water

½ cup bulgur

½ cup lentils, picked over, drained, and rinsed

½ tsp. salt

2 TB. lemon juice

1 TB. extra-virgin olive oil

⅛ tsp. ground black pepper

3 large plum tomatoes, chopped

1 medium cucumber, chopped

2 green onions, thinly sliced

½ cup fresh mint leaves, chopped

1. In a covered 3-quart saucepan over high heat, bring water to a boil.

2. In a medium bowl, cover bulgur with 2 cups boiling water. Let stand for 30 minutes, and drain well.

3. Meanwhile, add lentils and ¼ teaspoon salt to remaining boiling water in the saucepan. Reduce heat to low, cover, and simmer for 15 to 20 minutes or until lentils are tender. Drain in colander.

4. In a large bowl, whisk lemon juice, extra-virgin olive oil, remaining ¼ teaspoon salt, and pepper until blended. Add warm bulgur and lentils, and stir to coat. Let stand for 15 minutes or until cool.

5. Stir in tomatoes, cucumber, and green onions, cover, and refrigerate for at least 2 hours. Stir in mint right before serving.

Bulgur with Apples and Walnuts

Fresh basil and yogurt add flavor to this grain and fruit salad.

Snack servings:	Yield:	Prep time:	Serving size:
4	4 cups	15 minutes plus 1 hour chill time	1 cup

Each serving has:			
195 calories	6g protein	29g carbohydrates	5g fiber
7g fat	1g saturated fat	glycemic index: low	glycemic load: 10

$\frac{1}{2}$ cup *bulgur,* soaked per pkg. directions

1 medium apple, your choice variety, cored and cut into $\frac{1}{2}$-in. pieces

1 tsp. lemon juice

3 TB. extra-virgin olive oil

1 cup celery, thinly sliced

1 cup red or green seedless grapes, halved lengthwise

$\frac{1}{2}$ cup low-fat Greek-style yogurt

2 tsp. fresh basil, chopped, or 1 tsp. dried

$\frac{1}{8}$ tsp. ground black pepper

2 TB. walnut pieces, toasted and chopped

1. In a large bowl, combine bulgur, apple, lemon juice, and extra-virgin olive oil. Add celery, grapes, yogurt, and basil, and mix thoroughly. Season with pepper. Cover and refrigerate for 1 hour or overnight to allow flavors to blend.

2. Sprinkle each serving with $\frac{1}{2}$ tablespoon walnuts, and serve.

GLYCO-LINGO

Bulgur is a form of whole wheat that's been par-boiled and then packaged. It's reconstituted by soaking in hot water. It's used in many Middle Eastern and Mediterranean recipes.

Bulgur, Feta, and Olive Salad

This delightful salad with many textures takes on the distinctive flavor of Mediterranean cuisine.

Snack servings:	Yield:	Prep time:	Serving size:
6	6 cups	30 minutes	1 cup

Each serving has:			
295 calories	8g protein	25g carbohydrates	7g fiber
19g fat	5g saturated fat	glycemic index: low	glycemic load: 9

1 cup bulgur

2½ cups boiling water

1 cup carrot, shredded

1 cup fennel, sliced thinly

½ cup kalamata olives, pitted

½ cup roasted pistachios, shelled and salted

1 cup feta cheese, crumbled

2 TB. red wine vinegar

¼ cup extra-virgin olive oil

½ cup fresh parsley, chopped

¼ cup fresh oregano, chopped, or 2 tsp. dried

1. In a medium bowl, combine bulgur and boiling water. Let sit for 15 to 20 minutes or until bulgur is tender. Pour off any remaining water.

2. Add carrot, fennel, olives, pistachios, feta cheese, red wine vinegar, extra-virgin olive oil, parsley, and oregano. Toss to combine, and serve immediately. Refrigerate any leftovers for up to 3 days.

HEALTHY NOTE

You can now purchase shelled, roasted, and salted pistachios in the fresh-food aisle of many grocery stores. It's a great time-saver.

Wheat Berry and Cabbage Salad

A perfect blend of sweet and tangy Asian flavors boosts this salad with sesame, ginger, and the sweetness of papaya and carrots.

Snack servings:	Yield:	Prep time:	Cook time:	Serving size:
8	about 8 cups	15 minutes	45 to 60 minutes	1 cup

Each serving has:			
178 calories	8g protein	32g carbohydrates	7g fiber
3g fat	1g saturated fat	glycemic index: low	glycemic load: 6

1¼ cups water

½ cup wheat berries

1 cup canned black beans, drained and rinsed

½ papaya, seeded, peeled, and chopped

¾ cup carrots, julienned

¼ cup Asian salad dressing

2 tsp. toasted sesame seeds

¼ tsp. ground ginger

¼ tsp. salt (optional)

4 cups cabbage, coarsely shredded

1. In a medium saucepan over high heat, combine water and wheat berries. Bring to a boil, reduce heat to medium-low, and simmer, covered, for 45 to 60 minutes or until tender. Drain liquid.

2. Stir in black beans, papaya, carrots, Asian salad dressing, sesame seeds, ginger, and salt (if using).

3. Arrange cabbage on 8 serving plates. Top with 1 cup wheat berry mixture, and serve.

Variation: You can substitute peaches, nectarines, or bananas for the papaya if you like.

Fruit Salad with Wheat Berries

This colorful salad is sweetened with dried fruit and tossed with a combination of legumes and green beans.

Snack servings:	Yield:	Prep time:	Cook time:	Serving size:
6	about 5 cups	15 minutes plus overnight soaking plus 1 hour cool time	45 to 60 minutes	$\frac{5}{6}$ cup

Each serving has:			
171 calories	7g protein	32g carbohydrates	9g fiber
3g fat	0g saturated fat	glycemic index: low	glycemic load: 6

1 cup wheat berries, drained and rinsed

3 cups water

Dash plus $\frac{1}{2}$ tsp. salt

1 (15-oz.) can your choice salad legumes, drained and rinsed

1 cup canned green beans, or 1 cup fresh or frozen green beans, cooked and drained

$\frac{1}{2}$ cup dried apricots, sliced

$\frac{1}{2}$ cup raisins

$\frac{1}{4}$ cup green onion, chopped

3 TB. toasted walnut oil

1 TB. lemon juice

$\frac{1}{2}$ tsp. ground black pepper

1. In a medium bowl, combine wheat berries, water, and dash salt. Cover and refrigerate overnight.

2. Transfer to a medium saucepan over high heat, and bring to a boil. Reduce heat to medium-low, and simmer, covered, for 45 to 60 minutes or until tender. Drain, and cool for 1 hour.

3. In a large bowl, combine wheat berries, salad legumes, green beans, apricots, raisins, and green onion. Add toasted walnut oil, lemon juice, remaining $\frac{1}{2}$ teaspoon salt, and pepper, and stir to coat. Serve at once, or cover and refrigerate for up to 24 hours.

HEALTHY NOTE

Wheat berries give you the full nutritional power of wheat—the fiber, starch, and protein. Because you're eating the whole grain, you'll have more appetite satisfaction.

Creamy Swiss Grits

Creamy Swiss cheese is melted into these grits to give them an elegant taste.

Snack servings:	Yield:	Prep time:	Cook time:	Serving size:
4	4 cups	10 minutes	20 minutes	1 cup

Each serving has:			
155 calories	9g protein	9g carbohydrates	1g fiber
9g fat	4g saturated fat	glycemic index: low	glycemic load: 10

3¼ cups water

½ tsp. salt

¾ cup uncooked quick-cooking grits

1 cup low-fat Swiss or Gruyère cheese, shredded

½ cup half-and-half

1 TB. extra-virgin olive oil

¼ tsp. ground black pepper

1 tsp. dried parsley

1. In a medium saucepan over medium-high heat, combine water and salt, and bring to a boil. Gradually whisk in grits, and return to a boil. Reduce heat to medium, and simmer, whisking occasionally, for about 12 to 15 minutes or until thickened.

2. Whisk in Swiss cheese, half-and-half, extra-virgin olive oil, pepper, and parsley, and stir until cheese is melted and mixture is blended. Serve with cut-up vegetables.

Polenta with Sausage and Mushrooms

These polenta rounds hold spicy sausage with vegetables and Parmesan cheese.

Snack servings:	Yield:	Prep time:	Cook time:	Serving size:
16	16 polenta rounds	10 minutes	18 to 22 minutes	1 round

Each serving has:			
223 calories	9g protein	25g carbohydrates	1g fiber
7g fat	2g saturated fat	glycemic index: low	glycemic load: 10

1 (16-oz.) tube refrigerated polenta with sun-dried tomatoes

2 medium zucchini, halved lengthwise

1 TB. extra-virgin olive oil

¼ tsp. salt

⅛ tsp. ground black pepper

1 lb. bulk Italian sausage

1 (8-oz.) pkg. sliced white or crimini mushrooms

1 cup grape tomatoes

1 tsp. dried Italian seasoning, crushed

¼ cup Parmesan cheese, shredded

1. Preheat the broiler to low. Lightly grease a baking sheet.

2. Cut polenta in 16 slices, and place polenta and zucchini on the baking sheet. Brush with extra-virgin olive oil, and sprinkle with salt and pepper. Broil 4 or 5 inches from heat for 8 to 10 minutes or until polenta is lightly browned and zucchini is crisp-tender, turning once.

3. Meanwhile, in large skillet over medium heat, add Italian sausage, and cook, breaking up any lumps, for 5 to 7 minutes or until sausage begins to brown. Drain off fat.

4. Add mushrooms, tomatoes, and Italian seasoning to the skillet, and cook for 5 minutes or until meat is no longer pink.

5. Slice zucchini crosswise, and add to meat. Spoon sausage mixture over polenta rounds, sprinkle with Parmesan cheese, and serve warm. Store leftovers in the refrigerator for up to 3 days. Leftovers can also be frozen.

TASTY BITE

You can easily make polenta with coarsely ground cornmeal. Follow the package directions—you'll cook it in boiling water and salt. Then add some sun-dried tomatoes, if you prefer.

Brown Rice Salad with Pecans

This brown rice is spiced with Italian dressing and mixed with apple and fresh vegetables.

Snack servings:	Yield:	Prep time:	Cook time:	Serving size:
8	about 8 cups	15 minutes	20 to 30 minutes	1 cup

Each serving has:			
199 calories	3g protein	26g carbohydrates	3g fiber
10g fat	1g saturated fat	glycemic index: low	glycemic load: 10

1 cup brown rice

½ cup Italian dressing

2 tsp. Dijon mustard

1 cup celery, sliced

1 cup carrots, shredded

1 medium red bell pepper, ribs and seeds removed, and thinly sliced

1 medium apple, your choice variety, cored and diced

½ cup fresh parsley, chopped

½ cup pecans, coarsely chopped

1. Cook brown rice according to package directions. Spread cooked rice on a large plate to cool quickly.

2. In a large serving bowl, whisk together Italian dressing and Dijon mustard. Add rice, celery, carrots, red bell pepper, apple, and parsley, and toss.

3. Stir in pecans just before serving.

HEALTHY NOTE

Go ahead and substitute any whole grain for another in these recipes. You may need to slightly change the cooking times, but you'll find full flavor for your favorite grains in each recipe.

Cajun Dirty Rice

The fragrant aroma of sausage, red beans, rice, and Cajun seasonings exudes from the flavors of this spicy stew.

Snack servings:	Yield:	Prep time:	Cook time:	Serving size:
10	about 10 cups	15 minutes plus over-night soak time	3 hours	1 cup

Each serving has:			
228 calories	11g protein	32g carbohydrates	5g fiber
7g fat	2g saturated fat	glycemic index: low	glycemic load: 7

1 cup brown rice

1 (7-oz.) pkg. smoked turkey sausage links

1 cup yellow onion, diced

1 green bell pepper, ribs and seeds removed, and diced

3 tsp. minced garlic

1¼ cups dried red beans, soaked overnight in water in a covered pot

1 bay leaf

3 cups water

2 tomatoes, finely chopped

1½ tsp. Cajun seasoning

½ tsp. salt

¼ tsp. ground black pepper

4 TB. fresh cilantro, minced

1. Cook brown rice according to package directions. Remove from heat and set aside.

2. Meanwhile, in a medium saucepan over high heat, cover sausage with 3 inches water. Bring to a boil, and boil for 10 minutes. Remove from heat, drain, cool for 5 minutes, and slice.

3. Lightly spray a large pot with cooking spray, and set over medium-high heat. Add onion, green bell pepper, and garlic, and sauté for about 5 minutes.

4. Drain soaked beans, and add to the pot with bay leaf and water. Boil for 20 minutes, reduce heat to medium-low, and cook for about 2 hours or until beans are soft, stirring occasionally and adding more water as needed.

5. Add tomatoes, and cook for 15 minutes.

6. Remove bay leaf. Stir in Cajun seasoning, rice, and sausage, and cook for 10 minutes.

7. Season with salt and pepper, garnish with cilantro, and serve.

TASTY BITE

You can cut this recipe in half if you want fewer snack servings. Half the recipe yields 5 snack servings.

Barley Pilaf with Shrimp

This hearty shrimp and barley snack is flavored with sage, mushrooms, and onions.

Snack servings:	Yield:	Prep time:	Cook time:	Serving size:
4	about 8 cups	15 minutes	78 to 83 minutes	2 cups

Each serving has:			
282 calories	19g protein	42g carbohydrates	9g fiber
5g fat	1g saturated fat	glycemic index: low	glycemic load: 7

1 cup pearl barley

2½ cups water

1 TB. extra-virgin olive oil

½ cup onions, chopped

2 cups white mushrooms, chopped

4 cups baby spinach

½ lb. cooked medium shrimp, peeled and chopped (about 8 to 10 shrimp)

¼ tsp. ground black pepper

¼ cup fresh sage, snipped, or 2 tsp. dried

½ tsp. salt

1. In a medium saucepan over high heat, bring barley and water to a boil. Cover, reduce heat to medium-low, and simmer for 50 minutes.

2. In a medium skillet over medium heat, heat extra-virgin olive oil. Add onions and mushrooms, and sauté for 5 minutes. Add spinach, and sauté for about 3 minutes or until bright green.

3. Drain cooked barley, and return the saucepan to medium-low heat. Add shrimp and pepper, and cook for 5 minutes.

4. Stir in onion-mushroom mixture, sage, and salt, and cook for 5 to 10 minutes. Serve at once or store in the refrigerator for 2 or 3 days. Or freeze for up to 6 months.

Barley with Asparagus and Thyme

The earthy taste of barley and thyme are accented with asparagus and Parmesan cheese.

Snack servings:	Yield:	Prep time:	Cook time:	Serving size:
4	about 4 cups	10 minutes	50 to 60 minutes	1 cup

Each serving has:			
293 calories	12g protein	41g carbohydrates	11g fiber
10g fat	4g saturated fat	glycemic index: low	glycemic load: 6

1 TB. extra-virgin olive oil

1 cup quick-cooking barley

$\frac{1}{2}$ cup yellow onion, chopped

1 TB. butter

1 tsp. minced garlic

1 (14-oz.) can chicken or vegetable broth

8 oz. fresh asparagus, cut into 1-in. pieces (8 to 10 spears, or 1$\frac{1}{4}$ cups pieces)

$\frac{1}{2}$ cup carrot, shredded

$\frac{1}{4}$ cup Parmesan or Asiago cheese, shredded

$\frac{1}{4}$ cup fresh thyme, snipped, or 2 tsp. dried

$\frac{1}{4}$ tsp. salt

$\frac{1}{8}$ tsp. ground black pepper

1. In a large saucepan over medium heat, heat extra-virgin olive oil. Add barley, and sauté for about 5 minutes or until lightly toasted.

2. Add onion, butter, and garlic, and cook for 5 to 10 minutes or until onion is tender.

3. In a small saucepan over medium-high heat, or in a microwave, heat chicken broth. Slowly add $\frac{3}{4}$ cup broth to barley mixture, stirring constantly. Cook, stirring, for 10 to 15 minutes or until liquid is absorbed. Add another $\frac{1}{2}$ cup broth, and cook and stir until liquid is almost all absorbed.

4. Add asparagus and carrot, and cook for 30 minutes or until liquid is absorbed and barley is tender.

5. Remove from heat. Stir in Parmesan cheese and thyme, season with salt and pepper, and serve.

Crackers, Breads, and Muffins

In This Chapter

- Perfectly packaged snacks
- Using nut and seed flours
- Baking flatbreads and crackers
- A wide variety of muffin flavors

Crackers, breads, and muffins have long been favorite snack options. Many available on the grocery store shelves, however, are high glycemic because they're made with white flour and white sugar.

The recipes in this chapter offer you more healthful snacks made with highly nutritious and low-glycemic ingredients, especially some different flours such as coconut flour, whole-wheat flour, nut flours, and seed meals. You'll love soothing your snack cravings with these treats—and enjoy the extra energy!

The flatbreads and crackers are crisp and satisfying while being easy to bake. And we've given you lots of muffin recipes—a muffin is a perfect size for a snack. The calorie tally ranges between 100 to 200 calories, and they come in snack size!

Spiced Flax Cracker

Add your favorite spice or herb to this easy-to-make cracker.

Snack servings:	Yield:	Prep time:	Cook time:	Serving size:
1	1 cracker	5 minutes	90 seconds	1 cracker

Each serving has:			
75 calories	3g protein	4g carbohydrates	4g fiber
6g fat	1g saturated fat	glycemic index: low	glycemic load: 0

2 TB. flaxseed meal   Dash ground black pepper

2 TB. water

1. In a small bowl, use a fork to mix flaxseed meal with water and pepper. Let rest for 2 or 3 minutes.

2. On a piece of parchment paper, press and gently spread mixture with a fork into a 4×8-inch cracker. Microwave on high for 90 seconds or until cracker is solid. Cool.

3. Top with your favorite dip, salsa, or tapenade, and enjoy.

Variation: Vary the taste of this cracker by using different spices in place of the black pepper. Try cayenne, red pepper flakes, cardamom, ginger, oregano, thyme, cinnamon, nutmeg, coriander, basil, curry, or another favorite.

Walnut Crackers

These walnut-studded crackers are flavored with almond flour.

Snack servings:	Yield:	Prep time:	Cook time:	Serving size:
24	24 crackers	10 minutes	10 to 12 minutes	1 cracker

Each serving has:			
70 calories	2g protein	5g carbohydrates	1g fiber
5g fat	0g saturated fat	glycemic index: low	glycemic load: 1

1 cup almond flour	$\frac{1}{2}$ cup walnuts, chopped
1 cup whole-wheat flour	1 large egg, beaten
1 tsp. salt	2 TB. extra-virgin olive oil

1. Preheat the oven to 350°F. Line two baking sheets with parchment paper.

2. In a large bowl, stir together almond flour, whole-wheat flour, salt, walnuts, egg, and extra-virgin olive oil until well blended.

3. Place $\frac{1}{2}$ of dough in the center of each prepared baking sheet. Cut another piece of parchment paper, and place it over dough. With a rolling pin, roll out dough between the 2 pieces of parchment paper until it's the desired thickness: thin for crispy crackers or thicker for flat bread. Using a knife or pizza cutter, cut dough into 12 crackers.

4. Bake for 10 to 12 minutes or until golden. Cool. Eat warm or store in an airtight container in the pantry.

Parmesan Crisps with Garlic and Pepper

These Parmesan crisps flavored with garlic and black pepper are so quick to make, and delicious to eat.

Snack servings:	Yield:	Prep time:	Cook time:	Serving size:
12	12 crisps	5 minutes	9 to 10 minutes	1 crisp

Each serving has:			
52 calories	5g protein	1g carbohydrates	0g fiber
3g fat	2g saturated fat	glycemic index: low	glycemic load: 0

2 cups Parmesan cheese, freshly grated	1 tsp. minced garlic
	$\frac{1}{2}$ tsp. ground black pepper

1. Preheat the oven to 350°F. Line a baking sheet with parchment paper.

2. In a small bowl, combine Parmesan cheese, garlic, and pepper, stirring well. Spread mixture in an even thickness on the prepared baking sheet.

3. Bake for 9 or 10 minutes or until golden. When cooled, break into 12 crisps.

Variation: Add basil, parsley, oregano, rosemary, thyme, or your favorite fresh or dried herb to the cheese mixture.

Oatmeal Flatbread Bars

This oatmeal flatbread is sweetened with honey and spiced with cinnamon.

Snack servings:	Yield:	Prep time:	Cook time:	Serving size:
15	15 bars	10 minutes	15 to 20 minutes	1 bar

Each serving has:			
121 calories	2g protein	12g carbohydrates	1g fiber
7g fat	4g saturated fat	glycemic index: low	glycemic load: 5

½ cup butter

¼ cup honey

½ tsp. ground cinnamon

2 large eggs

2 cups long-cooking old-fashioned oats

1. Preheat the oven to 350°F. Line the base and sides of a 9×13-inch baking pan with parchment paper.

2. With an electric mixer on low to medium speed or in a food processor fitted with a chopping blade, beat butter, honey, cinnamon, and eggs. Stir in oats until blended.

3. Turn mixture into the prepared pan, and level the surface. Bake for 15 to 20 minutes or until just beginning to turn golden. Cool slightly, cut into 15 bars, and remove from the pan. Store in an airtight container.

Brie Biscuits

Onion flavors these buttery biscuits highlighted with pieces of elegant Brie cheese.

Snack servings:	Yield:	Prep time:	Cook time:	Serving size:
8	8 biscuits	10 minutes	15 to 20 minutes	1 biscuit

Each serving has:			
107 calories	5g protein	1g carbohydrates	0g fiber
10g fat	6g saturated fat	glycemic index: low	glycemic load: 0

4 large eggs	$\frac{1}{3}$ cup sifted coconut flour
$\frac{1}{4}$ cup butter, melted	$\frac{1}{4}$ tsp. baking powder
$\frac{1}{4}$ tsp. salt	$\frac{1}{2}$ cup low-fat Brie cheese, cut into small cubes
$\frac{1}{4}$ tsp. onion powder	

1. Preheat the oven to 400°F. Line a baking sheet with parchment paper.

2. In a large bowl, whisk eggs. Add butter, salt, and onion powder.

3. In a small bowl, combine coconut flour and baking powder. Fold into batter until no lumps remain. Gently stir in Brie cheese.

4. Drop batter by the spoonful onto the prepared baking sheet to make 8 biscuits. Bake for 15 to 20 minutes. Cool and store in an airtight container.

TASTY BITE

In these recipes, we give you a range for the baking time, as with the 15 to 20 minutes in this recipe. The time variance is based on the altitude where you live and the precision of your oven. Check the biscuits at 15 minutes to determine if they need more baking time.

Ham and Cheddar Scones

These moist and delicious scones are flavored with ham, cheddar, and dill.

Snack servings:	Yield:	Prep time:	Cook time:	Serving size:
24	24 scones	15 minutes	18 to 20 minutes	1 scone

Each serving has:			
93 calories	3g protein	8g carbohydrates	1g fiber
6g fat	4g saturated fat	glycemic index: low	glycemic load: 5

1½ cups whole-wheat flour

½ cup oat bran

2 tsp. baking powder

½ tsp. baking soda

⅛ tsp. salt

½ cup butter

½ cup shredded sharp cheddar cheese

¼ cup cooked ham, diced

1 tsp. dried dill weed

¾ cup lite sour cream

1 large egg, lightly beaten

1 TB. Dijon mustard

1. Preheat the oven to 375°F. Line 2 baking sheets with parchment paper.

2. In a large bowl, combine whole-wheat flour, oat bran, baking powder, baking soda, and salt. Using a pastry blender or 2 knives, cut in butter until mixture resembles coarse crumbs. Stir in cheddar cheese, ham, and dill weed.

3. In a small bowl, combine sour cream, egg, and Dijon mustard. Add to flour mixture, and using a fork, stir just until moistened. Do not overwork.

4. Turn dough out onto a lightly floured surface, and knead by folding and gently pressing dough 4 to 6 times or until dough holds together. Pat or lightly roll dough ¾ inch thick. Cut dough with a floured 2½- to 3-inch biscuit cutter. Reroll scraps as necessary; dip cutter into flour between cuts.

5. Place circles 1 inch apart on the prepared baking sheet. Bake for 18 to 20 minutes or until golden. Cool slightly on a wire rack. Serve warm. Scones will stay fresh for 3 or 4 days in your pantry. You can also freeze them and defrost them for convenient snacks.

Blueberry Banana Walnut Bread

This moist banana bread is sweetened with blueberries and enhanced with extra protein and flaxseed.

Snack servings:	Yield:	Prep time:	Cook time:	Serving size:
18	18 (1-inch) slices	15 minutes	45 to 50 minutes	1 slice

Each serving has:			
124 calories	4g protein	16g carbohydrates	4g fiber
5g fat	0g saturated fat	glycemic index: low	glycemic load: 5

1 ripe banana, peeled and mashed	$\frac{1}{2}$ tsp. salt
$\frac{3}{4}$ cup flaxseed meal	$\frac{3}{4}$ cup whole-wheat flour
2 egg whites	$\frac{3}{4}$ cup oat bran
$\frac{1}{3}$ cup honey	2 TB. chickpea flour
1 cup low-fat buttermilk	1 cup fresh or frozen blueberries
1 tsp. baking soda	$\frac{1}{2}$ cup walnuts, chopped

1. Preheat the oven to 375°F. Line a 9×5×3-inch loaf pan with parchment paper.

2. In a large bowl, stir together banana, flaxseed meal, egg whites, honey, and buttermilk.

3. In a separate bowl, mix baking soda, salt, whole-wheat flour, oat bran, and chickpea flour. Fold dry ingredients into banana mixture, and stir in blueberries and walnuts.

4. Pour mixture into the prepared loaf pan. Bake for 45 to 50 minutes. Cool and store in an airtight container.

Zucchini Apple Bread

Cinnamon sparkles up this zucchini bread made with yogurt and honey.

Snack servings:	Yield:	Prep time:	Cook time:	Serving size:
12	12 slices	15 minutes	40 to 45 minutes	1 slice

Each serving has:			
90 calories	3g protein	18g carbohydrates	2g fiber
1g fat	1g saturated fat	glycemic index: low	glycemic load: 8

1 cup whole-wheat flour

¼ cup coconut flour

¼ cup oat bran

2 tsp. baking powder

½ tsp. baking soda

½ TB. ground cinnamon

¼ tsp. salt

1 medium apple, your choice variety, grated

1 zucchini, grated

1 large egg

½ cup low-fat plain Greek-style yogurt

¼ cup honey

1. Preheat the oven to 350°F. Line a 9×5-inch or 8×4-inch loaf pan with parchment paper.

2. In a medium bowl, stir together whole-wheat flour, coconut flour, oat bran, baking powder, baking soda, cinnamon, and salt.

3. In a large bowl, stir together apple, zucchini, egg, yogurt, and honey.

4. Add apple mixture to flour mixture, and fold until just combined. Spread batter into the prepared pan, and bake for 40 to 45 minutes or until golden brown. Cool on a wire rack, and store in an airtight container.

Corn and Honey Muffins

Corn bread as you like it—sweet and gently flavored with honey.

Snack servings:	Yield:	Prep time:	Cook time:	Serving size:
6	6 muffins	10 minutes	12 to 15 minutes	1 muffin

Each serving has:			
138 calories	3g protein	14g carbohydrates	0g fiber
8g fat	4g saturated fat	glycemic index: low	glycemic load: 7

3 large eggs	¼ tsp. salt
3 TB. butter, melted	2 TB. whole-wheat flour
3 TB. honey	¼ tsp. baking powder
¼ tsp. vanilla extract	3 TB. cornmeal

1. Preheat the oven to 400°F. Fit a muffin pan with 6 muffin cup liners.

2. In a large bowl, and using an electric mixer on low to medium speed or by hand, whisk eggs, butter, honey, vanilla extract, and salt. Fold in whole-wheat flour, baking powder, and cornmeal until no lumps remain.

3. Divide batter among 6 muffin cups, filling ½ full with batter. Bake for 12 to 15 minutes. Cool on a wire rack, and store in an airtight container.

Lemon Poppy Seed Muffins

Poppy seeds and lemon flavor these buttery muffins.

Snack servings:	Yield:	Prep time:	Cook time:	Serving size:
8	8 muffins	10 minutes	15 to 20 minutes	1 muffin

Each serving has:			
101 calories	3g protein	10g carbohydrates	0g fiber
6g fat	2g saturated fat	glycemic index: low	glycemic load: 5

3 large eggs	2 tsp. lemon extract
2 TB. butter, melted	¼ cup whole-wheat flour
2 TB. skim milk	¼ tsp. baking powder
3 TB. honey	1 tsp. lemon zest
¼ tsp. salt	2 TB. poppy seeds

1. Preheat the oven to 400°F. Line a muffin pan with 8 muffin liners.

2. In a large bowl, whisk together eggs, butter, skim milk, honey, salt, and lemon extract. Fold in whole-wheat flour, baking powder, lemon zest, and poppy seeds, and mix thoroughly.

3. Divide batter among 8 muffin cups. Bake for 15 to 20 minutes. Store in an airtight container.

HEALTHY NOTE

You can purchase poppy seeds in jars or cans in the spice section of your grocery store. You may also find poppy seeds in the bulk food bins of the health food store at a lower price.

Cranberry Pumpkin Seed Muffins

Cranberries and orange flavor these muffins made with pumpkin seed and chickpea flour.

Snack servings:	Yield:	Prep time:	Cook time:	Serving size:
12	12 muffins	10 minutes	25 to 30 minutes	1 muffin

Each serving has:			
234 calories	8g protein	18g carbohydrates	1g fiber
16g fat	5g saturated fat	glycemic index: low	glycemic load: 6

2 cups pumpkin seed flour

1/4 cup whole-wheat flour

2 TB. chickpea flour

1 1/2 tsp. baking soda

1/2 tsp. salt

2/3 cup skim milk

1/4 cup butter, melted

1/4 cup honey

3 large eggs

1 TB. orange zest

1/2 cup dried cranberries

1. Preheat the oven to 350°F. Line a muffin pan with 12 paper liners.

2. In a medium bowl, stir together pumpkin seed flour, whole-wheat flour, chickpea flour, baking soda, and salt.

3. In a large bowl, whisk together skim milk, butter, honey, eggs, and orange zest. Fold into flour mixture, and stir in cranberries.

4. Divide batter among 12 muffin cups. Bake for 25 to 30 minutes. Remove muffins from the pan, and cool on a wire rack.

TASTY BITE

The pumpkin and cranberry flavors in these muffins are perfect for the holiday season.

Date and Sunflower Seed Muffins

Dates and honey flavor these sunflower seed flour muffins.

Snack servings:	Yield:	Prep time:	Cook time:	Serving size:
12	12 muffins	10 minutes	25 to 30 minutes	1 muffin

Each serving has:			
102 calories	3g protein	16g carbohydrates	1g fiber
4g fat	1g saturated fat	glycemic index: low	glycemic load: 5

¾ cup whole-wheat flour

¾ cup sunflower seed meal

½ tsp. baking soda

¼ tsp. salt

2 large eggs

1 TB. extra-virgin olive oil

2 TB. honey

¾ cup skim milk

¾ cup dates, chopped

1. Preheat the oven to 375°F. Line a muffin pan with 12 muffin liners.

2. In a medium bowl, combine whole-wheat flour, sunflower seed meal, baking soda, and salt.

3. In a large bowl, beat eggs and add extra-virgin olive oil, honey, milk, and dates. Fold flour mixture into egg mixture.

4. Divide batter among 12 muffin pans. Bake for 25 to 30 minutes. Store in an airtight container.

Sweet Treats

When your sweet tooth beckons, give it what it wants—a sweet snack—while you give yourself what you need—a healthy, low-glycemic, and low-calorie snack.

Take along the trail mix snacks you'll find in Part 4 for outdoor excursions and car trips. Enjoy choosing cookie and cake recipes from a wide assortment of tastes and textures. Desserts range from elegant to homespun with year-round seasonal choices.

Finally, I offer a wide variety of beverages as delicious alternatives to calorie-laden sodas. Yum!

Nuts and Trail Mixes

14

In This Chapter

- A wide variety of nuts, seeds, and fruit
- High energy for on-the-go snacking
- Mixing and matching favorite tastes
- Portable and nutritious bars

Nuts combined with fruit are an ideal snack. In ancient times, desert nomads ate dates right from the tree for sustained energy. And as today's hikers and outdoor aficionados know, trail mix and energy bars are excellent for boosting stamina.

All-natural nuts, seeds, and fruit supply essential nutrition in terms of protein, good fats, and low-glycemic carbohydrates, plus a healthy amount of vitamins and minerals. Eating them together creates an ideal balance of nutritional energy, but also offers an ideal combination of tastes, textures, and flavors. The recipes in this chapter add in small amounts of spices and sweeteners to give these basic nuts, seeds, and fruit a little something extra to love.

Almonds with Rosemary and Cayenne

Rosemary and cayenne add spice to these slightly sweetened almonds.

Snack servings:	Yield:	Prep time:	Cook time:	Serving size:
8	2 cups	15 minutes	15 minutes	¼ cup

Each serving has:			
144 calories	5g protein	6g carbohydrates	3g fiber
12g fat	1g saturated fat	glycemic index: low	glycemic load: 0

2 cups raw almonds	1 tsp. brown sugar
1½ tsp. butter	¼ tsp. salt
1 TB. fresh rosemary, finely snipped, or 1 tsp. dried	¼ tsp. cayenne

1. Preheat the oven to 350°F.

2. Spread almonds in a single layer on a baking sheet, and bake for about 10 minutes or until almonds are lightly toasted and fragrant.

3. Meanwhile, in a medium saucepan over medium heat, melt butter until sizzling. Remove from heat, and stir in rosemary, brown sugar, salt, and cayenne.

4. Add almonds, and toss gently to coat. Cool slightly before serving. If desired, store cooled nuts in an airtight container in refrigerator.

KITCHEN ALERT

Be sure to use real butter in this recipe. Don't substitute butter-type spreads or oils. The flavor of real butter is what makes this snack taste so good.

Orange Cashews

These cashews are roasted with jerk seasoning and orange zest.

Snack servings:	Yield:	Prep time:	Cook time:	Serving size:
8	2 cups	10 minutes	24 minutes	¼ cup

Each serving has:			
203 calories	5g protein	11g carbohydrates	1g fiber
17g fat	4g saturated fat	glycemic index: low	glycemic load: 1

1½ tsp. butter	¼ tsp. salt
2 cups whole cashews	2 tsp. Caribbean jerk seasoning
2 tsp. orange zest	

1. Preheat the oven to 350°F.

2. In an 8-inch cake pan, heat butter in the oven for 3 or 4 minutes or until melted. Stir in cashews, orange zest, salt, and Caribbean jerk seasoning.

3. Bake for 20 minutes, stirring occasionally. Store in an airtight container.

Variation: For a tangier taste, substitute lemon zest for the orange zest. If you're not a fan of cashews, pecans or almonds also work.

Berries with Pistachios

You'll love the special tastes of pistachios combined with dried berries and chocolate-covered raisins.

Snack servings:	Yield:	Prep time:	Cook time:	Serving size:
16	6 cups	10 minutes	10 to 15 minutes	$\frac{1}{3}$ cup

Each serving has:			
195 calories	4g protein	16g carbohydrates	3g fiber
14g fat	4g saturated fat	glycemic index: low	glycemic load: 6

2 TB. butter

1¼ cups pecan halves

1¼ cups shelled pistachio nuts

⅛ tsp. salt

⅛ tsp. ground nutmeg

1½ cups chocolate-covered raisins

2 cups dried berry mix

1 TB. fresh orange peel slivers

1. In a large skillet over medium heat, melt butter. Add pecan halves, pistachios, salt, and nutmeg. Cook, stirring every 1 or 2 minutes, for 10 to 15 minutes or until nuts are toasted and fragrant. Cool.

2. Store nut mixture in an airtight container at room temperature for up to 1 week. Before serving, transfer to a bowl and add chocolate-covered raisins, dried berry mix, and orange peel slivers, and stir to mix.

HEALTHY NOTE

You can purchase dried berry mix, which includes many different types of berries such as strawberries, cherries, blackberries, blueberries, and cranberries. For this recipe, you can also use your favorite type of dried berry.

Spicy Pecan Nut Mix

This hearty combination of pecans, pine nuts, peanuts, and sesame seeds are flavored with sage and cinnamon.

Snack servings:	Yield:	Prep time:	Cook time:	Serving size:
18	6 cups	5 minutes	20 to 25 minutes	⅓ cup

Each serving has:			
161 calories	3g protein	6g carbohydrates	2g fiber
15g fat	1g saturated fat	glycemic index: low	glycemic load: 2

1 large egg white	¼ tsp. cayenne
2 TB. honey	½ tsp. salt
1 TB. sesame seeds	1¾ cups hulled sunflower seeds
4 tsp. dried sage	1¾ cups raw pecan halves
¾ tsp. ground cinnamon	1 cup pine nuts

1. Preheat the oven to 300°F. Line 2 baking pans with parchment paper.

2. In a small bowl, whisk egg white until frothy. Whisk in honey, sesame seeds, sage, cinnamon, cayenne, and salt. Stir in sunflower seeds, pecans, and pine nuts.

3. Divide mixture between the prepared baking pans (or nonstick baking pans without parchment paper) and spread evenly.

4. Bake, stirring often, for 20 to 25 minutes or until nuts are golden and fragrant. To prevent sticking, turn mixture often as it cools. Store in an airtight container in the refrigerator or pantry.

Variation: Substitute peanuts, walnuts, hazelnuts, or your favorite nuts for the pecans and pine nuts in this recipe.

Apricot Trail Mix

Apricots flavor this tasty mixture of nuts and seeds for a quick snack.

Snack servings:	Yield:	Prep time:	Cook time:	Serving size:
14	7 cups	15 minutes	8 to 10 minutes	½ cup

Each serving has:			
254 calories	9g protein	13g carbohydrates	4g fiber
21g fat	3g saturated fat	glycemic index: low	glycemic load: 2

2 cups raw almonds

1 cup pumpkin seeds

1 cup sunflower seeds

1 cup cashews or other nuts

2 cups dried apricots, coarsely chopped

1. Preheat the oven to 350°F.

2. Place almonds, pumpkin seeds, and sunflower seeds on a baking sheet, and roast for 8 to 10 minutes. Cool for 5 minutes.

3. In a large bowl, place cashews and apricots. Add roasted nuts and seeds, and mix. Store in airtight containers.

Peanut and Cracker Snack Mix

This peanut and cracker mix is coated with Italian seasoned butter and baked.

Snack servings:	Yield:	Prep time:	Cook time:	Serving size:
8	4 cups	10 minutes	45 minutes	½ cup

Each serving has:			
195 calories	6g protein	12g carbohydrates	2g fiber
15g fat	3g saturated fat	glycemic index: low	glycemic load: 5

1 (4.25-oz.) box Blue Diamond Natural Hazelnut Nut-Thins, or another flavor

1 cup peanuts

1 TB. butter, melted

2 tsp. Italian seasoning, crushed

Dash garlic salt

Dash ground black pepper

1. Preheat the oven to 300°F.

2. Break crackers into 2 or 3 pieces each. In a roasting pan, combine crackers and peanuts.

3. In a small bowl, stir together melted butter, Italian seasoning, garlic salt, and pepper. Drizzle over cracker mixture, and stir to coat evenly.

4. Bake, uncovered, for 45 minutes, stirring every 15 minutes. Spread snack mix on large sheet of aluminum foil to cool. Store in airtight container.

HEALTHY NOTE

This recipe calls for Nut-Thins, which you can find in the health food or gluten-free section of your grocery store. These crackers are low glycemic. Be careful not to substitute other crackers because most of them are high glycemic.

Peanut Butter Cranberry Wraps

These wraps are sweet and crunchy with the rich taste of peanut butter.

Snack servings:	Yield:	Prep time:	Cook time:	Serving size:
4	4 wraps	5 minutes	3 to 4 minutes	1 wrap

Each serving has:			
269 calories	10g protein	24g carbohydrates	4g fiber
17g fat	4g saturated fat	glycemic index: low	glycemic load: 10

½ cup smooth or chunky peanut butter

4 (6-in.) corn tortillas

¼ cup celery, finely diced

¼ cup dried cranberries

1. Spread peanut butter over one side of each tortilla. Sprinkle celery and cranberries over peanut butter, pressing lightly.

2. Microwave on high for 20 seconds or until peanut butter is warm. Roll up loosely, and serve.

Variation: You can also substitute cashew, almond, pecan, or hazelnut butter for the peanut butter. Or try cut-up dried apricots, dates or figs, or raisins instead of the dried cranberries. You can also add other crunchy vegetables such as carrots, bean sprouts, or jicama.

High-Energy Protein Bars

These delectable energy bars contain honey, almonds, chocolate chips, and dates.

Snack servings:	Yield:	Prep time:	Cook time:	Serving size:
16	16 bars	15 minutes	30 to 35 minutes	1 bar

Each serving has:			
218 calories	5g protein	26g carbohydrates	4g fiber
19g fat	10g saturated fat	glycemic index: low	glycemic load: 10

¾ cup butter, softened	2 large eggs
¾ cup honey	1 cup almonds, chopped
1 tsp. lemon juice	½ cup semisweet chocolate chips
2 cups coconut flour	½ cup dates, chopped
1 cup old-fashioned oats	½ cup dried apricots, chopped
½ cup wheat germ	2 TB. sesame seeds
½ cup chickpea flour	

1. Preheat the oven to 350°F.

2. In a medium bowl, mix together butter, honey, and lemon juice until well blended. Stir in coconut flour, old-fashioned oats, wheat germ, and chickpea flour. Spread evenly into the bottom of an ungreased 9×13-inch baking pan.

3. In a medium bowl, beat eggs. Stir in almonds, chocolate chips, dates, apricots, and sesame seeds. Spread over crust in the baking pan.

4. Bake for 30 to 35 minutes or until center is set and top is lightly browned. Cool completely before cutting into bars.

HEALTHY NOTE

These protein snack bars are highly nutrient dense. All the ingredients are healthy and packed with power. Eat them slowly to enjoy and absorb all the energy available!

Oats and Walnut Protein Bars

These hearty protein bars are filled with walnuts, raisins, and butterscotch chips.

Snack servings:	Yield:	Prep time:	Cook time:	Serving size:
16	16 bars	15 minutes	20 to 25 minutes	1 bar

Each serving has:			
285 calories	5g protein	36g carbohydrates	4g fiber
15g fat	8g saturated fat	glycemic index: low	glycemic load: 9

4 cups old-fashioned oats	²/₃ cup butter, softened
1 cup coconut flour	¹/₂ cup honey
¹/₂ cup chickpea flour	¹/₂ cup butterscotch chips
1 tsp. baking soda	1 cup raisins
1 tsp. ground cinnamon	¹/₂ cup walnuts, coarsely chopped
1 tsp. vanilla extract	

1. Preheat the oven to 325°F. Line a 9×13-inch baking pan with parchment paper.

2. In a large bowl, combine old-fashioned oats, coconut flour, chickpea flour, baking soda, and cinnamon. Add vanilla extract, butter, and honey, and beat with an electric mixer on low speed for 1 minute. Batter will be very heavy.

3. Using a wooden spoon, stir in butterscotch chips, raisins, and walnuts until well combined.

4. Press dough into the prepared pan. Bake 20 to 25 minutes or until golden brown. Cool in the pan for 10 minutes before cutting into 16 bars. Lift parchment paper out of the pan and place on a cooling rack. Store in an airtight container.

Variation: Chocolate chips work well in this recipe in place of the butterscotch chips.

No-Bake Cranberry Balls

Molasses flavors these balls made with nut butter and pumpkin seeds.

Snack servings:	Yield:	Prep time:	Serving size:
12	24 balls	10 minutes	2 balls

Each serving has:			
209 calories	10g protein	24g carbohydrates	1g fiber
9g fat	3g saturated fat	glycemic index: low	glycemic load: 10

¼ cup honey

¼ cup molasses

½ cup peanut, cashew, or almond
  butter

½ cup dried cranberries

½ cup pumpkin seeds

1 cup nonfat milk powder (not
  instant)

½ cup shredded coconut (optional)

1. In a large bowl, combine honey, molasses, peanut butter, cranberries, and pump-kin seeds. Knead together, adding enough milk powder to form a stiff but not crumbly dough.

2. Shape into 24 balls, roll in coconut (if using), and chill.

TASTY BITE

Either light or dark molasses works in this recipe, so choose what you like best. If you don't like the taste of molasses, use ½ cup honey instead.

Puddings, Pies, and Cheesecakes

In This Chapter

- Sweet low-glycemic desserts
- Make-ahead treats to eat later
- Cutting down on the honey and sugar
- Satisfying your sweet tooth!

You may find yourself craving something sweet to eat, but you're worried you might ruin your diet. With the low-glycemic desserts in this chapter, you can stop worrying. You know exactly how many calories you're eating, along with other pertinent nutritional information.

So go ahead, try a few—or all!—of the recipes in this chapter that make your mouth water!

Sweet Snack Savvy

Satisfying your sweet tooth doesn't always mean eating lots of sugar or high-fructose corn syrup. Nor do you need to rely on the questionable safety and odd aftertastes of artificial sweeteners. The recipes in this chapter use low to moderate amounts of honey and table sugar to add sweetness. If you prefer to use another form of sweetener, feel free to modify the recipe.

Most recipes can be made for the future, stored in the refrigerator or freezer, and eaten whenever you're ready for a sweet treat. We added many healthful ingredients using mostly low-fat dairy and high-fiber starches.

Be sure to check out the recommended serving sizes of the desserts, and eat them slowly and savor every bite. You'll be glad you did!

Bread Pudding with Chocolate and Cherries

This rich bread pudding is baked in individual ramekins and flavored with vanilla and bittersweet chocolate.

Snack servings:	Yield:	Prep time:	Cook time:	Serving size:
8	8 puddings	20 minutes plus 15 min-utes stand time	30 minutes	1 pudding

Each serving has:			
201 calories	7g protein	26g carbohydrates	1g fiber
7g fat	4g saturated fat	glycemic index: low	glycemic load: 6

1 cup dried cherries	2 large egg yolks
¼ cup brandy or apple juice	1 tsp. vanilla extract
3 cups skim milk	6 slices bread, cubed
⅓ cup sugar	⅔ cup bittersweet chocolate, coarsely chopped
2 large eggs	

1. Preheat the oven to 350°F.

2. Lightly coat 8 (6-ounce) ramekins with olive oil cooking spray, and place cups in a large roasting pan.

3. In a small bowl, combine dried cherries with brandy. Set aside.

4. In a medium saucepan over medium heat, combine skim milk and sugar. Cook, stirring, for 2 or 3 minutes or until sugar is dissolved.

5. In a large bowl, whisk together eggs and egg yolks. Slowly add milk mixture to beaten egg mixture, whisking constantly. Whisk in vanilla extract, and stir in bread cubes. Let stand at room temperature for 15 minutes.

6. Stir in dried cherry-brandy mixture, and divide batter among custard cups. Evenly distribute chopped chocolate on top of cups.

7. Place the roasting pan on the oven rack, and pour boiling water into the pan to halfway up the sides of the ramekins. Bake for 25 to 30 minutes or until a knife inserted near pudding centers comes out clean.

8. Remove cups from the water. Serve warm or chill, you can reheat in microwave before serving.

Variation: You can omit the chocolate, or use white chocolate chips for a different taste.

Vanilla Pudding with Grilled Bananas

Grilled bananas are topped with nutmeg-flavored pudding and cookie crumbles.

Snack servings:	Yield:	Prep time:	Cook time:	Serving size:
8	8 parfaits	15 minutes	2 minutes	1 parfait

Each serving has:			
119 calories	2g protein	17g carbohydrates	2g fiber
5g fat	3g saturated fat	glycemic index: low	glycemic load: 6

½ (3.4-oz.) pkg. vanilla instant pudding mix

1 cup low-fat milk

¼ cup low-fat sour cream

1 tsp. vanilla extract

¼ tsp. ground nutmeg

4 medium firm bananas, peeled

2 TB. butter, melted

8 vanilla wafers or gingersnaps, crumbled

1. In a large bowl, prepare pudding mix according to package directions using low-fat milk. Whisk in sour cream, vanilla extract, and nutmeg until smooth. Cover surface with plastic wrap.

2. Cut each banana in ½ crosswise, and cut each ½ in ½ lengthwise (16 pieces).

3. In a large skillet over medium heat, melt butter. Add bananas, and sauté for about 2 minutes or until bananas are browned and softened, turning once.

4. To serve, place 2 banana quarters in each of 8 parfait or dessert dishes, cutting bananas as necessary to fit. Top with ⅛ pudding and crumbled vanilla wafers.

HEALTHY NOTE

Sautéing the bananas in butter brings out their sweetness.

Crustless Lemon Cheesecake

This sweet, crust-free cheesecake is flavored with lemon juice and lemon peel.

Snack servings:	Yield:	Prep time:	Cook time:	Serving size:
12	1 (10-inch) cake	10 minutes	50 minutes	1 slice

Each serving has:			
148 calories	7g protein	7g carbohydrates	0g fiber
11g fat	6g saturated fat	glycemic index: low	glycemic load: 1

1 cup 2 percent cottage cheese

1 (8-oz.) pkg. cream cheese

1 cup sour cream

4 large eggs

2 TB. lemon juice

1 TB. fresh lemon zest or 1 tsp. dried

6 TB. firmly packed brown sugar

1. Preheat the oven to 350°F. Lightly spray a 10-inch springform pan with cooking spray.

2. In a food processor fitted with a chopping blade, or in a blender, combine cottage cheese, cream cheese, sour cream, eggs, lemon juice, lemon zest, and brown sugar. Pulse for 1 or 2 minutes or until well blended.

3. Pour batter into the prepared springform pan, and bake for 50 minutes. Remove to a wire rack to cook. Store in airtight container in refrigerator.

Variation: For **Crustless Chocolate Cheesecake,** omit the lemon juice and lemon zest and instead add 2 (1-ounce) squares baking chocolate, melted, and an additional 1 tablespoon brown sugar (so 7 tablespoons total). *(Each serving has 162 calories, 7g protein, 10g carbohydrates, 1g fiber, 12g fat, 7g saturated fat, glycemic index: low, glycemic load: 1.)*

No-Bake Chocolate Ricotta Cheesecake

Orange flavors this richly dark no-bake chocolate cheesecake.

Snack servings:	Yield:	Prep time:	Cook time:	Serving size:
12	12 ramekins	20 minutes plus 15 minutes stand time	5 minutes	1 ramekin

Each serving has:			
127 calories	7g protein	14g carbohydrates	1g fiber
5g fat	3g saturated fat	glycemic index: low	glycemic load: 6

Zest of 1 medium navel orange (1 or 2 TB.)

Juice of 1 medium navel orange (⅓ to ½ cup)

¼ cup skim milk

¼ cup honey

1 (3.4-oz.) pkg. gelatin (about 2½ tsp.)

3 oz. dark bittersweet chocolate, chopped (about ½ cup)

1½ cups low-fat ricotta cheese

¾ cup low-fat cream cheese, softened

1 TB. unsweetened cocoa powder

1. In a small saucepan, add orange zest, orange juice, skim milk, and honey. Stir in gelatin, and let rest for 15 minutes at room temperature.

2. Set over medium-high heat, and bring to a boil, stirring continuously. Reduce heat to low, and stir for 2 minutes or until gelatin is dissolved. Remove from heat.

3. In a medium bowl over a double boiler or in a microwave, melt dark chocolate. Set aside.

4. In a large bowl, using an electric mixer on medium speed, beat ricotta cheese and cream cheese until combined and fluffy. With the mixer running, slowly pour in orange mixture until combined. Slowly pour in dark chocolate until combined.

5. Pour cheesecake mixture into 12 custard cups or ramekins. Refrigerate for 2 hours or overnight before serving. Dust tops lightly with unsweetened cocoa powder before serving.

Variation: This recipe prepares individual servings, but if you want to make this into a full cheesecake, prepare as directed, but pour filling into 1 No-Bake Cocoa Oatmeal Piecrust (recipe later in this chapter). Refrigerate and dust with unsweetened cocoa powder before serving.

HEALTHY NOTE

This cheesecake makes an excellent low-glycemic snack. It contains high-quality protein, has a glycemic load of 6, and is low in fat when made with low-fat dairy products.

No-Bake Cocoa Oatmeal Piecrust

Hazelnuts and honey sweeten this icebox piecrust.

Snack servings:	Yield:	Prep time:	Serving size:
12	1 (9- or 10-inch) crust	10 minutes	$\frac{1}{12}$ of crust

Each serving has:			
68 calories	2g protein	11g carbohydrates	2g fiber
3g fat	0g saturated fat	glycemic index: low	glycemic load: 4

$\frac{1}{4}$ cup unsweetened cocoa powder	$\frac{1}{4}$ cup honey
$\frac{1}{2}$ cup hazelnut flour	Dash salt
$\frac{3}{4}$ cup old-fashioned oats	

1. In a food processor fitted with a chopping blade, combine unsweetened cocoa powder, hazelnut flour, and old-fashioned oats, and pulse for 30 to 60 seconds or until combined and almost smooth.

2. Add honey and salt, and pulse for 30 to 60 seconds or until combined.

3. Press mixture evenly into the bottom of a 9- or 10-inch springform pan or 12 ramekins. Cover and refrigerate for 1 hour. Crust may be prepared ahead and kept, covered and refrigerated, for 24 hours.

Variation: For 12 nutty and sweet "cookies," press the dough into a 9×9-inch baking dish and score into 12 rectangles before baking.

Almond Nut Piecrust

This sweet and slightly crunchy piecrust made without flour or other high-glycemic ingredients really dresses up a pie.

Snack servings:	Yield:	Prep time:	Cook time:	Serving size:
12	1 (9-inch) crust	10 minutes	8 minutes	$\frac{1}{12}$ of crust

Each serving has:			
45 calories	1g protein	3g carbohydrates	1g fiber
3g fat	0g saturated fat	glycemic index: low	glycemic load: 0

¾ cup almonds   2 TB. sugar

1 tsp. butter, at room temperature

1. Preheat the oven to 400°F.

2. In a food processor fitted with a chopping blade, finely chop almonds. Add butter, and briefly pulse 1 or 2 times to blend. Stir in sugar.

3. Using the back of a tablespoon or your fingers, press mixture against the bottom and sides of an ungreased 9-inch pie plate.

4. Bake for about 8 minutes or until lightly browned. Cool.

Variation: Substitute hazelnuts, Brazil nuts, or pecans for the almonds in this recipe.

Tarragon Custard

Tarragon adds an elegant flavor to this classic custard.

Snack servings:	Yield:	Prep time:	Cook time:	Serving size:
4	4 ramekins	15 minutes plus 30 min- utes stand time	40 minutes	1 ramekin

Each serving has:			
119 calories	9g protein	5g carbohydrates	0g fiber
7g fat	3g saturated fat	glycemic index: low	glycemic load: 6

1½ cups whole milk

1 TB. fresh tarragon, coarsely
   chopped

4 large eggs

⅛ tsp. salt

⅛ tsp. ground black pepper

4 sprigs fresh tarragon

1. In a medium saucepan over medium heat, combine whole milk and tarragon.
   Bring to a simmer, remove from heat, cover, and let stand for 30 minutes.

2. Preheat the oven to 325°F. Lightly coat 4 custard cups or ramekins with olive oil
   cooking spray. Place custard cups in a large baking dish.

3. In a large bowl, whisk together eggs, salt, and pepper. Whisk in milk mixture,
   and divide among prepared cups.

4. Place the baking dish on the oven rack, and pour boiling water into the dish to
   a 1-inch depth. Bake for 40 minutes or until a knife inserted near centers comes
   out clean.

5. Cool cups on a rack for 30 minutes. Cover surface of custards with plastic wrap,
   and chill for 4 hours.

6. To serve, run a knife around the edges of the cups, and invert onto a serving
   dish, or serve in cups, garnished with 1 sprig tarragon each.

Variation: Substitute fresh basil or rosemary for the tarragon in this recipe.

Berry Ginger Tofu Mousse

This ginger-flavored mousse is sweetened with dates and honey and topped with fresh berries.

Snack servings:	Yield:	Prep time:	Serving size:
8	8 mousses	15 minutes plus 1 hour chill time	1 mousse or $\frac{1}{8}$ recipe

Each serving has:			
159 calories	9g protein	26g carbohydrates	5g fiber
4g fat	1g saturated fat	glycemic index: low	glycemic load: 8

$1\frac{2}{3}$ cups fresh strawberries, stems removed and quartered

$1\frac{2}{3}$ cups fresh blueberries

$1\frac{2}{3}$ cups fresh raspberries

1 (1-in.) piece fresh ginger, peeled and minced

$\frac{1}{2}$ cup pitted dates

3 cups firm silken tofu

$\frac{1}{3}$ cup honey

1. In a food processor fitted with a chopping blade, purée 1 cup strawberries, 1 cup blueberries, 1 cup raspberries, and ginger for 30 to 60 seconds or until smooth. Add dates, and purée for 30 to 60 seconds or until smooth. Add tofu and honey, and purée for 30 to 60 seconds or until smooth and creamy.

2. In a medium bowl, gently mix remaining $\frac{2}{3}$ cup strawberries, $\frac{2}{3}$ cup blueberries, and $\frac{2}{3}$ cup raspberries.

3. Scoop $\frac{1}{2}$ cup tofu mixture into each of 8 small glass dishes or glasses. Top each with $\frac{1}{4}$ cup mixed berries. Cover and refrigerate for 1 hour to set. Serve chilled. Mousse will keep, covered, in refrigerator for up to 2 days.

Variation: For **Peach Mousse,** add the seeds of 1 vanilla bean, 3 cups fresh peaches, diced, and 2 tablespoons lemon juice. Omit the berries and ginger. Use peaches in the food processor and garnish individual mousses with a sprig of fresh mint. The nutritional counts will be the same.

Chocolate and Espresso Mousse

This rich chocolate mousse is flavored with deep espresso taste.

Snack servings:	Yield:	Prep time:	Serving size:
6	6 servings	15 minutes plus 3 hours chill time	1/6 recipe

Each serving has:			
228 calories	7g protein	17g carbohydrates	1g fiber
15g fat	9g saturated fat	glycemic index: low	glycemic load: 6

1 cup semisweet chocolate chips	2 TB. butter
3 TB. freshly brewed espresso or strong coffee	4 large eggs, separated

1. Put chocolate chips and espresso into a bowl, set over a pan of hot water, and melt, stirring until smooth and liquid. Stir in butter a little at a time. Remove the bowl from the pan, and stir in egg yolks.

2. In a large bowl, whisk egg whites until stiff but not dry. Fold into chocolate mixture.

3. Pour mixture into a bowl, and chill for at least 3 hours or until set.

4. Scoop chilled mousse into 6 individual serving cups or ramekins, and serve.

TASTY BITE

Yes, you can eat low glycemic and enjoy your chocolate, too! The espresso or coffee in this recipe accentuates the chocolate flavor, making it taste stronger.

Baked Berry Ricotta Puffs

Individual ricotta cheese puffs are sweetened with honey and topped with a berry sauce.

Snack servings:	Yield:	Prep time:	Cook time:	Serving size:
4	4 ramekins	10 minutes	20 minutes	1 ramekin

Each serving has:			
185 calories	9g protein	27g carbohydrates	3g fiber
5g fat	3g saturated fat	glycemic index: low	glycemic load: 4

1 rounded cup low-fat ricotta
   cheese

2 egg whites, beaten

3 TB. honey

2½ cups mixed fresh or frozen berries (strawberries, raspberries, blackberries, cherries, etc.)

1. Preheat the oven to 350°F. Lightly grease 4 ramekins.

2. In a large bowl, place ricotta cheese. Using a wooden spoon, break up ricotta. Add beaten egg whites and honey, and mix thoroughly until smooth and well combined.

3. Spoon ricotta mixture into the prepared ramekins and level tops. Bake for 20 minutes or until ricotta puffs are golden.

4. Meanwhile, in a small saucepan over low heat, warm fruit, adding a little water if fruit is fresh, until softened. Let cool slightly.

5. Serve sauce warm or cold with ricotta puffs.

HEALTHY NOTE

A rounded cup isn't an accurate measurement. Rather, it means to add an additional tablespoon or so to the top of a cup so the ricotta forms a small heap at the top of the cup.

Frozen Blackberry Coconut Dessert

Blackberries and toasted coconut are wrapped in vanilla ice cream.

Snack servings:	Yield:	Prep time:	Cook time:	Serving size:
12	12 slices	20 minutes	16 minutes	1 slice

Each serving has:			
192 calories	4g protein	23g carbohydrates	3g fiber
10g fat	5g saturated fat	glycemic index: low	glycemic load: 6

3 cups fresh or frozen blackberries, thawed and drained

¼ cup sugar

1½ tsp. cornstarch

¼ cup water

¾ cup flaked coconut

1 qt. premium or low-fat vanilla ice cream

1 Almond Nut Piecrust (recipe earlier in this chapter)

1. Preheat the oven to 350°F.

2. In a food processor fitted with a chopping blade, process 1½ cups blackberries for 30 to 60 seconds or until smooth.

3. In a small saucepan over medium heat, combine sugar and cornstarch. Add berry purée and water. Cook, stirring, until thickened and bubbly, and cook and stir for 2 more minutes. Cool slightly.

4. Gently stir in remaining 1½ cups blackberries. Cover and cool.

5. In a shallow baking pan, spread coconut in a single layer. Bake for about 8 minutes, stirring once, or until lightly brown. Cool.

6. In a large, chilled bowl, stir ice cream to soften. Add ¾ cup blackberry mixture and 1 cup coconut mixture, and stir. Spoon over baked Almond Nut Piecrust, and sprinkle with remaining coconut mixture.

7. Cover and freeze for at least 4 hours or until firm. Cover and chill remaining berry mixture.

8. Before serving, let pie stand at room temperature for 10 minutes. Spoon some remaining blackberry mixture onto each piece, and serve.

Variation: For individual servings, omit the crust, divide the ice cream mixture among 12 ramekins or parfait glasses, and freeze.

Raspberry Yogurt Freezer Pops

These frosty cold pops feature yogurt, honey, and raspberries.

Snack servings:	Yield:	Prep time:		Cook time:		Serving size:
10	10 pops	10 minutes plus 6 hours freeze time		8 minutes plus 30 minutes chill time		1 pop

Each serving has:			
110 calories	2g protein	26g carbohydrates	4g fiber
1g fat	0g saturated fat	glycemic index: low	glycemic load: 6

1 cup low-fat Greek-style yogurt	1 tsp. vanilla extract
1 banana, peeled and cut into chunks	3 cups fresh or frozen raspberries
	1 TB. honey

1. In a food processor fitted with a chopping blade, or in a blender, process yogurt, banana, and vanilla extract for 30 seconds or until smooth.

2. In a medium saucepan over medium heat, bring raspberries and honey to a boil. Reduce heat to low, and simmer for 5 minutes. Cover and chill for 30 minutes.

3. Pour yogurt mixture evenly into 10 (2-ounce) pop molds. Top with raspberry mixture, and swirl, if desired. Top with lid of pop mold, and insert craft sticks, leaving $1\frac{1}{2}$ to 2 inches sticking out of pop.

4. Freeze for 6 hours or until sticks are solidly anchored and pops are completely frozen.

Variation: Substitute your favorite fresh or frozen fruit for the raspberries. Choose from peaches, cherries, apricots, and blueberries.

Cookies, Brownies, Bars, and More

In This Chapter

- Low-glycemic baked snacks
- All-natural cookies
- Brownies baked with healthy ingredients
- Flavorful nut macaroons

Good news! You don't have to give up cookies, pastries, and other baked goods when you eat low glycemic! You can prepare the recipes in this chapter with confidence, knowing you'll be eating low glycemic while savoring a sweet treat.

Low-Glycemic Baking

As you page through the recipes in this chapter, you'll find many interesting and delicious types of flours and flour substitutes, including nut flours, chickpea flour, whole-wheat flour, cornmeal, and oat bran. What you won't find is white all-purpose flour. It's too high glycemic.

But you will find regular white sugar. It's medium glycemic, and quite honestly, no sugar substitute comes close to tasting as good. Some recipes call for honey, and some have sweet ingredients, like dried fruits. In designing these recipes, we were very careful to keep the total carbohydrate count and the glycemic load in a healthy range.

Why no stevia-type sweeteners? We tested them in the oven-baked cookies and cake recipes and were left with a bitter aftertaste. Yuck. However, we found that the stevia taste was quite acceptable for both cold and hot beverages. If you like stevia for baking, go ahead and use it in these recipes.

TASTY BITE

Many of the recipes in this chapter call for nut flours. You can often find these at the grocery or health food store, but it's also easy to make your own. For 1 cup of flour, place 1 scant cup nuts in a food processor fitted with a chopping blade. Pulse or process nuts until they turn into flour. If you process for too long, you'll end up with nut butter. You don't need to process coconut into flour, but you can if you like.

Oatmeal Cookies with Shaved Chocolate

Chocolate chips and pecans flavor this chewy and moist cookie.

Snack servings:	Yield:	Prep time:	Cook time:	Serving size:
16	16 cookies	10 minutes	9 to 10 minutes	1 cookie

Each serving has:			
91 calories	2g protein	14g carbohydrates	1g fiber
3g fat	1g saturated fat	glycemic index: low	glycemic load: 4

7 TB. honey ($\frac{1}{2}$ cup less 1 TB.)

1 large egg white

1 TB. butter

1 tsp. vanilla extract

1$\frac{1}{4}$ cups quick-cooking old-fashioned oats

$\frac{1}{2}$ cup pecan flour

2 TB. chickpea powder

2 tsp. flaxseeds

$\frac{1}{2}$ tsp. baking powder

$\frac{1}{4}$ tsp. salt

1 (1-oz.) square baking chocolate

1. Preheat the oven to 350°F. Line 2 baking sheets with parchment paper.

2. In a large bowl, stir together honey, egg white, butter, and vanilla extract. Add quick-cooking old-fashioned oats, pecan flour, chickpea powder, flaxseeds, baking powder, and salt, and fold until well blended.

3. Using a sharp chef's knife, shave baking chocolate into fine shavings. (Some shavings will be larger than others.) Fold into batter.

4. Divide batter equally into 16 mounds (about 1 rounded tablespoon each), and place 8 on each prepared baking sheet. Use the back of a slightly dampened spoon to flatten each mound into a 2$\frac{1}{2}$-inch circle.

5. Bake for 9 or 10 minutes or until golden. Transfer parchment paper and cookies to racks to cool. Store in an airtight container. Cookies will stay fresh for 3 or 4 days.

Pecan Coffee Cookies

You'll appreciate the rich taste of pecans flavored with coffee and lemon in these cookies.

Snack servings:	Yield:	Prep time:	Cook time:	Serving size:
24	24 cookies	15 minutes	25 minutes	1 cookie

Each serving has:			
82 calories	1g protein	6g carbohydrates	1g fiber
7g fat	1g saturated fat	glycemic index: low	glycemic load: 2

2 cups pecans	½ tsp. salt
1 TB. instant coffee powder or granules	4 large egg whites
¾ cup firmly packed brown sugar	1 tsp. vanilla extract
1 tsp. lemon zest	

1. Preheat the oven to 325°F. Place racks in the center of the oven. Line 2 baking sheets with parchment paper.

2. In a food processor fitted with a chopping blade, process pecans, coffee powder, brown sugar, lemon zest, and salt for 45 to 90 seconds or until fine.

3. In a large bowl, beat egg whites until stiff.

4. Fold nut mixture gently into egg whites. Add vanilla extract, and mix until blended.

5. Drop by the spoonfuls onto the prepared baking sheets, giving cookies lots of room to spread.

6. Bake for 25 minutes or until golden on top. Cool on a wire rack, and store in an airtight container.

HEALTHY NOTE

If you like macaroons, you'll like these cookies. They have the same consistency.

Gingerbread Drop Cookies

Spiced with cinnamon, ginger, and cloves, and wrapped in a batter of coconut flour and molasses, these cookies are perfect for serving during the holidays.

Snack servings:	Yield:	Prep time:	Cook time:	Serving size:
24	24 cookies	10 minutes	12 to 14 minutes	1 cookie

Each serving has:			
91 calories	2g protein	12g carbohydrates	0g fiber
5g fat	3g saturated fat	glycemic index: low	glycemic load: 5

⅓ cup butter	1 tsp. ground ginger
¾ cup sugar	1 tsp. ground cinnamon
½ cup molasses	¼ tsp. ground cloves
6 eggs	¼ tsp. salt
¾ cup sifted coconut flour	

1. Preheat the oven to 400°F. Line 2 baking sheets with parchment paper.

2. In a large bowl, and using an electric mixer on medium speed, cream butter and sugar. Add molasses and eggs, 1 at a time, and beat well after each addition.

3. Stir in coconut flour, ginger, cinnamon, cloves, and salt, and mix thoroughly. Batter will thicken slightly as flour absorbs moisture.

4. Drop batter by spoonfuls onto the prepared baking sheet. Bake for 12 to 14 minutes.

Ricotta Pistachio Cookies

These rich cookies offer a taste of Italy, thanks to the ricotta cheese and pistachios.

Snack servings:	Yield:	Prep time:	Cook time:	Serving size:
36	36 cookies	15 minutes	10 to 12 minutes	1 cookie

Each serving has:			
114 calories	2g protein	12g carbohydrates	1g fiber
6g fat	4g saturated fat	glycemic index: low	glycemic load: 4

1 cup butter, softened	$\frac{1}{2}$ cup wheat bran
1 cup sugar	$\frac{1}{2}$ tsp. salt
2 eggs	$\frac{1}{2}$ tsp. baking soda
$\frac{3}{4}$ cup low-fat ricotta cheese	$\frac{1}{2}$ cup pistachios, chopped
$1\frac{3}{4}$ cups whole-wheat flour	$\frac{1}{3}$ cup golden raisins

1. Preheat the oven to 350°F. Line 2 baking sheets with parchment paper.

2. In a large bowl, and using an electric mixer on medium speed, cream butter and sugar. Beat in eggs, followed by ricotta cheese.

3. Beat in whole-wheat flour, wheat bran, salt, and baking soda. Dough will be stiff. Stir in pistachios and raisins.

4. Drop dough by the teaspoonful onto the prepared baking sheets, 2 inches apart.

5. Bake for 10 to 12 minutes, or until set and light brown on bottom. Transfer to a wire rack, and cool completely.

Chocolate-Chip–Lace Cookies

These crisp, buttery cookies are a delicious alternative to the standard chocolate-chip cookie.

Snack servings:	Yield:	Prep time:	Cook time:	Serving size:
36	36 cookies	10 minutes	15 to 25 minutes	1 cookie

Each serving has:			
108 calories	2g protein	10g carbohydrates	1g fiber
7g fat	3g saturated fat	glycemic index: low	glycemic load: 3

²/₃ cup butter	2 TB. chickpea flour
1 cup sugar	¹/₂ tsp. salt
1 large egg	1 cup semisweet or milk chocolate chips
1 tsp. vanilla extract	¹/₂ cup chopped walnuts
1 cup almond flour	
2 TB. cornstarch	

1. Preheat the oven to 350°F. Line 2 baking sheets with parchment paper.

2. In a large bowl, and using an electric mixer on medium speed, cream butter and sugar. Add egg and vanilla extract, and mix well.

3. Fold in almond flour, cornstarch, chickpea flour, and salt. Stir in chocolate chips and walnuts.

4. Drop dough by the spoonful onto the prepared baking sheets, leaving plenty of room for cookies to spread.

5. Bake for 10 to 15 minutes until browned and cooked throughout.

TASTY BITE

These cookies come out of the oven browned and crispy. They may not look great, but the taste is utterly wonderful. They taste like toffee sprinkled with chocolate chips and nuts.

Mint Chocolate Cookies

These crisp cookies are flavored with mint chocolate chips and given a deeper chocolate flavor with the addition of unsweetened chocolate.

Snack servings:	Yield:	Prep time:		Cook time:	Serving size:
36	36 cookies	10 minutes plus 2 hours chill time		8 to 10 minutes	1 cookie

Each serving has:			
98 calories	2g protein	13g carbohydrates	1g fiber
5g fat	3g saturated fat	glycemic index: low	glycemic load: 5

1¾ cups mint-flavored chocolate chips

2 (1-oz.) squares unsweetened chocolate, chopped

¼ cup butter, cut into chunks

1 cup sugar

3 large eggs

¾ cup whole-wheat flour

¾ tsp. baking powder

¼ tsp. salt

1. In a medium microwave-safe bowl, combine chocolate chips, unsweetened chocolate, and butter. Microwave on high for 60 seconds, stir, and microwave for 30 more seconds. Stir well, and repeat microwave process until mixture is melted. Let cool slightly.

2. Stir in sugar. Whisk in eggs until combined. Stir in whole-wheat flour, baking powder, and salt. Chill dough, covered, for about 2 hours or until firm.

3. Preheat the oven to 350°F. Line 2 baking sheets with parchment paper.

4. Let dough stand at room temperature for 15 minutes. Drop batter by the spoonful onto the prepared baking sheets. Flatten with the bottom of a glass or spoon.

5. Bake for 8 to 10 minutes.

No-Bake Chocolate Chip Cookies

These quick-energy cookies are flavored with dates, honey, and vanilla.

Snack servings:	Yield:	Prep time:	Serving size:
30	30 cookies	10 minutes	1 cookie

Each serving has:			
56 calories	1g protein	10g carbohydrates	2g fiber
1g fat	1g saturated fat	glycemic index: low	glycemic load: 6

½ cup dates, pitted	1 tsp. vanilla extract
2 cups old-fashioned oats	Dash salt
½ cup oat bran	½ cup semisweet or milk chocolate chips
4 TB. honey	

1. In a food processor fitted with a chopping blade, add dates and chop into small pieces. Add old-fashioned oats, oat bran, honey, vanilla extract, and salt, and process to mix well.

2. Remove mixture to a medium bowl, and stir in chocolate chips.

3. Drop by the tablespoon onto a baking sheet. Enjoy immediately, or chill before serving for firmer texture.

Variation: For **No-Bake Oatmeal Raisin Cookies,** substitute 2 teaspoons cinnamon for the vanilla extract and ½ cup raisins for the chocolate chips.

Oatmeal Raisin Cookies

Raisins, cinnamon, and allspice flavor these nutritious cookies.

Snack servings:	Yield:	Prep time:	Cook time:	Serving size:
16	16 cookies	10 minutes	9 to 10 minutes	1 cookie

Each serving has:			
99 calories	3g protein	15g carbohydrates	2g fiber
4g fat	1g saturated fat	glycemic index: low	glycemic load: 4

7 TB. honey

1 large egg white

1 TB. butter, melted

$\frac{1}{2}$ tsp. vanilla extract

1$\frac{1}{4}$ cups quick-cooking old-fashioned oats

$\frac{1}{2}$ cup almond flour

2 TB. chickpea flour

2 tsp. flaxseeds

1 tsp. ground cinnamon

$\frac{1}{2}$ tsp. allspice

$\frac{1}{2}$ tsp. baking powder

$\frac{1}{4}$ tsp. salt

$\frac{1}{4}$ cup raisins

$\frac{1}{4}$ cup walnuts, chopped

1. Preheat the oven to 350°F. Line 2 baking sheets with parchment paper.

2. In a large bowl, stir together honey, egg white, butter, and vanilla extract. Add oats, almond flour, chickpea powder, flaxseeds, cinnamon, allspice, baking powder, and salt, and fold until well blended. Stir in raisins and walnuts.

3. Divide batter equally into 16 mounds (about 1 rounded tablespoon each), and place 8 on each prepared baking sheet. Use the back of a slightly dampened spoon to flatten each mound into a 2$\frac{1}{2}$-inch circle.

4. Bake for 9 or 10 minutes or until golden. Transfer parchment paper and cookies to racks to cool. Store in an airtight container. Cookies will stay fresh for 3 or 4 days.

Lemon Drop Cookies with Cornmeal

These sweet yellow cookies are flavored with lemon and cornmeal.

Snack servings:	Yield:	Prep time:	Cook time:	Serving size:
36	36 cookies	10 minutes	6 to 8 minutes	1 cookie

Each serving has:			
99 calories	1g protein	11g carbohydrates	0g fiber
6g fat	3g saturated fat	glycemic index: low	glycemic load: 4

1 cup butter, softened	2 tsp. lemon peel
½ cup sugar	1 TB. lemon juice
½ cup light-brown sugar, firmly packed	1 cup whole-wheat flour
½ tsp. baking soda	¾ cup yellow cornmeal
¼ tsp. salt	¾ cup oat bran
2 large eggs	

1. Preheat the oven to 350°F. Line 2 baking sheets with parchment paper.

2. In a large bowl, and using an electric mixer on medium speed, beat butter, sugar, brown sugar, baking soda, and salt until pale and fluffy. Beat in eggs, lemon peel, and lemon juice until well blended.

3. Reduce speed to low, and gradually beat in whole-wheat flour, cornmeal, and oat bran just until blended.

4. Drop dough by the rounded teaspoonful onto the prepared baking sheets, 2 inches apart.

5. Bake for 6 to 8 minutes or until golden brown around edges. Cool cookies on baking sheets for 1 minute before removing cookies to wire rack to cool completely.

Coconut Pecan Cookies

Coconut flour and pecans flavor these good-for-you cookies.

Snack servings:	Yield:	Prep time:	Cook time:	Serving size:
16	16 cookies	10 minutes	9 to 10 minutes	1 cookie

Each serving has:			
107 calories	1g protein	11g carbohydrates	1g fiber
7g fat	3g saturated fat	glycemic index: low	glycemic load: 3

½ cup honey	2 TB. chickpea flour
1 large egg	2 tsp. flaxseeds
1 TB. butter, melted	½ tsp. baking powder
½ tsp. vanilla extract	¼ tsp. salt
1¼ cups coconut flour	¼ cup pecans, chopped
½ cup pecan flour	

1. Preheat the oven to 350°F. Line 2 baking sheets with parchment paper.

2. In a large bowl, stir together honey, egg, butter, and vanilla extract. Add coconut flour, pecan flour, chickpea powder, flaxseeds, baking powder, and salt, and fold until well blended. Stir in pecans.

3. Divide batter equally into 16 mounds (about 1 rounded tablespoon each), and place 8 on each baking sheet. Use the back of a slightly dampened spoon to flatten each mound into a 2½-inch circle.

4. Bake for 9 or 10 minutes or until golden. Transfer parchment paper and cookies to racks to cool. Store in an airtight container. Cookies will stay fresh for 3 or 4 days.

Hazelnut Macaroons

These delectable almond macaroons are flavored with brown sugar and ginger.

Snack servings:	Yield:	Prep time:	Cook time:	Serving size:
16	16 cookies	10 minutes	20 minutes	1 cookie

Each serving has:			
53 calories	2g protein	6g carbohydrates	1g fiber
3g fat	0g saturated fat	glycemic index: low	glycemic load: 2

1 large egg white	1 cup hazelnuts, ground
Scant ½ cup brown sugar, firmly packed	1 tsp. ground ginger

1. Preheat the oven to 350°F. Line 2 baking sheets with parchment paper.

2. In a large, grease-free bowl, whisk or beat egg white until stiff and standing in peaks, but not dry and crumbly. Then whisk or beat in brown sugar.

3. Sprinkle ground hazelnuts and ginger over egg whites, and fold in.

4. Drop dough by the spoonfuls on the prepared baking sheets, leaving plenty of space between each.

5. Bake for about 20 minutes or until pale golden brown and just turning crisp. Let cool slightly on the baking sheets before transferring to a wire rack to cool completely.

Variation: To make **Anise Almond Macaroons,** substitute almonds for the hazelnuts, and replace the ginger with anise seed.

TASTY BITE

When beating egg whites, be sure the bowl is very clean and doesn't contain any grease or oil. The grease or oil will prevent the whites from getting frothy and standing in peaks.

Pine Nut Coriander Macaroons

Coriander flavors these scrumptious macaroons.

Snack servings:	Yield:	Prep time:	Cook time:	Serving size:
24	24 cookies	15 minutes	20 to 25 minutes	1 cookie

Each serving has:			
99 calories	3g protein	8g carbohydrates	1g fiber
7g fat	1g saturated fat	glycemic index: low	glycemic load: 2

1 (8-oz.) can or 1 (7-oz.) pkg. almond paste (not marzipan)

²⁄₃ cup sugar

2 egg whites

½ tsp. lemon zest

1 tsp. coriander

¾ cup pine nuts

1. Preheat the oven to 325°F. Line 2 baking sheets with parchment paper.

2. Crumble almond paste into a food processor fitted with a chopping blade, and pulse into fine crumbs. Add sugar, egg whites, lemon zest, and coriander, and process until smooth.

3. Remove mixture to a medium bowl, and stir in pine nuts.

4. Drop dough by the heaping teaspoonful onto the prepared baking sheets, 1 inch apart.

5. Bake for 20 to 25 minutes or until tops feel firm and dry when lightly pressed. Cool completely on baking sheets on a wire rack.

Variation: Add your favorite spice or herb in place of the coriander. Rosemary, black pepper, cardamom, lemon peel, basil, anise seed, fennel seed, and cinnamon all would work.

TASTY BITE

Find almond paste in the baking section of your grocery store. Its main ingredients are ground almonds and sugar. This is the main ingredient in marzipan candy.

Fudgy Brownies

You'll enjoy the distinctly chocolate taste and texture of these coconut flour brownies.

Snack servings:	Yield:	Prep time:	Cook time:	Serving size:
15	15 brownies	10 minutes	20 to 30 minutes	1 brownie

Each serving has:			
227 calories	3g protein	21g carbohydrates	2g fiber
16g fat	9g saturated fat	glycemic index: low	glycemic load: 8

¾ cup butter	1 tsp. vanilla extract
¼ cup extra-virgin olive oil	½ cup coconut flour
1 cup sugar	½ cup whole-wheat flour
¼ cup honey	½ cup cocoa powder
4 large eggs	¼ tsp. salt

1. Preheat the oven to 350°F. Line a 9×9-inch baking pan with parchment paper.

2. In a large bowl, and using an electric mixer on medium speed, cream butter, extra-virgin olive oil, sugar, and honey. Add eggs, 1 at a time, beating well with each addition. Add vanilla extract.

3. In a medium bowl, sift together coconut flour, whole-wheat flour, cocoa powder, and salt. Fold into butter mixture.

4. Pour batter into the prepared baking pan. Bake for 20 to 30 minutes.

TASTY BITE

These brownies have a crumbly consistency, so you may want to eat them with a fork.

Sweet Potato and Cinnamon Brownies

These moist brownies are flavored with honey and cinnamon.

Snack servings:	Yield:	Prep time:	Cook time:	Serving size:
8	16 brownies	15 minutes	16 to 18 minutes	2 brownies

Each serving has:			
218 calories	43g protein	38g carbohydrates	4g fiber
6g fat	4g saturated fat	glycemic index: low	glycemic load: 10

¼ cup butter	½ cup unsweetened cocoa powder
½ cup honey	1 TB. ground cinnamon
1 cup cooked sweet potato	1 tsp. baking powder
1 tsp. vanilla extract	¼ tsp. salt
1 cup whole-wheat flour	6 egg whites

1. Preheat the oven to 350°F. Line a 9×9-inch baking pan with parchment paper.

2. In a food processor fitted with a chopping blade, or in a large bowl and using electric mixer on medium speed, combine butter, honey, sweet potato, and vanilla extract, and pulse until combined and smooth. If using a food processor, remove mixture to a large bowl.

3. Stir in whole-wheat flour, cocoa powder, cinnamon, baking powder, and salt.

4. In a separate large bowl, whisk egg whites until fluffy. Using a rubber spatula, gently fold egg whites into batter.

5. Pour batter into the prepared baking pan. Bake for 16 to 18 minutes or until a toothpick inserted into the center comes out clean. Remove the pan from the oven and allow brownies to cool for about 30 minutes or until they're room temperature. Cut into 16 squares.

Variation: To make **Sweet Potato and Cinnamon Blondies** instead, omit the cocoa powder and add ½ cup chickpea flour.

High-Protein Chocolate Bars

Black beans add texture and protein to these rich and healthy chocolate bars.

Snack servings:	Yield:	Prep time:	Cook time:	Serving size:
16	16 bars	15 minutes	30 minutes	1 bar

Each serving has:			
142 calories	6g protein	23g carbohydrates	4g fiber
4g fat	2g saturated fat	glycemic index: low	glycemic load: 5

1 oz. dark chocolate (70 percent cocoa or greater)	¼ heaped cup unsweetened cocoa powder
1½ cups black beans, drained and rinsed	1 tsp. baking powder
2 eggs	1 tsp. vanilla extract
1 egg white	¼ cup unsweetened applesauce
2 TB. butter	½ cup honey
	¼ cup walnuts, chopped

1. Preheat the oven to 350°F. Line an 8×8-inch baking dish with parchment paper.

2. In a small saucepan over low heat, melt dark chocolate.

3. In a food processor fitted with a chopping blade, combine melted dark chocolate, black beans, eggs, egg white, butter, cocoa powder, baking powder, vanilla extract, applesauce, and honey, and process for 30 to 60 seconds or until smooth.

4. Stir in walnuts, and pour batter into the prepared baking dish.

5. Bake for about 30 minutes or until top is dry and edges start to pull away from the dish. Let cool thoroughly and cut into 16 bars.

HEALTHY NOTE

Pack along these snack bars when biking or hiking, and you'll be rewarded with renewed energy and great taste.

Fruit and Nut Sticks

These breadsticks are coated with peanut butter and rolled in golden raisins and peanuts.

Snack servings:	Yield:	Prep time:	Serving size:
8	8 sticks	10 minutes	1 stick

Each serving has:			
53 calories	2g protein	5g carbohydrates	1g fiber
3g fat	1g saturated fat	glycemic index: low	glycemic load: 2

3 TB. golden raisins, snipped	8 (4-in.) sesame seed breadsticks
3 TB. peanuts, chopped	4½ tsp. creamy peanut butter

1. In a shallow bowl, combine golden raisins and peanuts.

2. Holding 1 breadstick with a paper towel, spread about ½ teaspoon peanut butter on ½ of breadstick.

3. Roll coated breadstick in raisin and peanut mixture.

4. Repeat with remaining breadsticks.

5. Eat right away. (These don't store well because peanut butter can get messy.)

Variation: Substitute your favorite nut butter for the peanut butter, dried cranberries or dates for the raisins, and your favorite nuts for the chopped peanuts. Choose from pecans, macadamia nuts, or hazelnuts.

Dried Fruit and Nut Cake

This very dense cake is packed with high-energy ingredients and flavored with brandy or rum.

Snack servings:	Yield:	Prep time:	Cook time:	Serving size:
36	36 slices	20 minutes	75 minutes	1 slice

Each serving has:			
162 calories	3g protein	16g carbohydrates	2g fiber
11g fat	4g saturated fat	glycemic index: low	glycemic load: 6

1 cup butter	¾ cup whole almonds
1 cup sugar	1 cup pecan halves
4 large eggs	1 cup dried apricots, halved
1½ tsp. almond extract	1 cup dried cherries
1½ cups whole-wheat flour	¾ cup dried blueberries
¾ tsp. baking powder	¾ cup dried cranberries
½ tsp. salt	¾ cup pitted whole dates, halved
⅓ cup orange juice	¼ cup brandy, rum, or apple juice
1¼ cups Brazil nuts, coarsely chopped	

1. Preheat the oven to 325°F. Grease and flour a 10-inch tube pan.

2. In a large bowl, and using an electric mixer on medium speed, cream butter and sugar. Add eggs, 1 at a time, beating well after each addition. Beat in almond extract.

3. Reduce speed to low, and beat in whole-wheat flour, baking powder, salt, and orange juice, beating well after each addition just until combined.

4. Stir in Brazil nuts, almonds, pecans, apricots, cherries, blueberries, cranberries, and dates until combined. Spoon batter into the prepared pan, spreading top evenly.

5. Bake for 75 minutes or until a toothpick inserted into cake comes out clean. If necessary, cover top of cake with aluminum foil during the last 15 to 20 minutes to prevent overbrowning. Cool cake in the pan on a wire rack for 15 minutes. Remove cake from the pan, and cool completely on the rack.

6. Wrap cake in cheesecloth that's been soaked in brandy. Wrap cheesecloth-wrapped cake in aluminum foil, and refrigerate for up to 1 month. Moisten cheesecloth every week with more brandy.

Variation: To make cupcakes, divide batter into 36 cupcake liners and place in muffin tins. Reduce baking time to 45 to 60 minutes. Omit wrapping in brandy.

Versatile Yellow Sponge Cupcakes

This simple yet elegant sponge cake is flavored with vanilla, or you can add your favorite flavorings.

Snack servings:	Yield:	Prep time:	Cook time:	Serving size:
15	15 cupcakes	15 minutes	25 to 30 minutes	1 cupcake

Each serving has:			
94 calories	2g protein	20g carbohydrates	0g fiber
1g fat	0g saturated fat	glycemic index: low	glycemic load: 8

3 large eggs	1 cup whole-wheat flour
1 cup sugar	1½ tsp. baking powder
¼ cup water	¼ tsp. salt
1 tsp. vanilla extract	

1. Preheat the oven to 350°F. Line a muffin tin or tins with 15 cupcake liners.

2. In a large bowl, and using an electric mixer on medium speed, or a wire whisk, beat eggs until light and frothy. Beat in sugar, followed by water and vanilla extract. Fold in whole-wheat flour, baking powder, and salt.

3. Divide batter among 15 cupcake cups. Bake for 25 to 30 minutes.

Variation: Instead of the water, you can use coffee, fragrant teas, juice, or coconut milk. You could also add spices and flavorings such as lemon or orange peel, cinnamon, ginger, cardamom, rosemary, or basil.

TASTY BITE

These quick and versatile cupcakes are delicious served alone or paired with your favorite low-glycemic topping such as unsweetened preserves, a dusting of cocoa powder, or fresh fruit.

Delicious Drinks

In This Chapter

- Healthy beverages with low to no sugar
- Exotic and traditional teas
- Hot or cold beverages for every time of day
- Super shakes and smoothies

Finding a healthy beverage is a big challenge for a person on a low-glycemic diet. You want to avoid the health risks associated with high-fructose corn syrup and artificial sweeteners, yet still want to enjoy a flavorful drink along with or in place of your snacks.

When you prepare a beverage from the recipes in this chapter, here's what you won't be sipping: large amounts of sugar, high-fructose corn syrup, or artificial sweeteners. Instead, you'll be enjoying small amounts of honey, sugar, or stevia added to interesting flavors.

You also won't find much if any fruit juice in these recipes. Fruit juice has been shown to stimulate the liver into releasing enzymes that cause the body to store fat, thus potentially increasing cholesterol and triglyceride levels.

Instead, you'll find ingredient lists calling for such herbs and fruit as apricots, tarragon, Earl Grey tea, chocolate, pumpkin, mango, nutmeg, and even spinach and green bell peppers. So prepare a cup, mug, or glass and relax while you sip a delicious snack!

Apricot Tea

Ginger spices up this green tea simmered with apricots.

Snack servings:	Yield:	Prep time:	Cook time:	Serving size:
8	8 mugs	10 minutes	10 minutes	1 mug

Each serving has:			
39 calories	1g protein	10g carbohydrates	1g fiber
0g fat	0g saturated fat	glycemic index: low	glycemic load: 3

8 cups water

12 dried apricot halves, finely diced

4 bags green tea or decaffeinated green tea

$\frac{1}{2}$ cup apricot nectar

2 tsp. honey

$\frac{1}{4}$ tsp. ground ginger

8 (2- or 3-in.) cinnamon sticks

1. In a large saucepan over medium-high heat, combine water, apricot halves, green tea bags, apricot nectar, honey, and ginger. Bring to a boil, reduce heat to low, and simmer, covered, for 10 minutes.

2. Place mixture in a blender, and purée until smooth.

3. Place 1 cinnamon stick in each mug. Pour in tea, and serve.

TASTY BITE

If you don't have apricot nectar on hand, you can use whatever other fruit juice you'd like. Good choices are apple, white grape, or pineapple.

Raspberry Lemon Tea

Raspberry tea is accented with lemon juice and sweetened with stevia.

Snack servings:	Yield:	Prep time:	Cook time:	Serving size:
4	4 cups	10 minutes	10 minutes	1 cup

Each serving has:			
8 calories	0g protein	3g carbohydrates	0g fiber
0g fat	0g saturated fat	glycemic index: low	glycemic load: 0

4 cups water

4 bags Raspberry Zinger tea or your favorite caffeine-free fruit or raspberry tea

1 TB. stevia, or to taste

½ cup lemon juice

Ice cubes

1. In a large saucepan over medium-high heat, bring water to a boil. Remove from heat, add tea bags, and steep for 5 minutes. Remove and discard tea bags.

2. Stir in stevia until dissolved, and add lemon juice. Test for sweetness and adjust amount of stevia, if necessary.

3. Serve over ice cubes.

TASTY BITE

When using stevia, add in the recommended amount first and let that dissolve. Taste, and if you require more sweetening, add it in small amounts, ¼ teaspoon at a time, tasting after each addition. With stevia, less often produces the desired taste.

Earl Grey Tea with Tarragon

Citrus juices and tarragon enhance the flavor of Earl Grey tea.

Snack serving:	Yield:	Prep time:	Cook time:	Serving size:
8	8 mugs	10 plus 15 minutes stand time	15 minutes	about 1 cup

Each serving has:			
28 calories	1g protein	7g carbohydrates	0g fiber
0g fat	0g saturated fat	glycemic index: low	glycemic load: 6

½ cup orange juice

2 TB. honey

8¼ cups water

3 TB. lemon juice

2 TB. lime juice

½ cup packed fresh tarragon leaves

4 bags Earl Grey tea

1. In a small saucepan over medium-high heat, combine orange juice, honey, ¼ cup water, lemon juice, and lime juice. Bring to a boil, stirring constantly. Remove from heat, and let stand for 15 minutes.

2. Place citrus mixture in a blender. Add tarragon leaves, and blend for 30 seconds. Strain citrus mixture and discard any solids.

3. In a large saucepan over high heat, bring remaining 8 cups water to a boil. Remove from heat, add Earl Grey tea bags, and steep for 5 minutes. Remove and discard tea bags.

4. Stir citrus mixture into tea, and serve.

TASTY BITE

Earl Grey tea is black tea flavored with bergamot, which is a citrus fruit grown in Italy. This recipe enhances the taste of the tea with the orange, lemon, and lime juice.

Mexican Hot Chocolate

Hot chocolate gets a spicy kick with tea and almond milk.

Snack servings:	Yield:	Prep time:	Cook time:	Serving size:
1	1 cup	10 minutes	3 minutes	1 cup

Each serving has:			
77 calories	3g protein	6g carbohydrates	3g fiber
6g fat	1g saturated fat	glycemic index: low	glycemic load: 1

1 bag Yogi Tea brand Mexican Sweet Chili tea or your favorite cinnamon tea	2 tsp. unsweetened cocoa powder
	½ tsp. stevia, or to taste
¾ cup boiling water	1 (2- or 3-in.) cinnamon stick (optional)
¾ cup unsweetened almond milk	

1. Place tea bag in a large mug. Pour boiling water over tea bag, and steep for about 2 minutes. Squeeze tea bag and remove from the mug.

2. While tea is steeping, heat almond milk in a small saucepan over medium heat until hot but *not* boiling.

3. Add to tea, and stir in cocoa powder and stevia. Mix with a spoon until cocoa powder and stevia are dissolved. Garnish with cinnamon stick (if using), and serve.

Variation: Other flavors of tea such as mint, black tea, or citrus work well here, too. You can also use dairy milk in place of the almond milk.

Chocolate Raspberry Cocoa

Raspberries and vanilla flavor this delicious hot cocoa.

Snack servings:	Yield:	Prep time:	Cook time:	Serving size:
3	3½ cups	5 minutes	6 to 8 minutes	1⅙ cups

Each serving has:			
124 calories	9g protein	22g carbohydrates	2g fiber
1g fat	0g saturated fat	glycemic index: low	glycemic load: 6

3 cups skim milk

½ cup frozen raspberries

2 TB. unsweetened cocoa

1 tsp. vanilla extract

½ tsp. stevia, or to taste

1. In a medium saucepan over medium heat, combine skim milk, raspberries, and unsweetened cocoa. Cook, stirring, for 1 or 2 minutes or until milk is hot.

2. Stir in vanilla extract and stevia, and serve in mugs with spoons to eat raspberries.

Variation: A nondairy milk, such as soy milk or almond milk, also works in this recipe. Or you can use reconstituted powdered milk.

Pumpkin Holiday Nog

This creamy nog has all the flavor of pumpkin pie served warm.

Snack servings:	Yield:	Prep time:	Cook time:	Serving size:
6	5 cups	5 minutes	10 minutes	$\frac{5}{6}$ cup

Each serving has:			
86 calories	6g protein	12g carbohydrates	1g fiber
2g fat	1g saturated fat	glycemic index: low	glycemic load: 5

4 cups low-fat milk	1 tsp. ground nutmeg
1 cup canned pumpkin	1 tsp. vanilla extract
1 tsp. stevia, or to taste	6 (2- or 3-in.) cinnamon sticks

1. In a large saucepan over medium-low heat, combine milk, pumpkin, stevia, and nutmeg. Heat through but do not boil, stirring often. Remove from heat.

2. Stir in vanilla extract, garnish with cinnamon sticks, and serve.

Variation: For **Pumpkin Soy Nog,** substitute soy milk for the low-fat milk in this recipe, and add 1 teaspoon ground cinnamon. *(Each serving has 106 calories, 6g protein, 14g carbohydrates, 2g fiber, 3g fat, 0g saturated fat, glycemic index: low, glycemic load: 7.)*

Coconut Berry Cooler

Raspberries, blueberries, and a trace of coconut flavor this cool lemonade.

Snack servings:	Yield:	Prep time:	Serving size:
4	4 cups	10 minutes plus 4 hours chill time	1 cup

Each serving has:			
60 calories	0g protein	10g carbohydrates	2g fiber
2g fat	2g saturated fat	glycemic index: low	glycemic load: 2

3 cups water	½ cup frozen blueberries
⅔ cup lemon juice	½ cup frozen red raspberries
1 TB. stevia, or to taste	Ice cubes (optional)
2 TB. cream of coconut	

1. In a large bowl, combine water, lemon juice, stevia, and cream of coconut. Stir until stevia dissolves. Cover and chill for 4 to 24 hours.

2. Transfer lemon juice mixture to a serving bowl or pitcher. Add blueberries and raspberries. Serve over ice (if using) in glasses.

TASTY BITE

It takes a minute or two of stirring to get the stevia to dissolve. This works best if the mixture is at room temperature rather than cold.

Blackberry Cream Smoothie

This rich vanilla blackberry smoothie is made with ice cream and yogurt.

Snack servings:	Yield:	Prep time:	Serving size:
4	4 cups	10 minutes	about 1 cup

Each serving has:			
129 calories	5g protein	22g carbohydrates	3g fiber
3g fat	2g saturated fat	glycemic index: low	glycemic load: 9

1 cup low-fat Greek-style yogurt

1 small ripe banana, peeled and cut into chunks

1 TB. honey

1 tsp. vanilla extract

1 cup fresh or frozen blackberries

½ cup vanilla ice cream

1. In a blender, purée yogurt, banana, honey, vanilla extract, blackberries, and ice cream for 30 to 60 seconds or until thick and smooth. If too thick, add up to 3 tablespoons water, 1 tablespoon at a time, to blender to thin smoothie.

2. Serve immediately.

Green Garden Smoothie

Green bell pepper and spinach add nutritional power to this smoothie sweetened with green grapes and banana.

Snack servings:	Yield:	Prep time:	Serving size:
6	6 cups	10 minutes	1 cup
Each serving has:			
45 calories	1g protein	11g carbohydrates	1g fiber
0g fat	0g saturated fat	glycemic index: low	glycemic load: 6

4 cups fresh spinach

2 cups seedless green grapes

1 medium banana, peeled and cut into chunks

¾ cup green bell pepper, chopped

½ cup water

1. In a blender or food processor fitted with a chopping blade, combine spinach, grapes, banana, green bell pepper, and water. Cover and blend or process for 30 to 60 seconds or until slightly pulpy and nearly smooth.

2. Serve immediately.

Variation: Kale or cabbage also work well in place of the spinach.

Piña Colada Smoothies

Coconut and pineapple pair up to flavor this banana smoothie.

Snack servings:	Yield:	Prep time:	Serving size:
5	about 5 cups	10 minutes	1 cup

Each serving has:			
77 calories	1g protein	15g carbohydrates	2g fiber
2g fat	2g saturated fat	glycemic index: low	glycemic load: 6

1 cup water

2 TB. lemon juice

2½ cups ripe fresh pineapple, diced

1 small ripe banana, peeled and
    cut into chunks

½ tsp. stevia, or to taste

2 TB. cream of coconut

1. In a blender or food processor fitted with a chopping blade, purée water, lemon juice, pineapple, banana, stevia, and cream of coconut for 30 to 60 seconds or until thick and smooth.

2. Serve immediately or chill for 4 or more hours.

HEALTHY NOTE

You can store cream of coconut in the refrigerator for a couple months. You can also freeze it and spoon out the amount you need without defrosting. You can do the same with frozen orange juice.

Thai Ginger Smoothie

Mango, pineapple, and coconut flavor this smoothie.

Snack servings:	Yield:	Prep time:	Serving size:
6	6 cups	10 minutes	1 cup

Each serving has:			
86 calories	3g protein	19g carbohydrates	1g fiber
2g fat	0g saturated fat	glycemic index: low	glycemic load: 9

2 cups frozen mango chunks

1 cup cubed fresh or canned
   pineapple

¾ cup coconut yogurt

½ cup low-fat milk

1 TB. honey

¼ tsp. ground ginger

1. In a blender, combine mango, pineapple, yogurt, milk, honey, and ginger. Cover and blend until smooth.

2. Serve immediately.

Dairy-Free Chocolate Mint Shake

This chocolate-y minty shake is made with soy milk and protein powder.

Snack servings:	Yield:	Prep time:	Serving size:
2	2 cups	5 minutes	1 cup

Each serving has:			
132 calories	7g protein	15g carbohydrates	5g fiber
6g fat	1g saturated fat	glycemic index: low	glycemic load: 4

1 cup low-fat soy milk

¼ cup protein powder

2 TB. unsweetened cocoa powder

2 TB. ground flaxseeds or flaxseed
　meal

1½ TB. fresh mint leaves

5 ice cubes

1. In a blender, combine soy milk, protein powder, unsweetened cocoa powder, flaxseeds, mint leaves, and ice cubes. Blend on high for about 1 or 2 minutes or until ice cubes are fully broken down and combined.

2. Serve immediately.

Variation: For **Chocolate Mint Cream Shake,** substitute low-fat milk for the soy milk and powdered milk for the protein powder. *(Each serving has 191 calories, 15g protein, 24g carbohydrates, 4g fiber, 5g fat, 2g saturated fat, glycemic index: low, glycemic load: 5.)*

Glossary

al dente   Italian for "against the teeth." Refers to pasta or rice that's neither soft nor hard, but just slightly firm against the teeth.

all-purpose flour   Flour that contains only the inner part of the wheat grain. Usable for all purposes from cakes to gravies.

allspice   Named for its flavor echoes of several spices (cinnamon, cloves, nutmeg), allspice is used in many desserts and in rich marinades and stews.

almonds   Mild, sweet, and crunchy nuts that combine nicely with creamy and sweet food items.

anchovies (also **sardines**)   Tiny, flavorful preserved fish that typically come in cans. Anchovies are a traditional garnish for Caesar salad, the dressing of which contains anchovy paste.

andouille sausage   A sausage made with highly seasoned pork chitterlings and tripe, and a standard component of many Cajun dishes.

artichoke hearts   The center part of the artichoke flower, often found canned in grocery stores.

arugula   A spicy-peppery garden plant with leaves that resemble a dandelion and have a distinctive—and very sharp—flavor.

au gratin   The quick broiling of a dish before serving to brown the top ingredients. When used in a recipe name, the term often implies cheese and a creamy sauce.

bake   To cook in a dry oven. Dry-heat cooking often results in a crisping of the exterior of the food being cooked. Moist-heat cooking, through methods such as steaming, poaching, etc., brings a much different, moist quality to the food.

balsamic vinegar   Vinegar produced primarily in Italy from a specific type of grape and aged in wood barrels. It is heavier, darker, and sweeter than most vinegars.

barbecue   To quick-cook over high heat, or to cook something long and slow in a rich liquid (barbecue sauce).

basil   A flavorful, almost sweet, resinous herb delicious with tomatoes and used in all kinds of Italian or Mediterranean-style dishes.

baste   To keep foods moist during cooking by spooning, brushing, or drizzling with a liquid.

beat   To quickly mix substances.

Belgian endive   A plant that resembles a small, elongated, tightly packed head of romaine lettuce. The thick, crunchy leaves can be broken off and used with dips and spreads.

black pepper   A biting and pungent seasoning, freshly ground pepper is a must for many dishes and adds an extra level of flavor and taste.

blend   To completely mix something, usually with a blender or food processor, more slowly than beating.

blue cheese   A blue-veined cheese that crumbles easily and has a somewhat soft texture, usually sold in a block. The color is from a flavorful, edible mold that's often added or injected into the cheese.

boil   To heat a liquid to a point where water is forced to turn into steam, causing the liquid to bubble. To boil something is to insert it into boiling water. A rapid boil is when a lot of bubbles form on the surface of the liquid.

bok choy (also **Chinese cabbage**)   A member of the cabbage family with thick stems, crisp texture, and fresh flavor. It's perfect for stir-frying.

bouillon   Dried essence of stock from chicken, beef, vegetable, or other ingredients. This is a popular starting ingredient for soups because it adds flavor (and often a lot of salt).

bouquet garni   A collection of herbs including bay leaf, parsley, thyme, and others traditionally tied in a bunch or packaged in cheesecloth for cooking and subsequent removal.

braise   To cook with the introduction of some liquid, usually over an extended period of time.

breadcrumbs   Tiny pieces of crumbled dry bread, often used for topping or coating.

Brie   A creamy cow's milk cheese from France with a soft, edible rind and a mild flavor.

broil   To cook in a dry oven under the overhead high-heat element.

broth   *See* stock.

brown   To cook in a skillet, turning, until the food's surface is seared and brown in color, to lock in the juices.

brown rice   Whole-grain rice, including the germ, with a characteristic pale brown or tan color; more nutritious and flavorful than white rice.

bulgur   A wheat kernel that's been steamed, dried, and crushed and is sold in fine and coarse textures.

Cajun cooking   A style of cooking that combines French and Southern characteristics and includes many highly seasoned stews and meats.

cake flour   A high-starch, soft, and fine flour used primarily for cakes.

canapés   Bite-size hors d'oeuvres usually served on a small piece of bread or toast.

capers   Flavorful buds of a Mediterranean plant, ranging in size from *nonpareil* (about the size of a small pea) to larger, grape-size caper berries produced in Spain.

caraway   A distinctive spicy seed used for bread, pork, cheese, and cabbage dishes. It's known to reduce stomach upset, which is why it's often paired with foods like sauerkraut.

carbohydrate   A nutritional component found in starches, sugars, fruits, and vegetables that causes a rise in blood glucose levels. Carbohydrates supply energy and many important nutrients, including vitamins, minerals, and antioxidants.

cardamom   An intense, sweet-smelling spice, common to Indian cooking, used in baking and coffee.

cayenne   A fiery spice made from (hot) chile peppers, especially the cayenne chile, a slender, red, and very hot pepper.

cheddar   The ubiquitous hard cow's milk cheese with a rich, buttery flavor that ranges from mellow to sharp. Originally produced in England, cheddar is now produced worldwide.

chickpea (or garbanzo bean)   A yellow-gold, roundish bean used as the base ingredient in hummus. Chickpeas are high in fiber and low in fat.

chiles Any one of many different "hot" peppers, ranging in intensity from the relatively mild ancho pepper to the blisteringly hot habañero.

chili powder A seasoning blend that includes chile pepper, cumin, garlic, and oregano. Proportions vary among different versions, but they all offer a warm, rich flavor.

chives A member of the onion family, chives grow in bunches of long leaves that resemble tall grass or the green tops of onions and offer a light onion flavor.

chop To cut into pieces, usually qualified by an adverb such as "coarsely chopped," or by a size measurement such as "chopped into $1/2$-inch pieces." "Finely chopped" is much closer to mince.

chorizo A spiced pork sausage that can be eaten alone or as a component in many recipes, usually Mexican cuisine.

chutney A thick condiment often served with Indian curries made with fruits and/ or vegetables with vinegar, sugar, and spices.

cider vinegar Vinegar produced from apple cider, popular in North America.

cilantro A member of the parsley family and used in Mexican cooking (especially salsa) and some Asian dishes. Use in moderation because the flavor can overwhelm. The seed of the cilantro is the spice coriander.

cinnamon A rich, aromatic spice commonly used in baking or desserts. Cinnamon can also be used for delicious and interesting entrées.

clove A sweet, strong, almost wintergreen-flavor spice used in baking and with meats such as ham.

coriander A rich, warm, spicy seed used in all types of recipes, from African to South American, from entrées to desserts.

count In terms of seafood or other foods that come in small sizes, the number of that item that compose 1 pound. For example, 31 to 40 count shrimp are large appetizer shrimp often served with cocktail sauce; 51 to 60 are much smaller.

couscous Granular semolina (durum wheat) that's cooked and used in many Mediterranean and North African dishes.

crimini mushrooms A relative of the white button mushroom, but brown in color and with a richer flavor. The larger, fully grown version is the portobello. *See also* portobello mushrooms.

croutons   Chunks of bread, usually between $\frac{1}{4}$ and $\frac{1}{2}$ inch in size, sometimes seasoned and baked, broiled, or fried to a crisp texture and used in soups and salads.

crudités   Fresh vegetables served as an appetizer, often all together on one tray.

cumin   A fiery, smoky-tasting spice popular in Middle Eastern and Indian dishes. Cumin is a seed; ground cumin seed is the most common form used in cooking.

curry   Rich, spicy, Indian-style sauces and the dishes prepared with them. A curry uses curry powder as its base seasoning.

curry powder   A ground blend of rich and flavorful spices used as a basis for curry and many other Indian-influenced dishes. Common ingredients include hot pepper, nutmeg, cumin, cinnamon, pepper, and turmeric. Some curry can also be found in paste form.

custard   A cooked mixture of eggs and milk popular as a base for desserts.

dash   A few drops, usually of a liquid, released by a quick shake; for example, a dash from a bottle of hot sauce.

devein   The removal of the dark vein from the back of a large shrimp with a sharp knife.

dice   To cut into small cubes about $\frac{1}{4}$-inch square.

Dijon mustard   Hearty, spicy mustard made in the style of the Dijon region of France.

dill   A herb perfect for eggs, salmon, cheese dishes, and, of course, vegetables (pickles!).

dollop   A spoonful of something creamy and thick, like sour cream or whipped cream.

double boiler   A set of two pots designed to nest together, one inside the other, and provide consistent, moist heat for foods that need delicate treatment. The bottom pot holds water (not quite touching the bottom of the top pot); the top pot holds the ingredient you want to heat.

dredge   To cover a piece of food with a dry substance such as flour or cornmeal.

drizzle   To lightly sprinkle drops of a liquid over food, often as the finishing touch to a dish.

dry   In the context of wine, a wine that contains little or no residual sugar, so it's not very sweet.

entrée   The main dish in a meal. In France, however, the entrée is considered the first course.

fennel   In seed form, a fragrant, licorice-tasting herb. The bulbs have a much milder flavor and a celery-like crunch and are used as a vegetable in salads or cooked recipes.

feta   A white, crumbly, sharp, and salty cheese popular in Greek cooking and on salads. Traditional feta is usually made with sheep's milk, but feta-style cheese can be made from cow's or goat's milk.

fillet   A piece of meat or seafood with the bones removed.

flake   To break into thin sections, as with fish.

floret   The flower or bud end of broccoli or cauliflower.

flour   Grains ground into a meal. Wheat is perhaps the most common flour. Flour can also be made from oats, rye, buckwheat, soybeans, chickpeas, etc. *See also* all-purpose flour; cake flour; whole-wheat flour.

fold   To combine a dense and light mixture with a circular action from the middle of the bowl.

frittata   A skillet-cooked mixture of eggs and other ingredients that's not stirred but is cooked slowly and then either flipped or finished under the broiler.

fritter   A food such as apples or corn coated or mixed with batter and deep-fried for a crispy, crunchy exterior.

fructose   Sugar naturally found in fruit, slightly sweeter than table sugar.

fry   *See* sauté.

fusion   To blend two or more styles of cooking, such as Chinese and French.

garlic   A member of the onion family, a pungent and flavorful element in many savory dishes. A garlic bulb contains multiple cloves. Each clove, when chopped, provides about 1 teaspoon garlic. Most recipes call for cloves or chopped garlic by the teaspoon.

garnish   An embellishment not vital to the dish but added to enhance visual appeal.

ginger   Available in fresh root or dried, ground form, ginger adds a pungent, sweet, and spicy quality to a dish.

glucose   The simplest natural sugar.

glycemic load   A numerical value that indicates the amount of carbohydrates in a meal or food that will affect a blood sugar rise. It's a calculation that includes the net amount of carbohydrates factored with the glycemic index value of the carbs. A healthy range of glycemic load for an average person is from 80 to 120 per day.

grate   To shave into tiny pieces using a sharp rasp or grater.

grind   To reduce a large, hard substance, often a seasoning such as peppercorns, to the consistency of sand.

grits   Coarsely ground grains, usually corn.

Gruyère   A rich, sharp cow's milk cheese made in Switzerland that has a nutty flavor.

handful   An unscientific measurement; the amount of an ingredient you can hold in your hand.

haute cuisine   French for "high cooking." Refers to painstakingly prepared, sometimes exotic, delicious, and complex meals.

hazelnuts (also **filberts**)   A sweet nut popular in desserts and, to a lesser degree, savory dishes.

herbes de Provence   A seasoning mix including basil, fennel, marjoram, rosemary, sage, and thyme, common in the south of France.

high-glycemic carbohydrates   A carbohydrate that triggers a quick rise in blood sugar levels and contributes to inflammation, mood swings, and weight gain.

hoisin sauce   A sweet Asian condiment similar to ketchup made with soybeans, sesame, chili peppers, and sugar.

hors d'oeuvre   French for "outside of work" (the "work" being the main meal), an hors d'oeuvre can be any dish served as a starter before a meal.

horseradish   A sharp, spicy root that forms the flavor base in many condiments, from cocktail sauce to sharp mustards. Prepared horseradish contains vinegar and oil, among other ingredients. Use pure horseradish much more sparingly than the prepared version, or try cutting it with sour cream.

hummus   A thick, Middle Eastern spread made of puréed chickpeas, lemon juice, extra-virgin olive oil, garlic, and often tahini (sesame seed paste).

infusion   A liquid in which flavorful ingredients such as herbs have been soaked or steeped to extract their flavor into the liquid.

Italian seasoning   A blend of dried herbs, including basil, oregano, rosemary, and thyme.

jicama   A juicy, crunchy, sweet, large, round Central American vegetable. If you can't find jicama, try substituting sliced water chestnuts.

julienne   A French word meaning "to slice into very thin pieces."

kalamata olives   Traditionally from Greece, these medium-small long black olives have a smoky, rich flavor.

Key limes   Very small limes grown primarily in Florida known for their tart taste.

knead   To work dough to make it pliable so it holds gas bubbles as it bakes. Kneading is fundamental in the process of making yeast breads.

kosher salt   A coarse-grained salt made without any additives or iodine.

lentils   Tiny lens-shape pulses used in European, Middle Eastern, and Indian cuisines.

low-glycemic carbohydrate   A carbohydrate that does not trigger a quick rise in blood sugar levels. Instead, it's digested slowly and provides the body with steady energy. Good examples are vegetables (except for potatoes) and most fruit.

marinate   To soak meat, seafood, or other food in a seasoned sauce, called a marinade, which is high in acid content. The acids break down the muscle of the meat, making it tender and adding flavor.

marjoram   A sweet herb, a cousin of and similar to oregano, popular in Greek, Spanish, and Italian dishes.

mascarpone   A thick, creamy, spreadable cheese, traditionally from Italy.

medallion   A small round cut, usually of meat or vegetables such as carrots or cucumbers.

meld   To allow flavors to blend and spread over time. Melding is often why recipes call for overnight refrigeration and is also why some dishes taste better as leftovers.

mince   To cut into very small pieces smaller than diced pieces, about $1/8$ inch or smaller.

miso   A fermented, flavorful soybean paste, key in many Japanese dishes.

mold   A decorative, shaped metal pan in which contents, such as mousse or gelatin, set up and take the shape of the pan.

mull (or **mulled**)   To heat a liquid with the addition of spices and sometimes sweeteners.

nutmeg   A sweet, fragrant, musky spice used primarily in baking.

olive oil   A fragrant liquid produced by crushing or pressing olives. Extra-virgin olive oil—the most flavorful and highest quality—is produced from the first pressing of a batch of olives; oil is also produced from later pressings.

olives   The fruit of the olive tree commonly grown on all sides of the Mediterranean. Black olives are also called ripe olives. Green olives are immature, although they are also widely eaten. *See also* kalamata olives.

oregano   A fragrant, slightly astringent herb used in Greek, Spanish, and Italian dishes.

oxidation   The browning of fruit flesh that happens over time and with exposure to air. Minimize oxidation by rubbing the cut surfaces with a lemon half. Oxidation also affects wine, which is why the taste changes over time after a bottle is opened.

paella   A grand Spanish dish of rice, shellfish, onion, meats, rich broth, and herbs.

paprika   A rich, red, warm, earthy spice that also lends a rich red color to many dishes.

Parmesan   A hard, dry, flavorful cheese primarily used grated or shredded as a seasoning for Italian-style dishes.

parsley   A fresh-tasting green leafy herb, often used as a garnish.

pâté   A savory loaf that contains meats, poultry, or seafood; spices; and often a lot of fat, served cold spread or sliced on crusty bread or crackers.

pecans   Rich, buttery nuts, native to North America, that have a high unsaturated fat content.

peppercorns   Large, round, dried berries ground to produce pepper.

pesto   A thick spread or sauce made with fresh basil leaves, garlic, extra-virgin olive oil, pine nuts, and Parmesan cheese. Some newer versions are made with other herbs.

pickle   A food, usually a vegetable such as a cucumber, that's been pickled in brine.

pilaf   A rice dish in which the rice is browned in butter or oil and then cooked in a flavorful liquid such as a broth, often with the addition of meats or vegetables. The rice absorbs the broth, resulting in a savory dish.

pinch   An unscientific measurement term, the amount of an ingredient—typically a dry, granular substance such as an herb or seasoning—you can hold between your finger and thumb.

pine nuts (also **pignoli** or **piñon**)   Nuts grown on pine trees that are rich (read: high fat), flavorful, and a bit pine-y. Pine nuts are a traditional component of pesto and add a wonderful, hearty crunch to many other recipes.

pita bread   A flat, hollow wheat bread often used for sandwiches or sliced, pizza style, into slices. Terrific soft with dips or baked or broiled as a vehicle for other ingredients.

pizza stone   Preheated with the oven, a pizza stone cooks a crust to a delicious, crispy, pizza-parlor texture. It also holds heat well, so a pizza or other food removed from the oven on the stone stay hot for as long as a half hour at the table.

poach   To cook a food in simmering liquid, such as water, wine, or broth.

porcini mushrooms   Rich and flavorful mushrooms used in rice and Italian-style dishes.

portobello mushrooms   A mature and larger form of the smaller crimini mushroom, portobellos are brownish, chewy, and flavorful. Often served as whole caps, grilled, and as thin sautéed slices. *See also* crimini mushrooms.

posole   A soup that originated in pre-Columbian Mexico. It has a spicy chili taste, interesting texture, and heart-warming healthfulness.

preheat   To turn on an oven, broiler, or other cooking appliance in advance of cooking so the temperature will be at the desired level when the assembled dish is ready for cooking.

prosciutto   Dry, salt-cured ham that originated in Italy.

purée   To reduce a food to a thick, creamy texture, usually using a blender or food processor.

quinoa   A whole grain, originally cultivated in the Andes Mountains of South America. It contains a good balance of essential amino acids, or protein, and it's high in dietary fiber while being gluten-free.

reduce   To boil or simmer a broth or sauce to remove some of the water content, resulting in more concentrated flavor and color.

reserve   To hold a specified ingredient for another use later in the recipe.

rice vinegar   Vinegar produced from fermented rice or rice wine, popular in Asian-style dishes. (It's different from rice wine vinegar.)

ricotta   A fresh Italian cheese smoother than cottage cheese with a slightly sweet flavor.

risotto   A popular Italian rice dish made by browning arborio rice in butter or oil and then slowly adding liquid to cook the rice, resulting in a creamy texture.

roast   To cook something uncovered in an oven, usually without additional liquid.

Roquefort   A world-famous French sheep's milk cheese that's creamy and contains blue lines of mold.

rosemary   A pungent, sweet herb used with chicken, pork, fish, and especially lamb. A little of it goes a long way.

roux   A mixture of butter or another fat and flour used to thicken sauces and soups.

saffron   A spice made from the stamens of crocus flowers, saffron lends a dramatic yellow color and distinctive flavor to a dish. Use only tiny amounts of this expensive herb.

sage   An herb with a musty yet fruity, lemon-rind scent and "sunny" flavor.

salsa   A style of mixing fresh vegetables and/or fresh fruit in a coarse chop. Salsa can be spicy or not, fruit-based or not, and served as a starter on its own (with chips, for example) or as a companion to a main course.

satay (also **sate**)   A popular Southeast Asian dish of broiled skewers of fish or meat, often served with peanut sauce.

sauté   To pan-cook over lower heat than what's used for frying.

savory   A popular herb with a fresh, woody taste.

sear   To quickly brown the exterior of a food, especially meat, over high heat to preserve interior moisture.

sesame oil   An oil made from pressing sesame seeds that's tasteless if clear and aromatic and flavorful if brown.

shallot   A member of the onion family that grows in a bulb somewhat like garlic and has a milder onion flavor. When a recipe calls for shallot, use the entire bulb.

shellfish   A broad range of seafood, including clams, mussels, oysters, crabs, shrimp, and lobster. Some people are allergic to shellfish, so take care with its inclusion in recipes.

shiitake mushrooms   Large, dark brown mushrooms with a hearty, meaty flavor. Can be used either fresh or dried, grilled or as a component in other recipes, and as a flavoring source for broth.

shred   To cut into many long, thin slices.

simmer   To boil gently so the liquid barely bubbles.

skewers   Thin wooden or metal sticks, usually about 8 inches long, used for assembling kebabs, dipping food pieces into hot sauces, or serving single-bite food items with a bit of panache.

skillet (also **frying pan**)   A generally heavy, flat-bottomed metal pan with a handle designed to cook food over heat on a stovetop or campfire.

skim   To remove fat or other material from the top of liquid.

slice   To cut into thin pieces.

steam   To suspend a food over boiling water and allow the heat of the steam (water vapor) to cook the food. A quick-cooking method, steaming preserves the flavor and texture of a food.

steep   To let sit in hot water, as in steeping tea in hot water for 10 minutes.

stew   To slowly cook pieces of food submerged in a liquid. Also, a dish that's been prepared by this method.

stir-fry   To cook small pieces of food in a wok or skillet over high heat, moving and turning the food quickly to cook all sides.

stock   A flavorful broth made by cooking meats and/or vegetables with seasonings until the liquid absorbs these flavors. This liquid is then strained and the solids discarded. Can be eaten alone or used as a base for soups, stews, etc.

succotash   A cooked vegetable dish usually made of corn and peppers.

tahini   A paste made from sesame seeds used to flavor many Middle Eastern recipes.

tapenade   A thick, chunky spread made from savory ingredients such as olives, lemon juice, and anchovies.

tarragon   A sweet, rich-smelling herb perfect with seafood, vegetables (especially asparagus), chicken, and pork.

teriyaki   A Japanese-style sauce composed of soy sauce, rice wine, ginger, and sugar that works well with seafood as well as most meats.

thyme   A minty, zesty herb.

toast   To heat something, usually bread, so it's browned and crisp.

tofu   A cheeselike substance made from soybeans and soy milk.

tomatillo   A small, round fruit with a distinctive spicy flavor, often found in south-of-the-border dishes. To use, remove the papery outer skin, rinse off any sticky residue, and chop like a tomato.

turmeric   A spicy, pungent yellow root used in many dishes, especially Indian cuisine, for color and flavor. Turmeric is the source of the yellow color in many prepared mustards.

veal   Meat from a calf, generally characterized by mild flavor and tenderness.

vegetable steamer   An insert for a large saucepan or a special pot with tiny holes in the bottom designed to fit on another pot to hold food to be steamed above boiling water. *See also* steam.

vinegar   An acidic liquid widely used as dressing and seasoning, often made from fermented grapes, apples, or rice. *See also* balsamic vinegar; cider vinegar; rice vinegar; white vinegar; wine vinegar.

walnuts   A rich, slightly woody flavored nut.

wasabi   Japanese horseradish, a fiery, pungent condiment used with many Japanese-style dishes. It's most often sold as a powder so you add water to create a paste.

water chestnuts   A tuber, popular in many types of Asian-style cooking. The flesh is white, crunchy, and juicy, and the vegetable holds its texture whether cool or hot.

whisk   To rapidly mix, introducing air to the mixture.

white mushrooms   Button mushrooms. When fresh, they have an earthy smell and an appealing soft crunch.

white vinegar   The most common type of vinegar, produced from grain.

whole-wheat flour   Wheat flour that contains the entire grain.

wild rice   Not a rice at all, this is actually a grass. It has a rich, nutty flavor and is popular as an unusual and nutritious side dish.

wine vinegar   Vinegar produced from red or white wine.

Worcestershire sauce   Originally developed in India and containing tamarind, this spicy sauce is used as a seasoning for many meats and other dishes.

yeast   Tiny fungi that, when mixed with water, sugar, flour, and heat, release carbon dioxide bubbles, which, in turn, cause the bread to rise.

zest   Small slivers of peel, usually from a citrus fruit such as lemon, lime, or orange.

zester   A kitchen tool used to scrape zest off a fruit. A small grater also works well.

Glycemic Index Values

In this appendix, I give you a list of common glycemic index values. Note this list includes only information on foods that contain carbohydrates. Animal proteins such as meats, seafood, and poultry don't contain carbohydrates, so their glycemic index and glycemic load are both 0. The same is true for butter and vegetable oils.

Food	Glycemic Index Value	Amount	Carbs (Grams)	Fiber (Grams)	Net Carbs	Glycemic Load
Almond flour	0	1 cup	21	11	10	0
Almonds	0	1 cup	28	15	13	0
Apple juice	40	1 cup	29	0	29	12
Apples	38	1 medium	22	5	17	6
Applesauce, unsweetened	40	½ cup	13	3	10	6
Apricots	57	3 medium	10	1	9	5
Apricots, dried	30	¼ cup	29	2	27	8
Artichokes	0	½ cup	6	4	2	0
Avocado, California	0	1 medium	12	9	3	0
Baked beans	50	½ cup	27	7	11	20
Banana	52	1 medium	29	4	25	12
Barley, pearl, uncooked	25	¼ cup	37	6	31	11
Basmati brown rice, cooked	58	½ cup	18	2	16	8
Black beans, boiled	30	½ cup	20	8	12	4
Black-eyed peas, canned	42	½ cup	16	4	12	5
Bouillon, chicken or beef	0	½ cup	2	0	0	0
Bran, whole-wheat	0	2 TB.	5	3	2	0
Brazil nut	0	6 large	4	2	0	0
Bread, white	80	1 slice	15	1	14	11
Bread, whole-wheat	77	1 slice	15	1	14	9
Bread, 100 percent whole-grain	51	1 slice	13	2	11	7
Broccoli, raw, chopped	0	½ cup	2	1	1	0
Brown sugar	59	1 oz.	28	0	28	17
Cabbage, raw, shredded	0	½ cup	2	1	1	0
Cantaloupe, cubed	65	1 cup	13	2	11	6
Capers	0	1 TB.	1	0	1	0
Carrots, raw, shredded	47	½ cup	6	2	4	3
Cashews	22	¼ cup	8	3	5	3
Cauliflower, 1-inch pieces	0	½ cup	3	2	1	0
Celery, diced	0	½ cup	2	1	1	0
Cheese, cheddar and Parmesan	0	1 oz.	0	0	0	0
Cheese, chèvre	0	1 oz.	1	0	1	0

Food	Glycemic Index Value	Amount	Carbs (Grams)	Fiber (Grams)	Net Carbs	Glycemic Load
Cherries, sweet with pits	22	½ cup	12	2	10	2
Chickpeas, canned	42	½ cup	18	7	11	7
Cocoa powder	55	1 TB.	3	1	2	1
Corn, sweet, boiled	60	½ cup	11	2	9	11
Cornmeal	68	¼ cup	25	3	22	5
Couscous	65	¼ cup	13	2	11	7
Cream, heavy	0	½ cup	3	0	3	0
Cucumber, sliced	0	½ cup	1.4	1	0	0
Dates	50	¼ cup	32	3	29	15
Donut, cake	76	1 small	23	0	23	17
Eggs, large	0	1 large	0.6	0	.6	0
Fennel, sliced	0	1 cup	6	2	4	0
Figs, dried	61	3 figs	31	5	26	15
Garlic	0	1 clove	1	0.1	1	0
Grapefruit	25	½ medium	16	6	10	3
Grapefruit juice	48	1 cup	20	0	20	9
Grapes, green	46	¾ cup	19	1	18	8
Green beans, cooked	0	½ cup	5	2	3	0
Green onions	0	¼ cup	2	1	1	0
Green peas, frozen	48	⅔ cup	12	4	8	6
Hazelnuts, diced	0	1 cup	18	7	11	0
Honey, varies widely	55–78	1 TB.	18	0	18	10–20
Ice cream, low-fat, vanilla	50	½ cup	9	0	9	5
Jicama	0	½ cup	5	3	2	0
Kidney beans, boiled	46	½ cup	20	7	14	6
Kiwi fruit	58	1 medium	11	3	9	5
Leafy vegetables, raw	0	1 cup	2	1	1	0
Lentils, cooked	29	½ cup	20	8	12	3
Lima beans, frozen	32	½ cup	22	5	17	7
Macadamia nuts	0	¼ cup	5	3	2	0
Mango, sliced	51	½	18	3	15	8
Milk, 2 percent	32	1 cup	13	0	13	4

continues

continued

Food	Glycemic Index Value	Amount	Carbs (Grams)	Fiber (Grams)	Net Carbs	Glycemic Load
Oat bran	55	2 TB.	10	5	5	3
Oatmeal, slow-cooking, cooked	42	½ cup	13	2	11	5
Orange, sections	42	½ cup	13	2	11	3
Orange juice	53	1 cup	18	0	18	9
Papaya, sliced	56	½ cup	11	3	8	5
Peach, sliced	42	1 cup	14	3	11	5
Peanuts, roasted	14	¼ cup	7	2	5	1
Pear	38	1 medium	25	4	21	4
Pecan flour	0	1 cup	15	15	0	0
Pecans, halves	0	¼ cup	5	5	0	0
Pepper, red or green bell, diced	0	¾ cup	4	2	2	0
Pine or piñon nuts	0	¼ cup	5	2	3	0
Pineapple, diced	66	½ cup	19	2	17	8
Pinto beans, canned	45	½ cup	18	6	12	7
Plums, sliced	39	½ cup	11	1	10	5
Popcorn, microwaved	72	1 ½ cups	14	3	11	8
Potato, white, baked in skin	85	4¾×2½	35	5	30	26
Potato chips	57	2 oz.	18	0	18	10
Raisins	64	¼ cup	31	2	29	14
Rice, brown, uncooked	50	¼ cup	37	3	35	16
Rice cakes	82	3 cakes	21	0	21	17
Salami	0	1 oz.	0	0	0	0
Split peas, cooked	32	¼ cup	27	11	16	2
Strawberries	40	½ cup	6	1	5	1
Sucrose, granulated table sugar	68	1 TB.	10	0	10	7
Sweet potato, mashed	44	½ cup	24	3	21	11
Tomato, chopped	0	1 cup	8	2	6	0
Tortilla chips, plain, salted	63	1 oz.	15	1	14	8
Walnuts, halves	0	¼ cup	3	3	0	0
Wild rice, uncooked	57	¼ cup	34	3	31	18
Yams, cooked, cubed	37	½ cup	39	3	36	13

Resources

Some of the recipes in this book call for specialty ingredients. If you live in a larger city, or near a well-stocked health food store, you'll be able to purchase them at your local health food stores. If you can't find them locally, try going online:

Chickpea flour: amazon.com, vitacost.com, and Whole Foods

Coconut flour: amazon.com, drugstore.com, and Whole Foods

Coconut cream: amazon.com, cubanfoodmarket.com, and Whole Foods

Coconut yogurt: foodservicedirect.com/product.cfm/p/210407/ Liberte-Coconut-Mediterranean-Yogurt-6-Ounce.htm and Whole Foods

Oat bran: amazon.com, drugstore.com, and Whole Foods

For more information on the glycemic index, check out the following:

Lucy Beale's website: lucybeale.com

Sign up for Lucy's free monthly e-mail newsletter: lucybeale.com/wellness/ newsletter.htm

Follow Lucy's blog: lucybeale-weight-loss.blogspot.com

Lucy's weight-loss book on the glycemic index: *The Complete Idiot's Guide to Glycemic Index Weight Loss*

For more of Lucy's low-glycemic recipes: *The Complete Idiot's Guide Glycemic Index Cookbook*, *The Complete Idiot's Guide to Low-Carb Meals*, and *The Complete Idiot's Guide to Terrific Diabetic Meals*

Index

A

activity level and glycemic load per day, 8
agave nectar, 14
almonds, 12
  almond milk, 277-278
  Almond Nut Piecrust, 243
  almond paste, 264
  Almonds with Rosemary and Cayenne, 224
  Cherry Almond Quiche, 168
  Frozen Cherry Almond Frosty, 60
  Green Bean and Almond Salad, 30
Anise Almond Macaroons, 263
apples, 61, 140, 169, 196, 215
Apricot Tea, 274
Apricot Trail Mix, 228
artichokes, 73, 89, 92, 165, 179
Asian Cakes with Cabbage, 37
Asian Chicken Lettuce Wraps, 133
Asian Tuna and Cabbage Salad, 149
Asian Vegetables with Peanuts, 23
avocados, 22, 117, 148, 188, 191

B

bacon, 25, 67, 173
Baja Fish Tacos, 144
Baked Apples with Yogurt, 61
Baked Berry Ricotta Puffs, 247
Baked Crab Enchiladas, 159-160
Baked Sweet Potato Skins, 35
baking equipment, 17
bananas, 58, 63, 214, 238
Barbecued White Beans, 185
Barley Pilaf with Shrimp, 205
Barley with Asparagus and Thyme, 206
bars. See cookies/cakes
basil, 16, 26, 53, 72, 82
beans, 15, 175-176
  Artichokes with Chickpeas, 179
  Barbecued White Beans, 185
  Beef and Black Bean Lettuce Wraps, 108
  Black Bean and Avocado Salad, 188
  Black Bean and Mango Dip, 69
  Black-Eyed Pea and Ham Salad, 184
  Cannellini Bean Dip, 71
  Chickpea, Basil, and Radish Dip, 72
  Chickpea Poppers, 182
  Chickpea Salad with Roasted Cumin, 183
  Curried Carrot Dip, 74
  digestive enzymes, 176
  Four-Cheese Black Bean Mash, 186
  glycemic index, 7
  glycemic load, 176
  Great Northern Bean and Mushroom Burgers, 190
  Green Bean Salad with Edamame and Chickpeas, 181
  Green Lentils with Feta, 177
  Guacamole with Green Peas and Tomato, 191

health benefits of, 31
Hummus with Lemon, 76
Lentil Tabbouleh, 195
Lentils with Spinach, Walnuts, and Parmesan, 178
Mozzarella and Black Bean Salad, 87
Quinoa and Lentil Salad, 194
Refried Bean–Stuffed Portobello Mushrooms, 192
Romaine Salad Tossed with Chickpeas, 180
Sweet Potato and Black Bean Wraps, 187
Tuna, Barley, and Black Bean Salad, 150
Turkey and Chickpea Burgers, 141
Tuscan Bean Soup, 189
beef
Beef and Black Bean Lettuce Wraps, 108
Beef and Blue Cheese Wraps, 114
Beef Gyros, 109
Hot Dogs with Avocado-Chili Relish, 117
Mediterranean Beef Wraps, 113
Mexican Beef Tostadas, 110
Moroccan Burgers, 115
Steak Sandwiches with Peppers and Onions, 116
Top Sirloin Kabobs, 112
Zucchini with Beef and Peppers, 111-112
Bengal grams. *See* chickpeas

berries. *See also specific berries*
Baked Berry Ricotta Puffs, 247
Berries with Pistachios, 226
Berry Ginger Tofu Mousse, 245
Coconut Berry Cooler, 280
berry mix, dried, 226
beverages, 273
Apricot Tea, 274
Blackberry Cream Smoothie, 281
Chocolate Mint Cream Shake, 285
Chocolate Raspberry Cocoa, 278
Coconut Berry Cooler, 280
Dairy-Free Chocolate Mint Shake, 285
Earl Grey Tea with Tarragon, 276
Green Garden Smoothie, 282
Mexican Hot Chocolate, 277
Piña Colada Smoothies, 283
Pumpkin Holiday Nog, 279
Pumpkin Soy Nog, 279
Raspberry Lemon Tea, 275
Thai Ginger Smoothie, 284
black beans, 69, 186-188
Black-Eyed Pea and Ham Salad, 184
Blackberry Cream Smoothie, 281

blender and kitchen equipment, 17
blood sugar levels, 4, 6
blue cheese. *See* cheese
Blueberry Banana Walnut Bread, 214
Brazil nuts, 12
Bread Pudding with Chocolate and Cherries, 236
breadcrumbs, 165
breads, 13. *See also* crackers; muffins
Blueberry Banana Walnut Bread, 214
Brie Biscuits, 212
glycemic index, 207
Ham and Cheddar Scones, 213
Oatmeal Flatbread Bars, 211
Zucchini Apple Bread, 215
Brie Biscuits, 212
Brie cheese. *See* cheese
Brie with Blueberry Preserves, 91
Broccoli and Corn Wraps, 46
Broccoli Salad with Blue Cheese, 29
brown rice, 202-204
brownies, 265-266
bulgur, 196-197
burgers
Chicken and Brie Burgers, 130
Chicken Italian Burgers, 130
Great Northern Bean and Mushroom Burgers, 190

Grilled Turkey and Cottage Cheese Burgers, 141

Ham, Corn, and Sweet Potato Patties, 123

Italian Sausage and Turkey Patties, 120

Lamb Patties Piccata, 127

lettuce wraps, 141

Moroccan Burgers, 115

Turkey and Chickpea Burgers, 141

Turkey and Pepperoni Burgers, 141

butter, 7, 16

butterscotch chips, 232

C

cabbage, 24, 37, 149, 198

Cabbage Pecan Slaw, 24

Cajun Catfish Po'Boy, 146

Cajun Dirty Rice, 203-204

cakes. *See* cookies/cakes

calories and snacks, 4, 6

canapés, 92

canned staples, 15, 22

cannellini beans, 71, 74, 185, 189

carbohydrates, effective, 176

Caribbean Pork and Fruit Salad, 125

ceci beans. *See* chickpeas

cheddar cheese. *See* cheese

cheese, 17

about low/reduced-fat, 85

Artichokes and Olives on Cucumber, 92

Bacon Cheddar Dip, 67

Baked Berry Ricotta Puffs, 247

Banana Cream Cheese Roll-Ups, 58

Beef and Blue Cheese Wraps, 114

Blue Cheese Iceberg Salad, 25

Blue Cheese Pitas, 96

Brie Biscuits, 212

Brie with Blueberry Preserves, 91

Broccoli Salad with Blue Cheese, 29

Bulgur, Feta, and Olive Salad, 197

Cheese and Fruit Kabobs, 95

Chicken and Brie Burgers, 130

Chicken Red Pepper Quesadillas, 131

choosing low/reduced-fat, 85

Corn, Red Pepper, and Monterey Jack Salad, 28

Creamy Artichoke Spinach Dip, 73

Creamy Salmon Spread, 78

Creamy Swiss Grits, 200

Eggplant Feta Rolls, 47

Feta, Fig, and Spinach Pizza, 88

Four-Cheese Black Bean Mash, 186

glycemic index, 7

Gorgonzola Bites with Fresh Fruit, 98

Green Lentils with Feta, 177

Green Olives with Feta and Celery, 94

Grilled Turkey and Cottage Cheese Burgers, 141

Ham and Cheddar Scones, 213

Ham and Cheese Pie, 166

Hot Chili Cream Cheese Dip, 66

Italian Pizza on a Pita, 97

Jalapeño Cheddar Cheese Pizza, 90

Layered Greek Pie, 99

Monterey Jack Tacos, 93

Mozzarella and Black Bean Salad, 87

Mushroom and Artichoke Camembert, 89

No-Bake Ricotta Cheesecake, 240

Olive and Pimiento Cheese Spread, 77

Olive Tapenade Roll-Ups, 100

Raspberry Cottage Cheese, 59

Ricotta Pistachio Cookies, 256

Spinach Cheese Squares, 164

Swiss Turkey Enchiladas, 139

Tomato, Basil, and Mozzarella Salad, 26

cheesecake, 239-240

Cherry Almond Quiche, 168

chicken, 129

Asian Chicken Lettuce Wraps, 133

Chicken and Brie Burgers, 130

Chicken Italian Burgers, 130

Chicken Red Pepper Quesadillas, 131
Chicken Satay with Peanut Sauce, 132
Chicken Wraps with Pears and Grapes, 134
Creamy Chicken Wraps, 135
Pecan Coconut Chicken Fingers, 137
Rosemary Honey Chicken Drumsticks, 136
Sesame Chicken Strips, 138
chickpea flour, 12, 32
chickpeas
Artichokes with Chickpeas, 179
Chickpea, Basil, and Radish Dip, 72
Chickpea Poppers, 182
Chickpea Salad with Roasted Cumin, 183
Hummus with Lemon, 76
Romaine Salad Tossed with Chickpeas, 180-181
Turkey and Chickpea Burgers, 141
Chili Sweet Potato Fries, 33
chocolate
Bread Pudding with Chocolate and Cherries, 236-237
Chocolate and Espresso Mousse, 246
Chocolate Mint Cream Shake, 285
Chocolate Raspberry Cocoa, 278
Chocolate-Chip-Lace Cookies, 257
Crustless Chocolate Cheesecake, 239
Dairy-Free Chocolate Mint Shake, 285
High-Protein Chocolate Bars, 267
Mexican Hot Chocolate, 277
Mint Chocolate Cookies, 258
No-Bake Chocolate Chip Cookies, 259
No-Bake Chocolate Ricotta Cheesecake, 240
Oatmeal Cookies with Shaved Chocolate, 253
chocolate chips, 15, 232
cholesterol, 161
cilantro, 16, 23
Classic Reuben with Pineapple, 121
coconut
Coconut Berry Cooler, 280
Coconut Island Shrimp, 155
Coconut Pecan Cookies, 262
cream of, 283
flour, 12, 32
Frozen Blackberry Coconut Dessert, 248
Pecan Coconut Chicken Fingers, 137
Piña Colada Smoothie, 283
cookies/cakes
Anise Almond Macaroons, 263
Chocolate-Chip-Lace Cookies, 257
Coconut Pecan Cookies, 262
Dried Fruit and Nut Cake, 269-270
Fruit and Nut Sticks, 268
Fudgy Brownies, 265
Gingerbread Drop Cookies, 255
Hazelnut Macaroons, 263
High-Protein Chocolate Bars, 267
Lemon Drop Cookies with Cornmeal, 261
low-glycemic, 251
macaroons, 254
Mint Chocolate Cookies, 258
No-Bake Chocolate Chip Cookies, 259
No-Bake Oatmeal Raisin Cookies, 259
Oatmeal Cookies with Shaved Chocolate, 253
Oatmeal Raisin Cookies, 260
Pecan Coffee Cookies, 254
Pine Nut Coriander Macaroons, 264
Ricotta Pistachio Cookies, 256
storing, 18
Sweet Potato and Cinnamon Blondies, 266
Sweet Potato and Cinnamon Brownies, 266
Versatile Yellow Sponge Cupcakes, 271
cooking and food preparation, 11, 17
corn, 28, 46, 123, 216

corn bran, 12
corn tortillas, 13
cornmeal polenta, 201
cortisol, 9
cottage cheese, 17, 59, 78, 141
crab, 158-160
crackers, 66, 207-210, 229
cranberries, 218, 230, 233
Cranberry Pumpkin Seed Muffins, 218
cream cheese, 57-58, 66, 73
Creamy Caraway Potato Salad, 42
Creamy Chicken Wraps, 135
Creamy Salmon Spread, 78
Creamy Swiss Grits, 200
Crustless Chocolate Cheesecake, 239
Crustless Lemon Cheesecake, 239
Cucumber, Bell Pepper, and Jicama Salad, 27
cucumbers, 27, 81, 84, 92
cup, rounded measure, 247
cupcake toppings, 271
Curried Carrot Dip, 74
custard cups, 17

D

dairy products, 16-17
Dairy-Free Chocolate Mint Shake, 285
Date and Sunflower Seed Muffins, 219
Deli Ham and Turkey Pitas, 122

desserts. *See also* cookies/cakes
Almond Nut Piecrust, 243
Baked Berry Ricotta Puffs, 247
Berry Ginger Tofu Mousse, 245
Bread Pudding with Chocolate and Cherries, 236-237
Chocolate and Espresso Mousse, 246
Crustless Chocolate Cheesecake, 239
Crustless Lemon Cheesecake, 239
Frozen Blackberry Coconut Dessert, 248
No-Bake Chocolate Ricotta Cheesecake, 240
No-Bake Cocoa Oatmeal Piecrust, 242
Peach Mousse, 245
Raspberry Yogurt Freezer Pops, 249
Vanilla Pudding with Grilled Bananas, 238
digestive enzymes, 176
dips and spreads, 65
Bacon Cheddar Dip, 67
Black Bean and Mango Dip, 69
Cannellini Bean Dip, 71
Chickpea, Basil, and Radish Dip, 72
Creamy Artichoke Spinach Dip, 73
Creamy Salmon Spread, 78
Curried Carrot Dip, 74
Five-Layer Mexican Dip, 70-71

Garlic Basil Pesto, 82
Greek Olive and Spinach Dip, 75
Hard-Boiled Egg Spread, 174
Hot Chili Cream Cheese Dip, 66
Hummus with Lemon, 76
Moroccan Ketchup, 83
Olive and Pimiento Cheese Spread, 77
Pepperoni Pizza Dip, 68
Salmon with Sun-Dried Tomatoes, 152
Sun-Dried Tomato Mediterranean Spread, 79
Sweet and Spicy Sesame Sauce, 83
Tzatziki, 84
dressing, salad, 54, 134
dried beans/fruits, 15
Dried Fruit and Nut Cake, 269-270
drinks. *See* beverages

E

Earl Grey tea, 276
Eggplant Feta Rolls, 47
eggs, 161-162
Apple Dutch Quiche, 169
Artichoke Squares, 165
Cherry Almond Quiche, 168
cooking methods, 162
Crustless Vegetable Quiche, 167
Egg and Bacon Salad Pitas, 173

egg substitutes, 162, 167
egg whites, beating, 263
glycemic index, 7, 161
Ham and Cheese Pie, 166
hard-boiled, 162
Hard-Boiled Egg Spread,
    174
Island Scrambled Eggs,
    170
Marinara Vegetable
    Frittata, 163
Norwegian Pancakes, 172
Spinach Cheese Squares,
    164
Sweet Potato Honey
    Kugel, 171
electric mixer and kitchen
    equipment, 17
enchiladas, 139, 159-160

F

Fennel, Apricot, and Carrot
    Wraps, 44
feta cheese. *See* cheese
Feta, Fig, and Spinach Pizza,
    88
fish. *See* seafood
Five-Layer Mexican Dip,
    70-71
flour, 12-13, 32, 252
food preferences for snacks, 6
food preparation. *See*
    cooking and food
    preparation
food processor and kitchen
    equipment, 17
Four-Cheese Black Bean
    Mash, 186
french fries, 33

Frozen Blackberry Coconut
    Dessert, 248
Frozen Cherry Almond
    Frosty, 60
frozen snacks, 60, 64,
    248-249
fructose, 49
fruit juice, 273
fruit preserves, 15
fruits, 15, 49. *See also specific*
    fruits
    Baked Apples with
        Yogurt, 61
    Banana Cream Cheese
        Roll-Ups, 58
    Caribbean Pork and Fruit
        Salad, 125
    Cheese and Fruit Kabobs,
        95
    Dried Fruit and Nut
        Cake, 269-270
    fresh vs. frozen, 16
    Frozen Cherry Almond
        Frosty, 60
    Fruit and Nut Sticks, 268
    Fruit Salad with Wheat
        Berries, 198-199
    glycemic index, 7, 49
    Gorgonzola Bites with
        Fresh Fruit, 98
    Granola Breakfast
        Sundaes, 50
    Grilled Pineapple Rings,
        60
    Mango and Pineapple
        Freeze, 64
    Minted Watermelon
        Salad, 56
    Orange Pistachio Parfait,
        51
    Papaya Basil Parfait, 53

    Peach and Pecan Stir-Fry,
        62
    Peach Parfait, 52
    Pineapple Broccoli Slaw,
        57
    Raspberry Cottage
        Cheese, 59
    Sautéed Bananas and
        Raisins, 63
    storing snacks, 18
    Strawberry Iceberg
        Wedges, 55
    Stuffed Dates, 57
    Waldorf Salad
        Vinaigrette, 54
Fudgy Brownies, 265

G

garbanzo bean flour, 12
garbanzo beans. *See*
    chickpeas
garlic
    Baked Crab Enchiladas,
        159-160
    Black-Eyed Pea and Ham
        Salad, 184
    Garlic Basil Pesto, 82
    Grilled Turkey and
        Cottage Cheese
        Burgers, 141
    minced, in jars, 26
    Parmesan Crisps with
        Garlic and Pepper, 210
    roasted, 24
Garlic Basil Pesto, 82
ginger, 133
Gingerbread Drop Cookies,
    255

glutamate, 108
glycemic index, 6-7
glycemic load, 4, 7-8
Gorgonzola Bites with Fresh Fruit, 98
grains, 14. *See also* whole grains
Granola Breakfast Sundaes, 50
Great Northern Bean and Mushroom Burgers, 190
Greek Olive and Spinach Dip, 75
Greek Salad Wraps, 45
Greek-style yogurt, 79
Green Bean and Almond Salad, 30
Green Bean Salad with Edamame and Chickpeas, 181
Green Garden Smoothie, 282
Green Lentils with Feta, 177
Green Olives with Feta and Celery, 94
Grilled Pineapple Rings, 60
Grilled Turkey and Cottage Cheese Burgers, 141
Guacamole with Green Peas and Tomato, 191

H

ham
    Black-Eyed Pea and Ham Salad, 184
    Classic Reuben with Pineapple, 121
    Deli Ham and Turkey Pitas, 122

Ham and Cheddar Scones, 213
Ham and Cheese Pie, 166
Ham, Corn, and Sweet Potato Patties, 123
New Orleans Quesadillas, 118
happy moods and low-glycemic eating, 8
hard-boiled eggs. *See* eggs
Hazelnut Macaroons, 263
hazelnuts, 12
health benefits of low-glycemic snacking, 8-9
health food stores, 12
healthy snacks, 3-5
herbs, fresh vs. dried, 15, 130
high-altitude cooking/baking, 177, 212
High-Energy Protein Bars, 231
high-fructose corn syrup, 14
high-glycemic food, 6
High-Protein Chocolate Bars, 267
honey, 13, 36, 136, 171, 216, 233
Honey-Baked Acorn Squash, 36
Hot Chili Cream Cheese Dip, 66
Hot Dogs with Avocado-Chili Relish, 117
Hummus with Lemon, 76
hunger pangs, 4

I

Indian peas. *See* chickpeas
inflammation, 9
insulin, 8
Island Scrambled Eggs, 170

Italian Pizza on a Pita, 97
Italian Sausage and Pesto Wraps, 119

J

Jalapeño Cheddar Cheese Pizza, 90
Jalapeño peppers, handling, 186
Japanese Tofu Skewers, 102
jars and canned staples, 15, 22
julienne, described, 37

K-L

kabobs, 95, 101, 112, 142

Lamb Patties Piccata, 127
Layered Greek Pie, 99
legumes. *See* beans
lemon, 145, 217, 239, 261, 275
lemon/lime juices, 14
Lemon Drop Cookies with Cornmeal, 261
Lemon Poppy Seed Muffins, 217
lemon zest, 225
Lentil Tabbouleh, 195
lentils, 177-178, 194-195
lettuce wraps, 44
lifestyle and snack choices, 5
lime/lemon juices, 14
Lobster Pitas, 160
low-fat staples to keep on hand, 16
low-glycemic food, 4, 8
low-glycemic ingredients, 11-27, 21-22

M

macaroons, 254, 263-264
mangoes, 64, 69, 80, 148
margarine, 16
Marinara Vegetable Frittata, 163
marzipan candy, 264
mayonnaise substitute, 54
measuring, rounded cup, 247
meat, 7, 18. *See also* beef; pork
Mediterranean Beef Wraps, 113
Mexican Beef Tostadas, 110
Mexican Hot Chocolate, 277
milk allergies, 50
Mint Chocolate Cookies, 258
Minted Watermelon Salad, 56
miso, 103
miso soup, 40, 103
mixer and kitchen equipment, 17
molasses, 14, 233
monosodium glutamate (MSG), 108
Monterey Jack cheese, 28, 93, 131
moods and food, 8
More-Than-Miso Soup, 40
Moroccan Burgers, 115
Moroccan Ketchup, 83
mousse, 245-246
mozzarella cheese, 26, 87
muffaletta sandwiches, 118
muffin tins and kitchen equipment, 17

muffins
    Corn and Honey Muffins, 216
    Cranberry Pumpkin Seed Muffins, 218
    Date and Sunflower Seed Muffins, 219
    glycemic index, 207
    Lemon Poppy Seed Muffins, 217
mushrooms
    Great Northern Bean and Mushroom Burgers, 190
    Mushroom and Artichoke Camembert, 89
    Polenta with Sausage and Mushrooms, 201
    Portobello Mushroom Pitas, 48
    Portobellos with Pepperoni and Walnuts, 39
    Refried Bean–Stuffed Portobello Mushrooms, 192

N

New Orleans Quesadillas, 118
New Orleans Turkey and Sausage Kabobs, 142
No-Bake Chocolate Chip Cookies, 259
No-Bake Chocolate Ricotta Cheesecake, 240
No-Bake Cocoa Oatmeal Piecrust, 242
No-Bake Cranberry Balls, 233

No-Bake Oatmeal Raisin Cookies, 259
nondairy milk, 278
Norwegian Pancakes, 172
Nut-Thins, 229
nuts, 15, 223. *See also specific nuts*
    Apricot Trail Mix, 228
    Berries with Pistachios, 226
    Dried Fruit and Nut Cake, 269-270
    flour substitute, 12
    Fruit and Nut Sticks, 268
    glycemic index, 7
    High-Energy Protein Bars, 231
    No-Bake Cranberry Balls, 233
    nut butter, 15
    nut flour, 12, 252
    Orange Cashews, 225
    Peanut and Cracker Snack Mix, 229
    Peanut Butter Cranberry Wraps, 230
    Ricotta Pistachio Cookies, 256
    toasting, 171

O

oat bran, 12
oatmeal, 211, 242, 253, 259-260
Oatmeal Flatbread Bars, 211
Oatmeal Raisin Cookies, 260
Oats and Walnut Protein Bars, 232

oils, 7, 15
olive oil, 15
olives, 160
  Artichokes and Olives on
    Cucumber, 92
  Bulgur, Feta, and Olive
    Salad, 197
  Greek Olive and Spinach
    Dip, 75
  Green Olives with Feta
    and Celery, 94
  Olive and Pimiento
    Cheese Spread, 77
  Olive Tapenade Roll-Ups,
    100
Open-Face Lemon Trout
  Sandwiches, 145
Orange Cashews, 225
Orange Pistachio Parfait, 51
orange zest, 137, 225
oregano, fresh, 16

P

Papaya Basil Parfait, 53
parchment paper and
  kitchen equipment, 17
parfaits, 51-53
Parmesan cheese, 17, 154,
  178, 210
parsley, 16, 23
patties. *See* burgers
Peach and Pecan Stir-Fry, 62
peaches, 52, 62, 126, 147, 245
Peanut and Cracker Snack
  Mix, 229
peanut butter, 15
Peanut Butter Cranberry
  Wraps, 230

pecans, 12
  Brown Rice Salad with
    Pecans, 202
  Cabbage Pecan Slaw, 24
  Coconut Pecan Cookies,
    262
  Peach and Pecan Stir-Fry,
    62
  Pecan Coconut Chicken
    Fingers, 137
  Pecan Coffee Cookies,
    254
  Spicy Pecan Nut Mix, 227
pepperoni, 39, 68, 141
peppers
  Bell Pepper and Tofu
    Kabobs, 101
  Chicken Red Pepper
    Quesadillas, 131
  Cucumber, Bell Pepper,
    and Jicama Salad, 27
  Green Garden Smoothie,
    282
  Red Pepper, Corn, and
    Monterey Jack Salad, 28
  Steak Sandwiches with
    Peppers and Onions, 116
  substitutes, 131
  Zucchini with Beef and
    Peppers, 111-112
Piña Colada Smoothie, 283
pine nuts, 112, 154, 264
pineapple
  canned, 15
  Classic Reuben with
    Pineapple, 121
  Grilled Pineapple Rings,
    60
  Mango and Pineapple
    Freeze, 64
  Piña Colada Smoothie,
    283

Pineapple Broccoli Slaw,
  57
Pineapple Broccoli Slaw, 57
pistachios, 51, 197, 226, 256
pita bread, 13
  Beef Gyros, 109
  Blue Cheese Pitas, 96
  Deli Ham and Turkey
    Pitas, 122
  Egg and Bacon Salad
    Pitas, 173
  Italian Pizza on a Pita, 97
  Lobster Pitas, 160
  Portobello Mushroom
    Pitas, 48
  Turkey and Apple
    Pockets, 140
pizza, 88, 90, 97
Po'Boys, 146-147
Polenta with Sausage and
  Mushrooms, 201
poppy seeds, 217
pork. *See also* ham; sausage
  Caribbean Pork and Fruit
    Salad, 125
  Pork Posole, 124
  Pulled Pork and Peach
    Wraps, 126
  tenderloin, 125
portobello mushrooms. *See*
  mushrooms
potatoes, 7, 22, 42. *See also*
  sweet potatoes
poultry, glycemic index, 7.
  See also chicken; turkey
pudding, 236-238
Pulled Pork and Peach
  Wraps, 126
Pumpkin Holiday Nog, 279
pumpkin seeds, 12
Pumpkin Soy Nog, 279

Q

quesadillas, 118, 131
quiche, 167-169
quinoa, 194
Quinoa and Lentil Salad, 194

R

radishes, 30
ramekins and kitchen equipment, 17
Raspberry Cottage Cheese, 59
Raspberry Lemon Tea, 275
Raspberry Yogurt Freezer Pops, 249
red new potatoes, 22, 42
red peppers. *See* peppers
Refried Bean–Stuffed Portobello Mushrooms, 192
rice. *See* brown rice
ricotta cheese, 240, 247, 256
rolls/roll-ups, 43, 47, 58, 100
Romaine Salad Tossed with Chickpeas, 180
Rosemary Honey Chicken Drumsticks, 136

S

sage, fresh, 16
salads
   Asian Tuna and Cabbage Salad, 149
   Black Bean and Avocado Salad, 188
   Black-Eyed Pea and Ham Salad, 184
   Blue Cheese Iceberg Salad, 25
   Bulgur, Feta, and Olive Salad, 197
   Bulgur with Apples and Walnuts, 196
   Caribbean Pork and Fruit Salad, 125
   Chickpea Salad with Roasted Cumin, 183
   Corn, Red Pepper, and Monterey Jack Salad, 28
   Cucumber, Bell Pepper, and Jicama Salad, 27
   Egg and Bacon Salad Pitas, 173
   Fruit Salad with Wheat Berries, 199
   Green Bean and Almond Salad, 30
   Lentil Tabbouleh, 195
   Minted Watermelon Salad, 56
   Mozzarella and Black Bean Salad, 87
   Quinoa and Lentil Salad, 194
   Romaine Salad Tossed with Chickpeas, 180-181
   Southwestern Salad, 31
   Southwestern Tuna Salad, 151
   storing, 27
   Strawberry Iceberg Wedges, 55
   Tofu Salad with Peanut Sauce, 104
   Tomato, Basil, and Mozzarella Salad, 26
   Tuna, Barley, and Black Bean Salad, 150
   Tuna Salad with Mangoes and Avocado, 148
   Waldorf Salad Vinaigrette, 54
   Wheat Berry and Cabbage Salad, 198
salmon. *See* seafood
Salmon with Orange Slices, 153
salsa, 80-81, 136
sandwiches, 145-147
saucepans and kitchen equipment, 17
sauces
   Chicken Satay with Peanut Sauce, 132
   Shrimp Tacos with Ginger Sauce, 157
   Sweet and Spicy Sesame Sauce, 83
   Tofu Salad with Peanut Sauce, 104
sausage
   Italian Sausage and Pesto Wraps, 119
   Italian Sausage and Turkey Patties, 120
   New Orleans Turkey and Sausage Kabobs, 142
   Polenta with Sausage and Mushrooms, 201
Sautéed Bananas and Raisins, 63
seafood, 7
   Asian Tuna and Cabbage Salad, 149
   Baja Fish Tacos, 144
   Baked Crab Enchiladas, 159-160
   Barley Pilaf with Shrimp, 205
   buying tips, 143

Cajun Catfish Po'Boy, 146
Coconut Island Shrimp, 155
Crab Cakes, 158
Creamy Salmon Spread, 78
Lobster Pitas, 160
Open-Face Lemon Trout Sandwiches, 145
Parmesan Shrimp with Pine Nuts, 154
Salmon with Orange Slices, 153
Salmon with Sun-Dried Tomatoes, 152
Shrimp Fajitas, 156
Shrimp Po'Boy with Peaches, 147
Shrimp Tacos with Ginger Sauce, 157
Southwestern Tuna Salad, 151
storing, 154
Tuna, Barley, and Black Bean Salad, 150
Tuna Salad with Mangoes and Avocado, 148
seeds, 7, 12, 15
serving size, 6
servings, daily, 21, 49
Sesame Chicken Strips, 138
Shoestring Carrot Patties, 32
shortening, 16
shrimp. See seafood
Shrimp Fajitas, 156
skewers, 102, 142
skillets and kitchen equipment, 17
smoothies, 7, 281-284
snacking, low-glycemic 3-8
snacks, calories, 4, 6

soup, 40, 103, 124, 189
Southwestern Salad, 31
Southwestern Tuna Salad, 151
soy milk, 278-279
Spaghetti Squash with Spinach, 38
Spiced Flax Cracker, 208
spices, 15, 115
Spicy Pecan Nut Mix, 227
spinach
    Creamy Artichoke Spinach Dip, 73
    Feta, Fig, and Spinach Pizza, 88
    Greek Olive and Spinach Dip, 75
    Green Garden Smoothie, 282
    Lentils with Spinach, Walnuts, and Parmesan, 178
    Spaghetti Squash with Spinach, 38
    Spinach Cheese Squares, 164
spreads. See dips and spreads
squash, 36, 38
staples (ingredients), 14-17
Steak Sandwiches with Peppers and Onions, 116
stevia, 14, 251, 275, 280
stew, Vegetable Curry, 41
storing snacks, 18, 27, 107, 154
Strawberry Iceberg Wedges, 55
stress and foods, 8
Stuffed Dates, 57
sugars, 13-14, 251, 273
Sun-Dried Tomato Mediterranean Spread, 79

sunflowers, 12
Sweet and Spicy Sesame Sauce, 83
sweet potatoes, 7, 22
    Baked Sweet Potato Skins, 35
    Chili Sweet Potato Fries, 33
    Ham, Corn, and Sweet Potato Patties, 123
    Sweet Potato and Black Bean Wraps, 187
    Sweet Potato and Cinnamon Blondies, 266
    Sweet Potato and Cinnamon Brownies, 266
    Sweet Potato Honey Kugel, 171
    Twice-Baked Sweet Potatoes, 34
sweeteners, 6, 13-14, 235, 251, 273
Swiss cheese, 139, 200

T

table sugar, 13
tacos. See tortillas
tahini, 138
tarragon, 16, 244, 276
Tarragon Custard, 244
taste buds, 108
tea, 14, 274-276
Thai Ginger Smoothie, 284
Thai Vegetable Rolls, 43
thyme, fresh, 16
toasting nuts, 171
tofu, 86, 101-104, 245
Tofu and Green Pea Soup, 103

Tofu Salad with Peanut Sauce, 104
tomatoes, 26, 79-80, 152, 191
Top Sirloin Kabobs, 112
tortillas, 13
Baja Fish Tacos, 144
Baked Crab Enchiladas, 159-160
Mexican Beef Tostadas, 110
Monterey Jack Tacos, 93
New Orleans Quesadillas, 118
pizza dough substitute, 88, 90
rolled, 100
Shrimp Tacos with Ginger Sauce, 157
Swiss Turkey Enchiladas, 139
trail mix, 226-229
Truvia, 14
tuna, 15. *See also* seafood
Tuna, Barley, and Black Bean Salad, 150
turkey, 129
Classic Reuben with Pineapple, 121
Deli Ham and Turkey Pitas, 122
Grilled Turkey and Cottage Cheese Burgers, 141
Italian Sausage and Turkey Patties, 120
New Orleans Turkey and Sausage Kabobs, 142
Swiss Turkey Enchiladas, 139
Turkey and Apple Pockets, 140
Turkey and Chickpea Burgers, 141

Turkey and Pepperoni Burgers, 141
Tuscan Bean Soup, 189
Twice-Baked Sweet Potatoes, 34
Tzatziki, 84

U-V

umami, 108
utensils and kitchen equipment, 17

Vegetable Curry, 41
vegetable scoopers, 65
vegetables, 15, 21-22
Asian Cakes with Cabbage, 37
Asian Vegetables with Peanuts, 23
Avocado Cups, 22
Baked Sweet Potato Skins, 35
Blue Cheese Iceberg Salad, 25
Broccoli and Corn Wraps, 46
Broccoli Salad with Blue Cheese, 29
Cabbage Pecan Slaw, 24
Chili Sweet Potato Fries, 33
Corn, Red Pepper, and Monterey Jack Salad, 28
Creamy Caraway Potato Salad, 42
Crustless Vegetable Quiche, 167
Cucumber, Bell Pepper, and Jicama Salad, 27
Eggplant Feta Rolls, 47

Fennel, Apricot, and Carrot Wraps, 44
fresh vs. frozen, 16
fresh vs. frozen/canned, 21
glycemic index, 7, 21
Greek Salad Wraps, 45
Green Bean and Almond Salad, 30
Honey-Baked Acorn Squash, 36
More-Than-Miso Soup, 40
Portobello Mushroom Pitas, 48
Portobellos with Pepperoni and Walnuts, 39
raw, with dip, 22
Shoestring Carrot Patties, 32
Southwestern Salad, 31
Spaghetti Squash with Spinach, 38
storing snacks, 18, 27
Thai Vegetable Rolls, 43
Tomato, Basil, and Mozzarella Salad, 26
Twice-Baked Sweet Potatoes, 34
Vegetable Curry, 41
Versatile Yellow Sponge Cupcakes, 271
vinegars, 15

W

Waldorf Salad Vinaigrette, 54
walnuts
Blueberry Banana Walnut Bread, 214

Bulgur with Apples and Walnuts, 196
Lentils with Spinach, Walnuts, and Parmesan, 178
Oats and Walnut Protein Bars, 232
Portobellos with Pepperoni and Walnuts, 39
Walnut Crackers, 209
watermelon, 8, 56
wheat berries, 198-199
wheat bran, 12
wheat flour, 13
white potatoes, glycemic index, 7, 22, 42
whole grains, 194, 219
Barley Pilaf with Shrimp, 205
Barley with Asparagus and Thyme, 206
Brown Rice Salad with Pecans, 202
Bulgur, Feta, and Olive Salad, 197
Bulgur with Apples and Walnuts, 196
Cajun Dirty Rice, 203-204
Creamy Swiss Grits, 200
Fruit Salad with Wheat Berries, 198-199
glycemic load, 193
Lentil Tabbouleh, 195
Polenta with Sausage and Mushrooms, 201
Quinoa and Lentil Salad, 194
Wheat Berry and Cabbage Salad, 198
whole-wheat pita bread, 13
whole-wheat tortillas, 13

wraps
Asian Chicken Lettuce Wraps, 133
Beef and Black Bean Lettuce Wraps, 108
Beef and Blue Cheese Wraps, 114
Broccoli and Corn Wraps, 46
Chicken Wraps with Pears and Grapes, 134
Creamy Chicken Wraps, 135
Eggplant Feta Rolls, 47
Fennel, Apricot, and Carrot Wraps, 44
Greek Salad Wraps, 45
Italian Sausage and Pesto Wraps, 119-120
Mediterranean Beef Wraps, 113
Pulled Pork and Peach Wraps, 126
Sweet Potato and Black Bean Wraps, 187

X-Y-Z

yogurt, 16. *See also* dips and spreads; smoothies
Baked Apples with Yogurt, 61
Greek-style, 79
Raspberry Yogurt Freezer Pops, 249
substitutes, 50

Zucchini Apple Bread, 215
Zucchini with Beef and Peppers, 111-112

CHECK OUT
THESE BEST-SELLERS

More than 450 titles available at booksellers and online retailers everywhere!

978-1-59257-115-4

978-1-59257-900-6

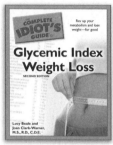

978-1-59257-855-9

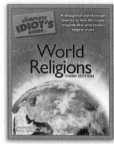

978-1-59257-222-9

978-1-59257-957-0

978-1-59257-785-9

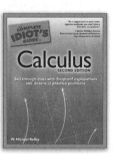

978-1-59257-471-1

978-1-59257-483-4

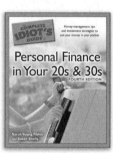

978-1-59257-883-2

978-1-59257-966-2

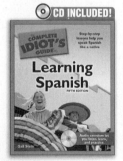

978-1-59257-908-2

978-1-59257-786-6

978-1-59257-954-9

978-1-59257-437-7

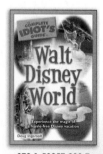

978-1-59257-888-7

ALPHA   idiotsguides.com